Dedicated to the memory of Donald E. Smith.

This book would have been impossible without the assistance of and encouragement from North Western personnel, the editorial staff, and a number of dedicated photographers and hobbyists. To everyone who has helped in various ways to make The 400 Story *a reality, I extend sincere appreciation and thanks.*
—*Jim Scribbins*

The 400 story

BY JIM SCRIBBINS

Charles Ost

3

© 1982 by Jim Scribbins. All rights reserved. This book may not be reproduced in whole or in part without permission in writing from the publisher, except in the case of brief quotations used in reviews. Published by PTJ Publishing, P.O. Box 397, Park Forest, IL 60466. Printed in U.S.A. Library of Congress Catalog Card Number: 82-81672. ISBN: 0-937658-07-3.

Front endpaper: Chicago & North Western; back endpaper: Alexander Maxwell

Contents

It's June 22, 1963, as the Twin Cities 400 arrives at Milwaukee's lakefront station en route to Chicago. A month later, the train will pause in this pleasant setting for the last time.

Jim Scribbins

Introduction

I THINK I KNOW why we've waited so long for a book-length study of the Chicago & North Western's *400* streamliners. They dwelled in the shadow of their long-haul, luxury sisters on the Overland Route; in their green-and-yellow format, they were late to the party monopolized by Milwaukee orange and Q silver; and once away from the columned, granite majesty of their Chicago terminal, they serviced a bucolic community which left its imprint upon consist and clientele. The *400*'s played to the salesman and student, farmer and fisherman, of Kenosha and Eau Claire, Mankato and Fond du Lac, an audience content with a reclining seat, a square meal, and a cool glass. Parlor car with drawing room; diner; tavern-lunch counter-lounge; coaches—that sufficed for most *400*'s, no matter if the prefix was *Commuter or Peninsula* or *Valley* or *Shoreland* or whatever.

I am not unmindful of the standard steam trains which coined the name *400*—of how North Western tweaked the noses of its Chicago-Twin Cities rivals by condensing approximately 400 miles into approximately 400 minutes beneath steam-driven, 79-inch Boxpok driving wheels propelling 12-wheel-trucked heavyweight cars in a splendid swan song of standard railroading. But that train lasted less than five years, bequeathed scarcely more than its route and three-digit name to posterity, and would not be duplicated in spirit again until Baltimore & Ohio's post-World War II *Cincinnatian*. (Our company librarian, George H. Drury, tells me that in the next life we can reinstate all the leaves on all the calendars and ride what and where we will. If so, an early journey of mine will be aboard that *400*'s frosty January 2, 1935, inaugural.)

No, the *400*'s most of the America remembers were the Pullman-Standard apple green and English stagecoach yellow streamliners of Electro-Motive propulsion which preoccupy this volume. (How appropriate that "English stagecoach yellow" was for a lefthanded rail*way*!) They were, well, pleasant trains . . . easy riding (Amtrak could study their trucks with profit), clean, swift (*400*'s had no trouble establishing a beachhead in Mr. Steffee's surveys), serviceable.

I remember the silky smoothness of their electropneumatically braked stops. How they were still serving bacon and eggs when the Milwaukee Road had descended to the depths of Continental breakfast. The call of their brakemen—"Next stop will be *Raay-ceeen!*" (Racine to you outlanders). A girl friend, Diane, telling me how the bartender of the *Twin Cities 400* always had her favorite drink mixed and poured when she swung aboard in Milwaukee Friday afternoons for the short ride to her hometown of Beaver Dam, Wis. My trepidation when the final *400*'s appeared in gallery shells all too readily convertible into commuter cars if the intercity trade continued its decline. Those strange bulbous air scoops on the ends of the roofs of the observation-parlors on the flagship Twin Cities trains.

You are in good hands as Jim Scribbins relates the story of these trains. He grew up with the *400*'s, rode them, timed them, photographed them. They frequently competed with the *Hiawathas*, the subject of the author's previous book, which lent Jim's curiosity a clinical value useful to all historians.

One concluding thought: The useful future for the passenger train is surely in the role played by the *400*'s so well in the 1940s and 1950s, in corridor-distance, high-frequency service. Once upon a time, in 1948, one could catch a *400* out of Chicago for Milwaukee on any weekday at 7:30 a.m., 9:45 a.m., 11:15 a.m., 1:30 p.m., 2:45 p.m., 4:10 p.m., and 10 p.m. These trains averaged 60 mph or better, downtown to downtown, inclusive of usually four intermediate population-center stops, mingling people in their passenger counts on errands of business, shopping, theater, vacation, and school. In the 1980s the cost and supply of oil could render that sort of service valid again. If so, this book can be read as prophecy as well as history.

David P. Morgan
Trains Magazine
Milwaukee, Wis.
November 1981

C&NW

400 miles in 400 minutes

For a train of social rank, a splendidly appropriate title

IN 1934, the Chicago, Burlington & Quincy and the Union Pacific were garnering the headlines in railroading, astonishing North Americans with an entirely new concept in passenger trains—the "streamliner." The Burlington's stainless-steel *Zephyr* and the UP's yellow-and-brown M-10000 both began their careers with extended publicity tours. They roamed the rails of their owners and connecting lines as well, bringing volumes of newspaper, radio, and motion picture attention to UP and Burlington—and to the railroad industry in general.

However, these diminutive lightweight consists did not initially provide specific improvements in speed. When the *Zephyr* finally settled down in 1934 to become the first streamliner in regular service, it averaged but 49 mph—certainly not a remarkable timing.

Actually, the first improvements in speed to regularly scheduled passenger trains during this era had been made on the Chicago-Milwaukee subdivisions of the Chicago-Twin Cities routes of the competing Chicago & North Western and Chicago, Milwaukee, St. Paul & Pacific—the Milwaukee Road. On July 15, 1934, both roads had begun operating 90-minute trains on 85-mile routes with steam locomotives and standard rolling stock, kicking off a hot rivalry between the two intensely competitive railroads that would last for nearly three decades. Unlike all other C&NW

trains, which had two or more stops, the 7:15 a.m. from Milwaukee and 3:35 p.m. from Chicago operated nonstop. Within a few weeks the Chicago-Milwaukee run was changed to a 9 a.m. departure as train 151 which, with opposite 152, was named the *Pacemaker*.

Shortly, the Burlington had shown its inclination to enter the competition between Chicago and St. Paul by operating its *Zephyr* on a demonstration trip over that route in just under six hours (stops deducted), for an average speed of 71 mph. Then, in mid-August, all three railroads announced their intention to drastically reduce the time of their day trains from the Twin Cities to Chicago, from 10½ to 6½ hours. Such improvement was a competitive necessity; automobiles were averaging 50 mph on recently improved highways.

CB&Q announced that its train would be of the *Zephyr* type: diesel-powered, articulated, three-car, stainless-steel. Neither of the other two roads specified equipment. The CMStP&P's train obviously would travel via Milwaukee. On the other hand, many C&NW terminals were connected by more than one principal route, so the selection of a route for its new Twin Cities-Chicago service was a matter for debate. The *Viking*, the North Western's existing daytime limited between those cities, operated via Madison, the capital of Wisconsin, without direct Milwaukee connections. Milwaukee's only C&NW link with the Twin Cities, therefore, was by overnight train: the *North Western Limited* in both directions, and the *Victory* eastbound only. These trains utilized the Adams Cutoff, a partially single-track route touching only small communities along its path between Milwaukee and the junction with the Madison route at Wyeville, Wis.

This route was selected for the new service. Quietly, right-of-way improvements were made north of Milwaukee while public attention was centered on the Chicago-Milwaukee section. Considerable new rail was laid during the summer of 1934, followed by reballasting, curve elevation and finally complete inspection of the route by a Sperry rail detector car during the fall. Every precaution was taken to insure the safety of high-speed operation; the North Western did not want to risk losing its top place for safety, a position it had earned among Class A roads for four consecutive years. It also wanted to provide a smooth journey for patrons.

According to newspaper accounts, the North Western was "reticent" to announce its plans, but in October 1934, tentative reports did appear of a departure from Chicago's Madison Street Station at 3 p.m., with arrival at St. Paul Union Depot 10 p.m. Work was progressing to meet the challenge of the Burlington *Zephyr*, expected to enter service by February, with 90-mph cruising speeds. Some 250 cars of ballast were spread between Milwaukee and Clyman Junction alone, a distance of 51 miles. Four locomotives—E-2-class Pacifics—were converted from coal to oil firing to eliminate engine changes at Adams and Altoona, Wis., and fuel and water stops at other intermediate points. Regular coaches were improved to provide the ultimate in comfort, with widely spaced seats, indirect lighting, and air conditioning. As the first coaches emerged from the North Western shops, they were placed in service temporarily on the *Viking*. (Eventually, air-conditioned stock would also operate on the *North Western Limited,* the *Victory,* and the *Rochester Minnesota Special,* as well as the transcontinental trains operated with the Union Pacific and Southern Pacific.)

Four days before Christmas, modest newspaper announcements noted that 90-mph service would be inaugurated between Chicago and St. Paul on January 2, 1935, in order to maintain a 63-mph average speed for that entire distance. The first mention of the new train's name—the *400*—appeared in newspaper advertisements on December 30, which boasted: "400 miles in 400 minutes . . . the fastest train on the American continent." The half-page ads spoke of powerful locomotives able to travel 100

mph over heavy steel rails, laid on an oiled, dust-free, newly ballasted roadbed. The *400* was touted as a speedster with spacious and comfortable standard-sized steel cars and a cooling system providing pure, clean, properly humidified air.

Also praised were reclining seats in the lounge coach, the "latest type" parlor car, and a select-your-own-price dining car. The *400* would offer smooth, safe riding over rails regularly inspected by an "electric eye," the ad stated. A closing sentence urged readers to watch for an upcoming contest with $1000 in cash prizes.

This ad surprised those who placed their faith in lightweight streamliners, because the *400* was to be a fully conventional train—standard heavyweight cars pulled by a steam locomotive. The introduction of trains 400 and 401 on the world's fastest schedule for distances exceeding 164 miles was a striking coup that stole the thunder from the new crop of lightweights. Schedules called for the 408.6 miles between Chicago and St. Paul to be completed in 420 minutes, including intermediate stops—an average of 58.4 mph. When the three intermediate stops of five minutes each were deducted, the new time of 405 minutes resulted in an average speed of 60.5 mph. An additional 30 minutes were used between St. Paul Union Depot and Great Northern Station in Minneapolis.

The name "400" was chosen to reflect the running time of approximately four hundred miles in four hundred minutes. Furthermore, in society circles, "the four hundred" was a group of distinction, signifying the most exclusive social rank. Thus *400* implied a conveyance of exceptionally fine quality—a splendidly appropriate title for a distinguished limited.

The *400*'s equipment had been operated to the Twin Cities on December 30 as a five-car passenger extra, steaming into St. Paul in one minute less than the seven hours allotted for the journey. Carl R. Gray Jr., vice-president and general manager of the Chicago, St. Paul, Minneapolis & Omaha—the C&NW subsidiary which would be the northern end of the *400*'s speedway—was aboard for the complete trip. He explained that the trial run was made to discover any last-minute impediments to the inauguration of high-speed service.

There were none. Equipment functioned as intended, and the locomotive demonstrated ample capacity to meet a strenuous schedule. Officials claimed that an even cruising speed was maintained, without the necessity of spurts—though the operating timetable for the new train would imply otherwise—and the

Pacific 2908, normally assigned to the Chicago-Milwaukee segment of 400-401, appears in Minneapolis in this scene from August 22, 1935, sporting an original, non-gyrating signal light that beamed at the sky at a 45-degree angle.

R. Graham

The crew of the first 400 was properly attired as the train is inaugurated at Chicago. Neil Neiglick, the first engineer on January 2, 1935, sits behind two unidentified men before taking the throttle himself. Note the removable "400" sign below the cab window.

All photos, unless otherwise credited, C&NW

An imposing quartet of dignitaries pose on the rear platform of the first Twin Cities-bound 400. From left to right: Illinois States Attorney Thomas Courtney, Illinois Gov. Henry E. Horner, C&NW President Fred W. Sargent and Chicago Mayor Ed Kelly.

Pacific 2907, normally part of the Milwaukee-Minneapolis power pool for the 400, shines in the gloom of the Chicago & North Western Terminal train shed, considerably more plain in appearance than sister 2908.

Some 15 minutes after leaving Chicago, No. 401 steams toward an appointment in Milwaukee, 85 miles distant. Engine 2907 accelerates a five-car heavyweight consist through Evanston, intent on keeping the demanding schedule.

Alexander Maxwell

14

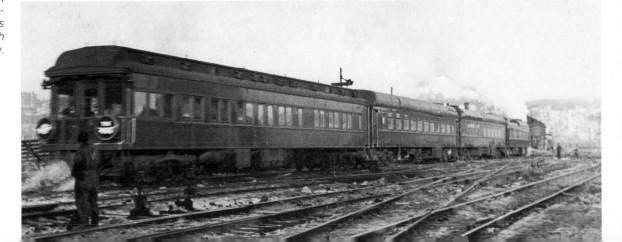

A crowd braves the cold January 2, 1935, weather of St. Paul as the first Chicago-bound 400 departs. Pacific 2902 steps out quickly for the 409-mile dash to the Windy City.

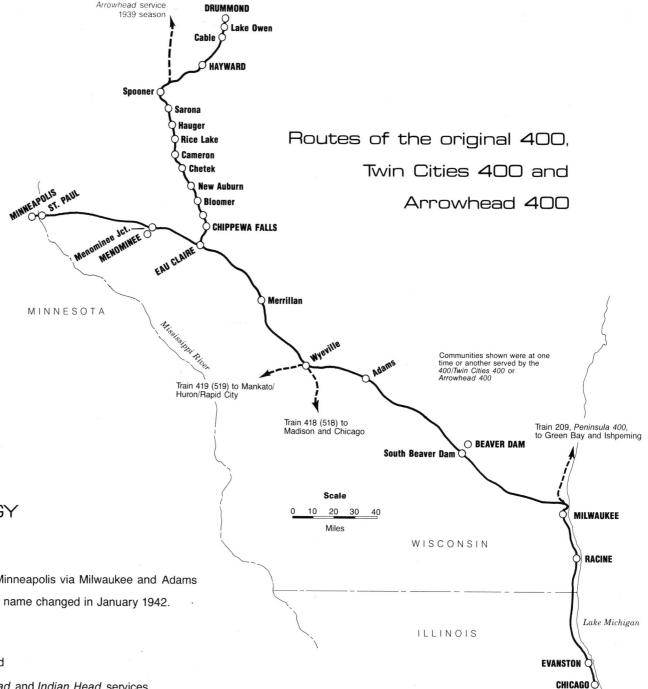

Routes of the original 400,
Twin Cities 400 and
Arrowhead 400

Arrowhead service
1939 season

DRUMMOND
Lake Owen
Cable
HAYWARD
Spooner
Sarona
Hauger
Rice Lake
Cameron
Chetek
New Auburn
Bloomer
CHIPPEWA FALLS
MINNEAPOLIS
ST. PAUL
Menominee Jct.
MENOMINEE
EAU CLAIRE
Merrillan

MINNESOTA

Mississippi River

Wyeville

Adams

Communities shown were at one
time or another served by the
400/Twin Cities 400 or
Arrowhead 400

Train 419 (519) to Mankato/
Huron/Rapid City

Train 418 (518) to
Madison and Chicago

Train 209, *Peninsula 400,*
to Green Bay and Ishpeming

Scale

0   10   20   30   40
Miles

BEAVER DAM
South Beaver Dam

WISCONSIN

MILWAUKEE

RACINE

Lake Michigan

ILLINOIS

EVANSTON

CHICAGO

ROUTE CHRONOLOGY

The 400/Twin Cities 400

January 1935-July 1963: Chicago-St. Paul/Minneapolis via Milwaukee and Adams

NOTE: Train streamlined in September 1939; name changed in January 1942.

Arrowhead 400

Summer season 1937: Eau Claire-Drummond

NOTE: See text for detail of related *Arrowhead* and *Indian Head* services.

test trip was described as thoroughly enjoyable. Near Hudson, 80 mph speeds were recorded, and the railroad admitted to 90 mph. (Railroad men talked privately of touching 100 mph, according to news articles.)

The *400's* made their first public departures from Chicago and St. Paul on Wednesday, January 2, 1935. Pacific 2907 departed from North Western Terminal at Madison and Canal Streets with a train distinguishable from others only by its luster, by the small rectangular plate attached below the locomotive's headlight with the words "THE 400" and by the drumheads on the railing of the solarium.

A few dozen spectators clustered at the far end of the platform, out beyond the Bush trainshed. Listeners to WBBM radio that afternoon heard the exhaust of the E-2-a Pacific as it departed from Chicago and again as it passed Glencoe, 19 miles out and about 19 minutes later. There, the 79-inch drivers churned in ever faster revolutions to break the festive ceremonial tape in front of a reviewing stand occupied by approximately one hundred businessmen, civic leaders, and railway officials, formally marking the commencement of the record-breaking train. When the markers and two drumheads of Pullman parlor-solarium *Odin* disappeared from view and No. 401's Pacific from hearing, WBBM broadcast a special program, which included speeches by Chicago's Mayor Edward J. Kelley and H. W. Beyers, North Western's traffic vice-president.

A similar radio presentation was aired as train 400 left from St. Paul—at 3:30 p.m., the same time as 401's departure from Chicago—with Twin Cities newsmen aboard. The C&NW Women's Club presented Omaha Road official Carl R. Gray, Jr., with a floral bouquet just before the highball from veteran conductor Jule Sontag. The first eastbound *400*, headed by Pacific 2902, consisted of combine, coach, lounge-coach (with reclining seats), diner, parlor and Pullman parlor-solarium *Viking*. There were 185 passengers aboard out of St. Paul, including a Twin Cities business delegation that returned from Eau Claire, Wis., on 401.

At the throttle on the momentous first run up the Lake Michigan shore from Chicago to Milwaukee was Neil Neiglick, who would also handle the southbound (eastbound in terms of railroad operations) *400* that evening. During his career as a *400* engineer, Neiglick would entertain several VIP's in the confines of his cab, one of the most notable being Viscount Falmouth, who would describe the ride aboard the "footplate"—as he, an Englishman would call the cab—of the 2908 between Chicago and Milwaukee as one of the thrills of his life. At one point, Neiglick would be featured on the cover of a small brochure outlining the crew requirements of the *400's* entitled "Every One of Them Tops at His Trade and Proud of the Famous *400*."

Over the Chicago-Waukegan (Ill.) and Waukegan-Milwaukee subdivisions, Neiglick, on that inaugural run and later, was faced with several speed restrictions: 60, 50, and 45 mph through interlockings in the north suburban area; a few 40-mph and 50-mph curves; and limits between 45 and 20 mph in Kenosha and Racine, Wis. To aid engineers in their struggle against these handicaps, the timetable prescribed no maximum speed; on tangents, the oil-burners could race as rapidly as necessary to maintain schedule.

A most important footnote in the timetable emphasized: "Nos. 400 and 401 are superior to all trains. Freight trains, transfer trains, and switch engines must clear the schedules of Nos. 400 and 401 fifteen (15) minutes." This special instruction remained in force throughout most of the *400's* lifetime and was expanded to cover the routes of the other members of the fleet during the streamliner years. This was something very special; the competing *Zephyrs* and *Hiawathas*, for example, received no such treatment.

Relieving Neiglick in Milwaukee with a fresh Pacific was Madison Divison engineman Ray E. "Rusty" Sherman, who would regularly handle 401 to Adams until his retirement in 1946. On that inaugural afternoon, Sherman and his steel steed had their work cut out for them, since 401 was delayed in Milwaukee while an extra coach was added to accommodate the heavy passenger demand. Later, about five hundred people—a phenomenal turnout—were present in the little railroad town of Adams, Wis., for 401's on-time meet with 400. In the early evening darkness, observers at trackside could appreciate the beautiful interiors of the cars and the roses adorning the tables in the diner.

Back on double track, on the right-hand-running Omaha Road—a change from C&NW's unique use of the left track—401 maintained an exhilarating pace, negotiating the 81 miles from Wyeville to the stop at Eau Claire in 67 minutes and touching 91 mph in the process, apparently the highest speed on the inaugural journey.

Though the advance newspaper coverage of the January 2 installation of the *400* was sparse, the event itself was well reported. Several accounts credited 400 and 401 with on-time completion of their runs. Even so, one daily relegated the speedster to page two, while a "runaway" locomotive in Pine Bluff, Ark., made the front page. Typical headlines along the route of the *400* in January 3 editions read: "New Train Hits 91 Miles an Hour," "Speedy Train Service Opens," and "The Iron Horse Isn't Through Yet."

The president of the North Western system, Fred W. Sargent, was interviewed while traveling on "the new aristocrat of the rails." His comments are extremely interesting in light of what actually would occur during the ensuing five years. According to

Coach 6180 typifies the deluxe reclining-seat coaches used for long-distance patrons.

Sargent, C&NW felt that, although diesels would be ideal for runs with frequent stops because of their excellent acceleration capabilities, the purchase cost of internal-combustion locomotives to pull heavyweight long-distance trains was too great. Steam locomotives, therefore, were ideally suited to the *400*. Though he acknowledged that streamlining would eventually come for all passenger trains, Sargent held that the practical route to that goal was to rebuild existing equipment, and then gradually acquire new streamlined cars and locomotives as earnings warranted. Articulation—at the time a universal corollary of streamlining—he deemed undesirable.

In a bit of high optimism, Sargent said that two more *400* trains were ready for use as soon as traffic would support them. He also predicted a tremendous amount of grade separation work to allow the trains to run at the speeds of which they were capable.

Candid comments from the chief executive emphasized that the 7-hour schedule only hinted at greater things to come, and that C&NW could do much better than the anticipated 6½-hour Chicago-St. Paul schedule contemplated by the CB&Q and the CMStP&P because it possessed two important physical advantages. First, C&NW's alternate Chicago-Milwaukee route, the freight line, bypassed all of Chicago's North Shore suburbs as well as Racine and Kenosha, where speeds would have to be restricted. Second, its line beyond Milwaukee passed through fewer and smaller towns, allowing higher speeds.

The freight subdivision—situated two or three miles west of and parallel to the existing passenger line—was well maintained and laid with the heavy rail necessary for freight trains. Because it was almost entirely in rural surroundings, it had no metropolitan speed restrictions. Consequently, high average speeds could be achieved without unduly fast cruising speeds. In fact, conversion of the line to a 100-mph speedway was under consideration. The Milwaukee Road was planning to place in service five 80-minute Chicago-Milwaukee trains on January 17, and the North Western was likely to do the same.

What people had only dreamed about was now an accomplished fact. The *400* was "the train that set the pace for the world"—a slogan quickly adopted for the service. The super-speed schedule, which placed North Western first in the world for sustained daily high-speed railway operation, was two hours and fifty minutes faster than the best previous Chicago-St. Paul running time. Between Chicago and Milwaukee, time was cut to 80 minutes, 10 minutes less than the already fast schedule introduced five and one-half months earlier. Only absolutely necessary intermediate stops were made. Thus 400 and 401 operated nonstop through three cities between Chicago and Milwaukee, but stopped at Adams and Eau Claire to change crews.

Between Clyman Junction and Wyeville, the junction with the Omaha Railway, was 102 miles of single track. When the *400's* had identical departure times from St. Paul and Chicago, both sides of the fast flyer met at Adams, where the mile between the depot and the yard office was double tracked. No. 401 would pull away from the depot at the precise moment 400 stopped. Considering that 401 had meets with two opposing freight trains between Clyman Junction and Adams, some sharp operation was required to maintain the timing of this meet.

In early planning, apparently, the *400* was expected to be a five-car train—baggage-coach (smoker), coach, reclining-seat coach, diner, and parlor-solarium. However, business in the first days of the *400's* defied all expectations, and the train routinely ran with

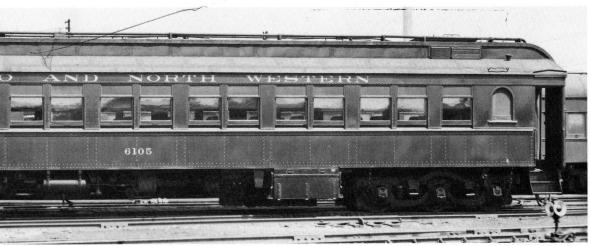

Coach 6105, a six-axle heavyweight, was one of the cars rebuilt for service on the original 400's. Some cars C&NW selected for the upgrading had been built as early as 1912. The seats in coach 3286 (below) like those in 6105 did not recline; these cars were designated for short-distance travelers.

C&NW

C&NW

six-car consists. Even seven-car trains were not uncommon.

Standard steel cars, some of them built in 1912, had been selected for the *400*. Air conditioning was installed; interiors were redecorated with brighter colors, re-upholstered seats, new shades, and new floor covering; hot water was provided in coach lavatories.

Considerable attention was paid to air conditioning, since it was one of the principal selling points of the new train. The system, designed by the railway, was ice-activated and used air-conditioning units manufactured by the Trane Company of La Crosse, Wis., and the Young Company of Racine, both "on-line" to C&NW.

Two ice chests of 1600-pounds capacity were located beneath the car, with a thirty-gallon sump pump between them to receive the frosty water after its passage over the ice. A one-half h.p. electric-motor-driven pump forced the water through thin copper pipe to the fin-type cooling coils of the air-conditioning unit, located at one end of the clerestory. Warm air passing the coils was cooled by transmission of its heat to the water, which then returned to the ice bunkers to repeat the process.

An electric blower of 2000-cubic-feet-per-minute capacity transmitted the air through the cooling unit and then through cork-insulated ducts along the clerestory to grills inside the car. Some of the cars in *400* service carried these air-conditioning ducts the full length of the roof on both sides—in part inoperative dummies—to provide a more streamlined appearance. What resulted was a roof contour similar to the well-known Harriman style used extensively by Union Pacific and Southern Pacific.

After passing through the car, air re-entered the cooling unit through a grill and filter in the ceiling, where it was mixed with

The 73-foot dining car (above) provided seating for 36 at tables for two and four. The menu on the table in the foreground (lower left) carries the slogan "400 miles, 400 minutes." A parlor car was not included in the planned consist, but one such as 6401 (below) was included from the inception of service due to heavy demand for first-class seats. The cars featured 23 swivel seats and a four-seat couch (right) plus additional capacity of 15 in the men's room and smoking lounge. Carpet, like that in the diner, was two-tone brown with double-diamond designs.

fresh air. To eliminate the musty odors common to some previous air-conditioning systems, a special machine was linked to the system to supply oxygen. By admitting steam to some of the coils in the air-conditioning unit, C&NW's cooling system could also be used to heat the cars in mild weather and to supplement the regular steam heat in cold weather. The heat took the chill off the cold fresh air admitted to the system and thereby prevented drafts.

Temperatures within the cars were controlled in relationship to exterior temperatures rather than at an arbitrary constant—approximately 73 degrees—as is generally the case today. The *400*'s system was intended to maintain a 71-degree temperature when the outside temperature was 75 to 80 degrees, 75 degrees for an outside range of 80 to 90, and 80 degrees when outdoor temperatures exceeded 90. If outside temperatures were below 75 degrees, fresh air was admitted and circulated, bypassing the cooling process.

The only major mechanical change to the cars other than the addition of air conditioning was the installation of special side bearings, designed by a C&NW employee, to the trucks. Already in use on the North Western for some four years and marketed through the Railway Products Company, they eliminated side-bearing pounding and provided sufficient take-up to assure a quiet and smooth ride. The total mechanical upgrading of the cars for the *400* was later reported to have cost "only a few thousand dollars" per unit.

The 70-foot-3-inch combine had a 29-foot baggage room and a passenger section seating 50. Its interior decoration and seats were approximately identical to those of the 54-foot 2-inch coach, which accommodated 60 and was intended for short-haul riders. Both cars retained their original lighting fixtures; these descended from the clerestory roof above the aisle and ended in clusters of four incandescent bulbs, each individually enclosed in a china shade, with one fixture above each four double seats.

The seats were of the conventional walkover type, their backs modified somewhat so that the tops had the contour of bucket seats. The cushions were resprung, and the entire seats reupholstered in a patterned brown Chase plush. Seat sides, parallel to the aisle, were painted a light color and topped with black wooden arm rests. The aisle of the combine, which was used as a smoker, and the entire floor of the full coach were covered with asbestos tile in a diamond pattern of light and dark tan. Water coolers and drinking-cup dispensers were provided. Narrow, open-frame metal luggage racks ran the entire length of the seating areas of the cars. Walls and ceilings were gray, with tan trim on moldings above the luggage racks where the ceiling curve commenced, in the clerestory, and at vertical window edges.

Greater effort was expended on reconditioning the 73-foot 4½-

inch lounge coach for through passengers. The car seated 38 in reclining seats in the forward section, with men's and women's lounges to the rear. Again, the floor covering throughout the car was a multi-hued tile, in this case predominantly green and black. Walls were aluminum and, in the mode of the time, stippled with varying shades of rose, resulting in a minimum amount of glare from the bright basic color. Narrow luggage racks of the same type as in the regular coach extended the length of the car, but here they were supplemented by luggage shelves—items the forthcoming streamlined competition would not have—on both sides of the aisle just inside the entrance from the vestibule at the forward end of the car.

The clerestory was brightly hued in aluminum stippled with ivory to enhance a novel system of indirect lighting. Seventy-six 15-watt incandescent bulbs were recessed in the base of the clerestory in the car's main section, bouncing their light against the bright surface, which reflected into the body of the car. The smoking rooms were also illuminated in this manner.

The ladies' lounge contained two armchairs and a sofa which, like the reclining seats in the body of the car, had a rose design. The men's lounge contained four armchairs and a sofa, all upholstered in green leather. Two fern-green wash basins were in each lounge. The sofas in each lounge seated three.

An electric water cooler was at the rear of the main passenger compartment. The car's windows were wide—4 feet, 3 inches, with foot-wide panels between them. This lounge coach, suitably luxurious for the long-haul passenger, was an exceptionally well renovated vehicle; porter service was offered.

The 73-foot dining car, when operated as usual with its kitchen to the rear, had tables for four on the train's left and for two on the right, with seats for 36 passengers in all. The clerestory and interior walls were finished in a light color. Chairs were upholstered in brown leather. The ceiling was squared off in the manner of the lounge coach, and large bowl-type fixtures were suspended from the top of the clerestory. Fixtures containing two individually shaded bulbs were mounted above each large window adjacent to a table. On the floor was a sponge-rubber pad covered by a two-tone brown carpet with a double-diamond design. One of the diners had photo murals mounted on each side of the exit to the pantry and kitchen. Menu covers carried the *400* emblem, and the slogan "400 miles in 400 minutes."

Although not contemplated in the original planning for the train, the 70-foot North Western parlor car was included from the initial departures because of the unforeseen demand for first-class seating. Its interior was light in tone, with walls and ceiling of blonde finish. Ceiling and clerestory were curved, and several large bowl lights, similar to those in the diner, descended from the clerestory. Double-bulb lights—the same type as in the diner—

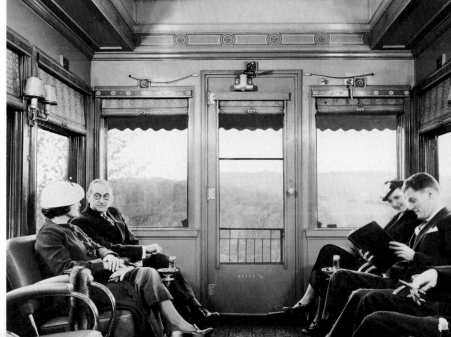

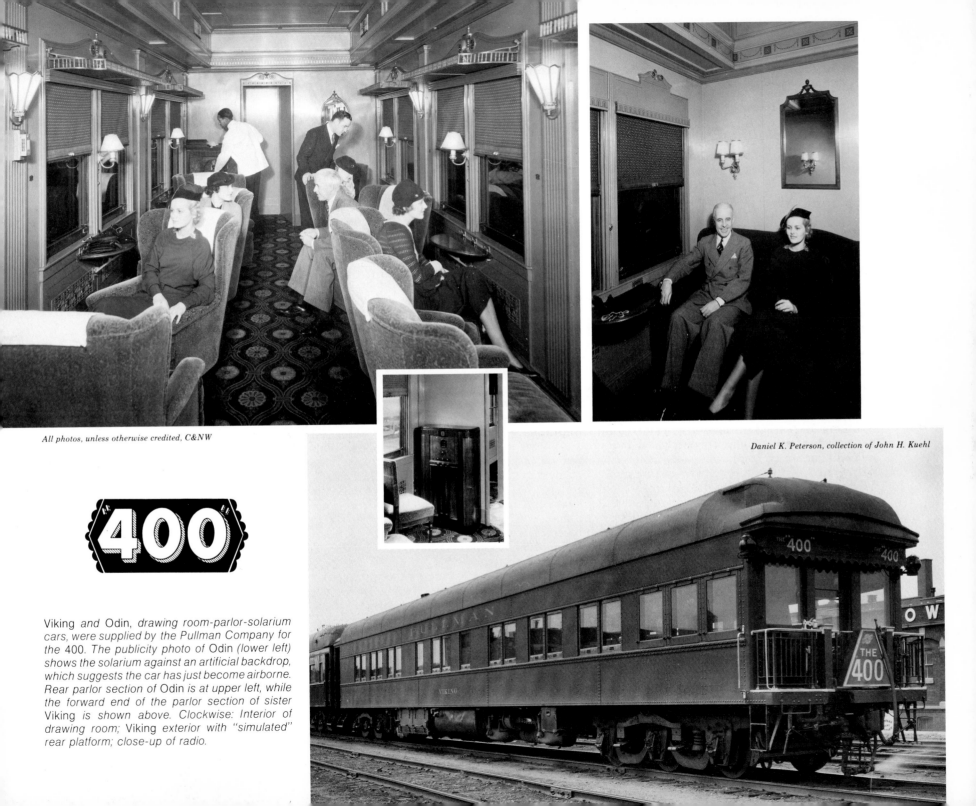

All photos, unless otherwise credited, C&NW

Daniel K. Peterson, collection of John H. Kuehl

Viking and Odin, drawing room-parlor-solarium cars, were supplied by the Pullman Company for the 400. The publicity photo of Odin (lower left) shows the solarium against an artificial backdrop, which suggests the car has just become airborne. Rear parlor section of Odin is at upper left, while the forward end of the parlor section of sister Viking is shown above. Clockwise: Interior of drawing room; Viking exterior with "simulated" rear platform; close-up of radio.

were mounted near the top of each panel separating the large windows. Above each window, immediately below the curving roof, were individual ornamental metal luggage racks.

Seats 1, 2, 3 and 4 were a couch across the bulkhead at the end of the car. Above them were a pair of photo murals, one of Mount Rushmore and one of a swift-flowing northwoods Wisconsin stream. The other 23 seats in the car were swivel chairs, high-backed, well padded, and non-reclining. They were upholstered in varying patterns—a circular design, a leafy vine, and plain—in shades of either brown or green, with five different mixtures of weave and color. The two-tone brown carpet was of the same double-diamond design as in the dining car. Total capacity of the car, including the men's room and smoking lounge, was 42.

Viking and *Odin*, the 78-foot 3½-inch drawing room-parlor-solarium cars, were supplied by the Pullman Company. Pullman seat accommodation tickets were required for travel aboard these cars, which were staffed by Pullman porters. Formerly, these cars had been the stars of the *Viking*, the *400*'s predecessor on a daytime Twin Cities-Chicago schedule, usually via Madison. The cars were basically identical in design, each containing 12 parlor seats forward, a drawing room accommodating five passengers, and 11 rear parlor seats, plus an eight-seat solarium graced with a railing to simulate an open platform.

Suspended from this railing in early operation were two drumheads, the left displaying the railroad's herald and the right proclaiming "THE 400." Later, they were replaced by a triangular, centrally mounted illuminated *400* sign. Right up until the end of heavyweight operations, this large blue sign was always wiped and the brass railing always polished. As soon as the train stopped in Milwaukee, a carman clambered onto the rear of *Viking* or *Odin* to perform this ritual.

Interiors of *Viking* and *Odin* were done in shades of green, including upholstery, with cream clerestory ceilings. Both cars had small ornamental metal luggage racks above each window and radios in their rear parlors. Their drawing rooms contained facing couches, with a pair of double candlestick lamps, separated by a rectangular mirror, above each.

There were slight differences in decor between the two cars. *Odin* had tubular-frame chairs in its sun room, and the light fixtures in its parlor rooms were of the bullet magnifying-lens type, both over the aisle and at the tops of the windows. Patterned upholstery adorned the front of the seats, but their backs were a solid color. Carpeting contained variations of lines, leaves, and flowers. *Viking* had wicker chairs in its solarium; illumination in its two parlor rooms was by candlestick-style lamps on the narrow center posts of its windows and large petal-type lamps reflecting toward the ceiling from the wide panels between the windows. Both front and back of the seats were covered with a flower-design

upholstery, and the car's carpet bore large whimsical flowers separated by wavy lines.

The normal six-car consist of the *400* weighed in at 457 tons, and the class E-2-a Pacific assigned to propel it weighed, with tender, 296 tons, making the complete tonnage of the train 753. The maximum capacity of the *400*, if all dining, smoking lounge, and solarium chairs were filled, was 275 persons. Thus, the weight of the train averaged out to slightly below three tons per passenger—considerably more than the lightweight streamliners. North Western felt this weight was justified, however, because of the low cost of readying the already existing equipment.

Despite the bitter, difficult Wisconsin winter, the *400* kept to schedule in its first month with only two minor delays due to extremely perverse weather, and a third, longer delay caused by a freight train ahead on the line. Later, there were other delays, of course, but the reliable 4-6-2's were normally able to regain as much as 30 minutes of lost time on their tight schedules. Subzero weather in itself did not prove to be much of a handicap. One incident indicative of time recovery was this: On March 31, high demand for passage on 401 required that an extra coach be cut into the train at Milwaukee. The Pacific that joined the train there not only handled the seven-car limited with ease but gained back the time lost in switching and arrived in St. Paul four minutes early.

Even before its first highball, the *400* had proved a success. The demand for parlor seats was so great that the C&NW first-class car was added, making a six-car train. The late afternoon departures, established for businessmen, were an instant hit. During the first days of operation, average passenger loading on 401 was 174 and on 400, 191. As many as 135 persons were served in the diner in the course of the journey, leading to speculation about increased dining facilities.

When the new train was not quite two weeks old, the railway announced an extraordinary 87 percent profit, with costs per trip $400 and receipts $750. Requests for parlor reservations were so numerous that several would-be rear-car patrons ended up ahead of the diner in the coach and passholders were prohibited from traveling on the *400*.

Patronage on the *400* that first January totaled 9,531 passengers. Earnings were even more stupendous than suggested by the earlier figures, exceeding direct operating costs by 100 percent. Furthermore, the success of the *400* was not gained at the expense of existing trains. Rather, its tremendous visibility and drawing power stimulated an increase in patronage on all passenger trains through Madison and Milwaukee. Though over two-thirds of the *400*'s passengers were through riders between the Twin Cities and Chicago, the North Western's share of

Milwaukee business improved too as a result of the super-speed steamster. Between the Beer City and Eau Claire, for instance, ridership increased an impressive 78 percent. Patrons were often driving as much as 40 miles by automobile to commence or conclude their rail trips, yet another indication of the *400*'s success.

During March, 10,000 passengers raced through Wisconsin behind the tenders of the *400*'s Pacifics. The average was 160 riders per day in each direction, with a new record of 257 persons aboard 401 on March 27. In its first three months of operation, the *400* had carried 28,000 clients. Contemporary accounts describe the speedster's being packed nearly every day, with as many as 50 prospective patrons turned away on occasion. Ridership remained high during the first three weeks of April, averaging between 150 and 175 in each direction, with more than 200 on each train on Easter.

A one-time special feature on train 401 was the showing of a new motion picture, "The Whole Town's Talking," to film critics and regular passengers as a preview prior to its Chicago opening. The film was screened between Chicago and Milwaukee with special equipment installed by Columbia Pictures. This was the first time a movie was previewed aboard a speeding train.

Coincident with the inauguration of the train, the railway initiated a contest in which passengers were asked to describe their impressions of their first ride aboard the *400*. Entry forms were distributed en route. By the end of March, some 500 contestants were hoping for one of the 28 cash prizes. The $500 first prize went to Mrs. Harriet H. Weeks of Detroit Lakes, Minn., who contrasted the *400* with her experiences on conveyances ranging from ox cart to airplane. Second prize of $200 was awarded E. E. Burke of Minneapolis, who emphasized the advantages of the new train for business travel. Lesser amounts were also given out, to a grand total of $1000.

With the April 28 change to daylight saving time, the schedule of the *400* was reduced 30 minutes for a running time of 6½ hours between Chicago and St. Paul. Five minutes were cut between Chicago and Milwaukee, bringing about the first 75-minute schedule and raising the average speed between the two cities to 68 mph. The 25-minute reduction between Milwaukee and the Minnesota capital raised the average speed across Wisconsin to 63 mph. Some experimentation had been done in anticipation of the expedited timings, reported in the trade press as prompted by the success of the Pacifics in maintaining the initial seven-hour operation. On one occasion 401, with its usual six-car consist, hurtled between Kenilworth and Highland Park in "less than five minutes," cruising at 97 mph, supposedly the fastest speed to that date on the North Western.

Normally, such exploits along the Lake Michigan shoreline were performed with the 2908 on the head end. That engine, with its attention-getting adornments—large front-end sign, Mars light, and air horns—was usually restricted to the heavily populated Chicago-Milwaukee route; the other three members of Class E-2-a operated between Minneapolis and Milwaukee.

The impetus for these service improvements came in part from the introduction of the *Twin Cities Zephyr* on April 21, 1935, even though the Budd Company and Electro-Motive product competed with the *400* only for business between the end points, sharing no intermediate stops. More serious competition began on May 29, when the Milwaukee Road inaugurated its *Hiawatha*, which paralleled more closely the route of the *400*. Then, on June 2, *Zephyr* service was expanded to two daily runs in each direction. From that time forward, the *400* was always to be pitted against formidable rivals.

During their first two months of operations, 400 and 401 had carried approximately 19,000 people, an average of 160 per trip. But during June and July, the first two months during which they were faced with tough competition, 15,500 riders were aboard, an average of 128 per trip. Receipts at this time totaled slightly more than $92,000, rail and parlor tickets and dining car service all included. Wages, fuel oil and its transportation, supplies such as water and lubricants, and car and locomotive repairs including enginehouse costs were under $59,000, leaving a net revenue of $33,000.

Dining car expenses were $3000 *more* than cash received, so meals on wheels were a large red-ink entry in the ledger, a situation typical throughout the industry. It would have been unthinkable to operate a quality train without food service, and the restaurant car certainly contributed to the attractiveness of the *400*. In any event, 400 and 401 were bringing 65 cents per mile to the North Western and Omaha treasuries, after expenses were deducted from gross revenues.

Because of its greater capacity, the C&NW train was able nearly to equal the ridership of the two *Zephyr* trips; the *Hiawatha* presented the larger problem, combining as it did the flexibility of nonarticulated full-sized equipment and the advantages of streamlining. Although the *400* carried over 30,000 passengers during the four months ended April 30—maintaining the average of about 160 per trip—the conventional train began to lose some of its initial advantage.

But even though the *400* may have lacked the modernity of its streamlined opponents, it remained a healthy and vigorous competitor. With some improvements of its own and aided by the general economic upswing, its patronage began to climb again. The *400* continued to attract attention. Faster schedules combined with spring and summer weather brought onlookers to witness its passage. Shorewood, just outside Milwaukee's northern limit, posted a police car at a principal grade crossing every day to control traffic when 401 passed. Sometimes as many as 50 automobiles were parked at the crossing, their occupants anticipating the Minneapolis-bound streak of black lightning.

In early summer, a parlor-lounge car was added to the *400*'s consist. Its squared-off clerestory—similar to that of the lounge coach, diner, and Pullman parlor—was of light wood with darker trim, and the balance of the interior was paneled in dark wood. The car's forward section, used for beverage service, had a leather couch across the vestibule end, with triangular vases of flowers above it. Adjacent were eight heavy chairs, four on each side of the aisle, upholstered in leather with wooden arm rests. A writing desk and radio were across the aisle from each other. Behind a shoulder-high wooden divider, the top portion of which was partially open and surmounted by a huge crosspiece, were booths and an enclosed service area. Beyond the service area were 13 high-back nonrevolving parlor seats. Large ash stands with napkins permitted beverage service in the parlor section, though a prominent sign proclaimed "Parlor car reserved seat section— lounge section ahead." Walls and ceilings were the same as in the forward portion of the car, and the entire car had carpet with a flowered pattern. Illumination was provided by vertical clusters of three unshaded bulbs between each window and groupings of six unshaded bulbs suspended from the ceiling.

A more modern "Cabana Lounge" emerged from the North Western's shops on July 15 and was added to the *400*'s consist in August. It had the same floor plan as the parlor-lounge it replaced but a brighter, cheerier decorative scheme. Entering from the dining car, just ahead, one's passage was deflected to the right by a vertical wooden "fence," which had a floor-model radio recessed into its lower portion, facing the interior of the lounge. A round, chrome-trimmed, Formica-topped table was nestled in the forward left end of the car.

Six tubular-framed chairs on the left and five on the right had their backs to the windows. The most modern furniture aboard the *400*, they were of two types: light brown chairs with dark lines in a contrasting pattern and square arm rests, and chairs with a vertical bright-colored striped pattern throughout and rounded arm rests. There were two small light bulbs in porcelain shades between each window and single-bulb fixtures at the ends of this portion of the lounge. A waist-high divider of solid wood isolated a single booth on each side of the aisle. The two tables, each with four chairs, were identical to the table near the radio. Tablecloths were spread when drinks were served.

Behind the tables was a bulkhead with a center archway. The bulkhead's lower portion echoed the divider between the table and lounge-chair areas; its upper portion had columns appearing to support an arch above the aisle. On the right bulkhead was a

The immediate popularity of the 400 *led to the addition of a parlor-lounge in early summer (immediate right), which was replaced in July 1935 by a more modern "Cabana Lounge" (center and far right). The cheerful car was used mostly for beverage service and was positioned between the diner and two parlor cars.*

photo mural of a Wisconsin north woods lake scene, and on the left one of South Dakota's Black Hills. Beyond the bulkhead, the aisle looped to the car's left to pass the bar—which had the same decorative arch treatment as the bulkhead—and service room.

In the parlor section were brightly upholstered chairs, a drape across the door to the service area, and a photo mural of a northwoods waterfall. There were large ash trays, without holes to steady glasses. Throughout the car, the carpet had a raised diamond pattern, and the ceilings were as in the C&NW parlor, with high clerestory and bowl-type lighting fixtures.

The addition of the lounge brought the regular consist of 400 and 401 to seven cars: baggage-smoker, coach, deluxe coach, diner, lounge, C&NW parlor, and Pullman parlor. Frequently, however, the C&NW parlor was excluded. On such occasions, as well as during holidays, the formal seating of the Cabana Lounge may have been used as assigned first-class space. (On Friday, October 11, 1935—apparently the only date on which the steam-powered *400* exceeded seven cars—the train operated with

All photos, C&NW

eight heavyweights behind its E-2-a on the occasion of a brewmaster's convention.)

On the August day when the Cabana Lounge was added to the consist, stops at South Beaver Dam, Wis., were inserted into 400 and 401's schedules—stops that afforded a bus connection to Green Lake. A bus connection destined to last longer was instituted at the same time between Adams and Nekoosa, Port Edwards, and Wisconsin Rapids, the two intermediate towns previously being served only by Milwaukee Road trains.

Despite competition, the *400* broke all previous patronage records in August, handling nearly 1100 more passengers than in its best previous month, February. The big steel train was clearly a match for its streamlined opponents. Furthermore, this success encouraged improvements of service on other trains, such as a 35-minute reduction in the running time of the *Victory*, between Chicago and Minneapolis, and, in September, the commencement of the coach-only *Fast Mail* for local business. These trains operated via Madison.

No. 2907 departs from Chicago's North Western Terminal on April 29, 1939 (right), and in a scene from August 27, 1938, hustles an eight-car consist through Highwood, Ill. Visible at left is CNS&M interurban equipment and North Shore Line's general offices.

Vincent Quayle

Paul Eilenberger, collection of Harold Stirton

At Juneau Park, just north of Milwaukee's lakefront station, 2903 backs onto a waiting 401. Crowds watch from the Prospect Ave. overlook as 2903 prepares to depart for the Twin Cities. Pacific 2907 (above), couples on while passengers board the combine and "short coach" at Milwaukee.

Alexander Maxwell

As the 400 posted ridership records, a
first anniversary birthday cake was cut
by Robert Thompson, passenger
traffic manager. Holding the cake is
Neil Neiglick, engineer of the first
400. Lurking in the background is
engine 2912, not a member of the
400 pool. At far right, C&NW's 1938
Chicago softball team, the "400's,"
accept a trophy.

C&NW

C&NW

30

It's December 19, 1947, and 2911 is at speed at Eau Claire, running as a passenger extra on train 400's schedule account of a derailment.

Forlorn Pacific 2909 rests on its side on September 10, 1939, after derailing with the Victory near Hudson, Wis., the day before. Later that afternoon, 2902 leads the first train through the scene of the wreck—the eastbound 400.

31

The Indian Head, *looking much like the original 400 and operating as the second section of train 400, blasts through Altoona, Wis., behind engine 2905 in July 1946, as the North Western, along with most other railroads, experiences a travel boom.*

32

Alexander Maxwell

Victor T. Fintak

Twin Cities-bound 401 (upper left) is moving quickly through Chicago's North Shore suburbs (possibly Wilmette). The wig-wag signal protects North Shore Line tracks. The baggage car behind No. 2903 (above) and the length of the consist cannot be explained, but the 400 sign seems to indicate that the Pacific has the 400 in tow.

As the *400* rolled into its second year of operation, North Western was modernizing its signal system between Wilmette interlocking plant and St. Francis tower, approximately 65 miles, and on 3½ miles of the westbound exit from Milwaukee. In both locations, Hall disc signals (sometimes called "banjo" signals), installed in 1905 and oil-lit, were replaced by four-indication color light and three-indication searchlight signals. Because of problems of visibility, which Lake Michigan fog made particularly acute, this modern system was needed to cope with the high speeds typical of the *400*.

The *400* celebrated its first anniversary with much hoopla. Advertisements claimed that, though train "birthdays" did not usually rate mention, the *400*'s was different, because it had established new records for sustained high-speed operation. The *400* was "the train that set the pace for the world."

When daylight-saving time took effect in the spring of 1936, the *400*'s times were moved 30 minutes earlier at all stations. (Wisconsin and Minnesota did not adopt daylight-saving time until many years later.) As a result, the connection at Milwaukee between train 209—which gathered local traffic from com-

munites north of Chicago—and 401 was broken. However, train 120 was rescheduled to maintain the southbound connection to points intermediate to Chicago. On June 14, stops were inserted in the schedules of 400 and 401 to connect at Wyeville with the new *Minnesota 400*, and 401 was given a conditional stop at Racine to receive for Eau Claire and beyond.

As part of a second annual Railroad Week which took place in Chicago in the summer of 1936, the participating railroads were invited to select a queen to represent each line. From among them, a girl would be chosen to reign over the entire celebration. Dorothy Whitt, of the Ravenswood Office Building, was North Western's entry, and, as a runner-up in the general contest, she served on the queen's court during the celebration.

Shortly thereafter, Miss Whitt participated in an event of more lasting significance: the introduction of hostesses aboard the *400*. She began in that role on Monday, August 10, on 401, while Ruby Williams worked out of Minneapolis on 400. On the 11th, a third hostess, Lee Hobbs, started on 401 from Chicago. Misses Williams and Hobbs had also been participants in the contest to name C&NW's queen. In addition to relieving Dorothy and Lee on their rest days, Ruby made trips on the *Flambeau*—a summer-only vacationers' train to the north woods—to fill out her work week. The young women, all from Chicago, wore the semi-military uniforms then in style for airline stewardesses: French blue gabardine, with "overseas" caps bearing the *400* insignia, white shirts, brilliant red ties, and brown walking shoes.

The hostesses helped mothers with children, assisted patrons in making train connections, sent their telegrams, arranged seats for them in the diner and buffet-lounge, and in Chicago helped them to the Parmelee Transfer loading area for movement to other rail terminals. In addition, hostesses were expected to be sure that passengers were not accidentally carried past their intended destinations.

A particularly important assignment was to see that un-accompanied children were met at their destinations. On one arrival in Minneapolis, for instance, no one appeared to pick up a little girl. The hostess put her in a cab and told the driver that, if no one were at home, the youngster should be brought to the hostess's hotel. This turned out to be the case, and the small traveler spent the night as a guest of C&NW before being successfully united with her relatives the next morning.

On May 4, 1939, hostess service was expanded when Neva Neander, of Concordia, Kan., was appointed nurse-stewardess aboard the *Minnesota 400*, between Mankato, Minn., and Wyeville, Wis. But in January 1942, as the *400* trains were being expanded into a fleet, the railroad announced that nurse-stewardess or hostess service would be confined to the Chicago-Rochester routing via the *Twin Cities 400* and *Minnesota 400*. It was retained here at least in part to serve the noted Mayo Clinic in Rochester. Some time later, this service too was quietly discontinued.

Most who patronized the *400* acknowledged its uniqueness. The train claimed to be the personification of speed, proving the right to its title by matching units of time with units of distance: "I must do this with regularity and safety. I shall accept the challenge of all comers. I shall acquit myself with honor. I shall never admit defeat. I am the *400*." A businessman who had made a visit to Great Britain called the conclusion of his international journey aboard 401 between Chicago and Minneapolis the finest transportation of the trip. Another patron described the *400* as a black knight of modern civilization, roaring on its way beneath a white plume rising to the sky.

Approximately one-third more passengers rode the *400* in 1936 than in its inaugural year. In June 1936, it posted a 47 percent increase over the same month of the preceding year. Wisconsin Dells tour business (reached by C&NW bus probing Milwaukee Road domain) was far ahead of 1935, and July saw average loads of 225 in each direction—the best yet for the "marvelous mile-a-minute *400*." The *400*'s honorable reputation instilled in C&NW employees great pride in their railway; 2500 of them, the most representing any railroad, marched in Chicago's second Railroad Week parade behind a float bearing a likeness of the *400*, with its distinctive front-end name sign.

Labor Day weekend in 1936 saw particularly heavy passenger traffic, with 401 operating in two sections on Friday, Saturday, and Monday—carrying 700 passengers on the holiday itself. The *400* dining cars were decorated for the Christmas season of 1936, beginning a custom of many years duration. It thrived aboard the train's streamlined incarnation, as cardboard wreaths adorned the *Twin Cities 400* diner and solarium windows right through the Second World War.

On completion of two years' service in January 1937, the *400* had rolled 536,000 miles, equal to 23 times around the world. In that time it had carried approximately 250,000 passengers, bringing in a gross of $2.35 per mile, and netting $1 for each of the 840 miles totaled by the two trains every day. By then, new connecting services had been added.

With the July 15, 1935, issue of the public timetable, a passenger extra had been established to depart Eau Claire at 8:35 p.m., receiving passengers from 401 and making stops at important resort communities up the Omaha Railway to Drummond, Wis., where it arrived at 11:59 p.m. This train departed Fridays only, through Labor Day weekend. On Sundays and Labor Day, the train left Drummond at 1:15 p.m. to connect with 400.

This operation was repeated in 1936, for the Memorial Day holiday and weekends from mid-June through the end of September. That year, the slightly expanded operation was given regular-train status as No. 1401 on Friday and No. 1400 on Sunday. Operation of this resort special was unchanged in 1937, with the trains making all stops between Eau Claire and Spooner, then Hayward, Cable, Lake Owen, and Drummond. The Omaha had the unique practice of naming all its trains, including freights, in the operating timetable, and the Eastern Division card in effect for the 1937 season designated 1400 and 1401 as the *Arrowhead 400*, even though they ran nowhere near the Arrowhead country of northeastern Minnesota.

In 1938, the *Arrowhead 400* was replaced by a new through train from Chicago to Drummond. Inaugurated for Memorial Day, it subsequently ran north on Fridays and south on Sundays from mid-June through Labor Day. It was named the *Indian Head,* for the section of Wisconsin it served. (The St. Croix River, forming the border between Wisconsin and Minnesota, can be imagined as an Indian's chin, mouth, and nose, with the straight, arbitrarily drawn portion of the border north of it to Lake Superior the forehead and the Bayfield peninsula the head dress.)

Friday-only train 403 left Chicago at 1 p.m. and took but 20

A close relative of the original 400-401 was the Indian Head *(402-403), which operated between Chicago and Drummond, in northwest Wisconsin, on summer weekends before and after World War II. Above, on Sunday, July 7, 1946, the train leaves Eau Claire as Second 400. At right, a pre-war* Indian Head *arrives at Eau Claire behind Omaha Railway No. 517, a Pacific.*

minutes more than 401 to reach Eau Claire. Ninety minutes with intermediate stops were allowed to Milwaukee, and beyond there a scant five minutes more than 401's time was required to Eau Claire. Eastbound, the *Indian Head* was listed in the folder as train 402, but it appears actually to have been operated as Second 400 between Eau Claire and Chicago. No. 402 (or Second 400) made the pick-up from the *Minnesota 400* at Wyeville on Sunday, enabling No. 400 to run nonstop to Adams. The *Indian Head* and train 401 normally met at Adams Yard, making for quite a lively 10 minutes or so every Sunday evening. Then, too, since there were only enough oil-burning E-2-a's for 400 and 401 themselves, coal-fired power such as E-2-b's were necessarily used, which required a coaling stop en route for which no timetable allowance was made. If this were not enough, 402 faced the possibility of having to stop at Racine, Kenosha, and Evanston (to discharge from Eau Claire and beyond) and still make the 85 miles from Milwaukee to Chicago in 75 minutes.

Equipment for the *Indian Head* was a parlor, diner, and coaches, all air-conditioned. North of Eau Claire, the *Indian Head* was powered by CStPM&O engines: Class E Pacifics—identical to C&NW's Class E's—or the even lankier Class K-2 Pacifics, of which No. 388 was often used on this crack train. On rare occasions, an Omaha Railway Ten-Wheeler would do the honors.

The *Indian Head* ran again in 1939, with the addition of a Spooner-Duluth leg called the *Arrowhead*, for the region in northeastern Minnesota known by that name. Intermediate stations served were Minong, Gordon, Solon Springs, and Superior, all in Wisconsin. The *Arrowhead* was the only daytime through train ever operated between Duluth and Chicago. Coaches, diner, and parlor car operated Chicago-Drummond on trains 402 and 403 (412 and 413 beyond Spooner). Coach and parlor-"dining car service" were also provided to and from Duluth on 402 and 403, though there was no true diner.

The northwestern Wisconsin resort train operations remained

As popular as the 400's were, the North Western realized that streamlining was inevitable, if its speedsters were to remain competitive. By the summer of 1939, new equipment ordered from Pullman-Standard was still several months away, but four new Electro-Motive E3's, costing $180,000 each, had arrived and were pressed into service on heavyweight consists. On July 1, 1939, the new and the old mix at Kenosha, Wis., while at Milwaukee's lakefront depot on another day, E3 set 5002A&B gleam under an afternoon sun.

Brad Kniskern

essentially unchanged through the last two peacetime summers but were cancelled during the years of the Second World War. The *Indian Head* but not the *Arrowhead* was revived from Memorial Day through Labor Day in 1946, but the brilliant running of prewar years was not restored, with the westbound train now taking 33 minutes longer than 401 to Eau Claire; the return trip was even slower. The consist was buffet-lounge, diner, and coaches.

In the next three years, *Indian Head* operations were further compromised. Between Chicago and Eau Claire, its passengers rode the *Mountaineer,* which was a Chicago-Vancouver summer-season train via C&NW, Soo Line, and Canadian Pacific, and the running time was approximately 50 minutes longer than it had been in the last season of through *Indian Head* service. On the return trip, passengers fared better, changing to the *Twin Cities 400* at Eau Claire. Trains 303 and 304 between Eau Claire and Drummond carried only coaches and a snack car. In the early fifties, operations remained unchanged except that 401 was used for Chicago-Eau Claire trips, since the *Mountaineer* was no longer operated. The final season of *Indian Head* service was 1953.

During all but a brief portion of its existence, the heavyweight steam-powered *400* was pitted against streamlined competition, which naturally drew much attention because of its novel design and bright colors. Since the *400* was not showy, North Western was obliged to emphasize other aspects of its appointments. The contribution of air conditioning to a pleasant journey was stressed; ads mentioned the general use of air conditioning by the North Western, which had 60 completely air-conditioned trains by 1936. Good food received plenty of attention, with the journey of the *400* often called "just a pleasant dinner trip." The roominess of substantial all-steel full-sized cars on a perfectly graded, well maintained roadbed ensured a smooth and comfortable ride.

Only the keeping to schedule indicated the swiftness of the train, and swift it was. North Western had set the pace, and the streamliners faced the task of equaling the conventional *400.* Eventually, though, the Chicago & North Western was to concede that streamlining would be necessary to uphold the fine reputation of the *400.*

C&NW

Yellow and green

Hot competition for the Hiawathas and Zephyrs

THE NORTH WESTERN'S heavyweight *400* was notably successful in combining steam-powered standard equipment with high speed, as were certain similar trains—the New York Central's Chicago-Detroit *Twilight Limited* and the Chicago-St. Louis trains of the Chicago & Eastern Illinois and the Wabash, among Midwestern examples. Nevertheless, streamlining clearly was the future direction of passenger railroading. Considering that the competing Burlington and Milwaukee Road trains were each in their second sets of streamlined equipment and that the streamlined *City* trains which C&NW operated with Union Pacific and Southern Pacific were highly successful, the North Western must have thought about dressing up its crack flyer even while the heavyweight *400* was "setting the pace for the world."

In January 1938 the railway told its employees that it was studying the prospect of streamlining the *400* in the near future, indicating that it would seek bids for twelve cars and three locomotives. Locomotive bids were requested for diesel, steam-turbine, and reciprocating steam, each to be fully streamlined to match the cars. (The proposal for three locomotives indicated that power would continue to be changed at Milwaukee.)

On December 14, 1938, C&NW's desire to update its Twin Cities speedster was confirmed, for on that date the railroad requested permission, since it was bankrupt, from the Federal District Court

in Chicago to purchase 20 streamlined cars and four diesel-electric units for the *400*. Exterior colors of yellow and brown were planned, to be in harmony with the *City* Streamliners operated by C&NW between Chicago and Omaha on their Overland Route journeys. The court authorized expenditure of $720,000 for the locomotives and $1,600,000 for the cars—a total of $2,320,000, which would bring the first streamlined train and the first diesels into the "northern territory" of the railway and on subsidiary Omaha Road.

By February 1939, Pullman-Standard had begun work on the new cars. It was none too soon, for the competition was getting hotter: The original *Hiawatha* was now in its *third* set of equipment—introduced the previous September—and late in January a new train, the *Morning Hiawatha,* had entered service. Happily, the North Western's new coaches—as well as the "power cars" from Electro-Motive—were expected by midsummer.

All would be streamlined throughout, the cars embodying the latest advances in exterior design as well as interior lighting, decoration, and appointments. Hundreds of fresh ideas were incorporated so the new *400* would emerge, in the words of one company communication to employees, as the "finest train anywhere." Exceptional imagination, research, care and study by carbuilder, railway, and locomotive manufacturer insured that

All photos, both pages, C&NW

Chosen speedsters for the new 400's were Electro-Motive E3A's. C&NW ordered two pairs, 5001A&B and 5002A&B, but judging by this photo, C&NW may have intended to number each unit separately without suffixes.

the pace-setting example of the original *400* would be continued in the new streamliner.

The diesels—two back-to-back sets of E3A's, each pair rated at 4000 h.p.—arrived before the cars. The first "growler" in *400* passenger service ran from Minneapolis to Chicago on train 400 on Friday, June 2, and, appropriately, arrived in Milwaukee six minutes early, with Ray Sherman at the throttle and the regular seven-car heavyweight consist trailing behind. The E3's were the first non-articulated road diesels in service northwest of Chicago. Delivery in back-to-back, "double-ended" configuration allowed these units in *400* service to routinely return overnight on the *North Western Limited* without wyeing.

Immediately after the introduction of diesels, the heavyweight *400*'s consist was filled out with nonrecliner coaches to ten or eleven cars. Patronage continued to be not only plentiful but prestigious: James Roosevelt, son of President Franklin D. Roosevelt, was photographed beside the illuminated tailsign of train 401, prior to departure from Chicago for Rochester, and the photo captioned, "The Roosevelts are frequent riders of North Western trains."

Mid-September was a joyous time indeed on the North Western, for the first set of new *400* cars—delayed several months by structural changes to make them heavier and stronger—was delivered in Milwaukee (rather than Illinois, for tax reasons) from Pullman-Standard, being taken from Chicago on Friday,

In the streamliner era, every classic train worth its name sported an observation car, and the 400 was no exception. Its creature comforts await travelers at North Western Terminal.

September 15, over the rails of the Milwaukee Road behind a *Hiawatha* engine, a startling combination of motive power and consist. The ten 82-foot-long cars were arranged in what would be standard order: a baggage-taproom-lounge followed by four 56-seat coaches, a 56-seat diner, three 27-seat parlors, and a club-observation car with 12 parlor seats, bar, and lounge.

After making its way to Chicago on its own rails, the streamlined consist on its first outing carried C&NW brass, Chicago Traffic Club members, and newsmen on a round trip to Milwaukee on Monday, September 18. Passengers described the trip as the nearest thing to a ride on a plane—floating and gliding, not swaying and bouncing. The drinks served on board only trembled, never spilling from their glasses.

The general public was impressed, too. With little advance notice of the occasion, thousands gathered along the right-of-way in cities, suburbs, and rural areas alike to watch the demonstration special pass. Eventually, an estimated 100,000 persons would witness the passage of the new train—either from trackside or aboard—when it went on an extended tour through *400* territory. The detailed count of those persons with patience to endure long lines shows that 19,965 toured the cars in Chicago, 16,804 in Milwaukee (where an additional 2,500 who were unable to enter the exhibit viewed the new train from adjacent Juneau Park), 12,278 in Minneapolis, and 9,610 in St. Paul. At each of these cities, the train was exhibited for one day. In briefer enroute

41

stopovers, the totals were 2,124 in two hours at Winona, 4,008 in three hours at Rochester, and 3,808 in two and one-half hours at Mankato (three cities which would be linked with the streamlined *400* only by connection from the *Minnesota 400*); and 3,000 in two hours at on-line Eau Claire.

During the exhibition tour, radio broadcasts were made from the train in Chicago, Rochester, and Eau Claire. Entire school classes were dismissed to watch the train as it passed; its diesels proved the main attraction with the students. The tavern-lunch counter car won particular praise from all who inspected it, and there was great interest in the speedometers in that car and in the solarium, particularly on the Chicago Traffic Club demonstration tour, when the needle climbed beyond 100 mph several times. In St. Paul, a nearly full-page newspaper ad invited local citizens to view the "amazing *400*," which would step into the miles as a champion should.

Tied into the exhibition in Eau Claire was a demonstration trip from the Twin Cities for local government executives and reporters. Two Omaha Road officials—Carl Gray, the innovative vice-president and general manager, and E. L. Pardee, passenger traffic manager—surprised the guests, who expected to board the sparkling streamliner, with a vintage steam-powered train with appointments including potbelly stove, gaslights, and open windows. The old coaches were painted in the traditional North Western yellow and green, which had been revived for the new train.

This nostalgic assemblage was the Omaha Road's Stillwater Lumberjack Train, which ran from the Twin Cities to Stillwater, Minn., for the Lumberjack Festival held there early each September during the late thirties and early forties. Number 136, a 4-4-0 with balloon stack and imitation oil headlight, pulled the yellow-and-green coaches, which were lettered for the Chicago, St. Paul, Minneapolis & Omaha. All were pre-1900 open-platform stock, with the baggage car and business car coming from the West Wisconsin Railroad, an 1870s predecessor of the Omaha.

Dorothy Whitt, *400* stewardess, was aboard, suitably attired in hoop-skirt gown and bonnet. At Hudson, Wis., after the party had transferred to the streamliner, she changed into modern uniform in the special compartment provided for stewardesses on the new *400*. Guests lunched on cold turkey or roast beef, potato salad, and apple pie a la mode during the run to Eau Claire, made at "somewhat reduced speeds," 80 mph being the maximum. There, approximately a thousand persons had to be turned away disappointed from the new *400* because host Omaha Railway simply ran out of exhibition time.

The streamlined *400* entered regular service on September 24, 1939. Pullman-Standard considered it to be the finest train to have rolled from its shops; according to one executive, "We shot the

Train 400 departs Minneapolis over the Mississippi River on the James J. Hill Bridge circa 1940. By 1982, the stone arch monument to the great rail empire builder of the Northwest no longer saw traffic.

C&NW

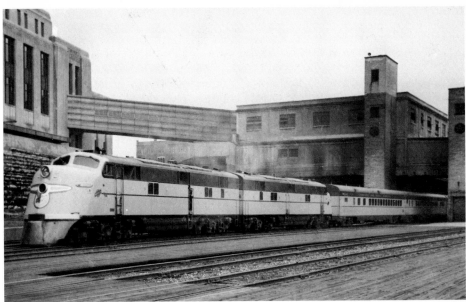

(Above) A rush of exhaust indicates that train 400 is beginning its trip to Chicago out of Great Northern's Minneapolis depot, a station C&NW also shared with Northern Pacific, Burlington, Chicago Great Western and Minneapolis & St. Louis. (Below) CStPM&O's promotion of the 400 in 1939 featured 4-4-0 No. 136 and 19th century rolling stock, shown here backing into St. Paul Union Depot in September 1939.

Both photos, collection of Alden E. Miller

works on this train and we are mighty, mighty proud of it." R. L. Williams, North Western's chief executive officer, boasted that the new *400* contained everything to a superlative degree: smoothness, swiftness, sleekness, and aesthetic delight in the interior and exterior colors. The comfort provided by the furnishings and illumination was the result of months of painstaking selection of fabrics, leathers, fixtures, and wall colors, during which time myriad combinations of hues, designs, and lighting effects were considered until a perfect harmony was achieved. Appealing aesthetic innovations included sepia-tint murals in tavern and parlor cars. The most modern mechanical devices were sought to produce the ultimate in riding quality and safety.

In the forward portion of the lead car, the tavern-lunch counter-lounge, was a 12-foot baggage room; its side doors, when fully closed, were flush with the exterior walls of the car. Immediately behind the baggageman's domain were the men's and women's toilets, then the taproom (sometimes referred to as the Rathskeller, in the best German-influenced Milwaukee beer-drinking tradition), the service area, the lunch counter, and the lounge. In the taproom or tavern were two booths for four on each side of the aisle. Their rectangular tables had tops of tan linen-finish formica with red-and-blue inlays, while their bench-type seats were upholstered in blue tufted leather with chrome buttons. Walls were natural cork, with photo murals of sporting and outdoor scenes above the windows, which were in line with the tables. There were both peach-colored venetian blinds and rust-colored drapes with horizontal yellow, blue, and brown stripes. Between the windows were large round mirrors.

The ceiling, of light peach hue, was low on the sides and higher in the center, approximating the design of the traditional clerestory. At the end toward the bar, mirrors extended from the ceiling to the seat backs. Pairs of round incandescent lighting fixtures were partially recessed into the lower portion of the ceiling over each booth, and identical fixtures were centered in the ceiling. Four more fixtures of the same style followed the curve of the bar, while three smaller lamps illuminated the back bar. Above the bar was the attention-getting speedometer.

From its blue linen-finish formica top to the footrail, the bar was fronted with red tufted leather. The back bar was lined with mirrors, which lent an illusion of increased length to the taproom. The aisle connecting the taproom with the lunch counter ran past the kitchen on the car's left. There were windows along the exterior of the aisle and a mirror on the bulkhead at its forward end.

The lunch counter ran lengthwise through the next section of the car. Three large circular mirrors were on the exterior wall above the back counter, and the wall at the kitchen end of the

room had mirrors between counter top and ceiling. (Here and throughout the train, flesh-colored mirrors were used to give a warm glow to the interiors.) Ten stools, upholstered in red leather with aluminum-edged backs, lined the counter. The ceiling in the lunch room was flat, with overhead lighting fixtures placed congruent to the shape of the counter and a pair of additional fixtures illuminating the back counter. The top of the counter protruded; under it was a shelf for gloves and purses. Above a solid footrest, the side of the counter was red leather, flat rather than tufted, and enhanced by four chrome stripes.

Dividers, identical to those between booths and bar, separated the lunch room from the lounge which completed the car's configuration. The lounge had the same clerestory-style ceiling as did the tavern and similar large square mirrors covering the upper two-thirds of its bulkheads. Photo murals above the windows depicted on-route cities, those on the left showing Milwaukee, St. Paul, and Chicago and those on the right Minneapolis, Chicago, and St. Paul. Like those in the taproom, the lounge windows had blinds; since they were less widely spaced, they were set off by drapes instead of mirrors.

Five lounge chairs upholstered in tweed of contrasting blue and coral colors stood on each side of the aisle, with their backs to the windows. The lounge and taproom shared carpeting in a brown and beige leaf motif, while the bar and lunch counter were floored in terra-cotta rubber tile with blue and cream inlays. There was a radio in the lounge. This pair of cars—Nos. 7500 and 7501—weighed more than any others in the train but the diner.

Next in line were four coaches, the first of which contained a stewardess's room adjacent to its smoking lounge, which reduced its seating capacity from 56 to 48. (In the descriptions which follow, the vestibule end will be considered the forward end, though C&NW most often ran its cars with vestibule ends together.) Just inside the vestibule, the men's toilet and the baggage shelves were on the right and the ladies' toilet and powder room on the left. The main section of each car except the one with the stewardess's room contained 56 reclining seats, the first four of which rode backward against the front bulkhead. The seats had curved chrome armrests, amply cushioned on the top and supported by two vertical bars. Footrests were fixed tubular bars an inch or two above the floor. At the rear of the coach was the smoking room; its availability to both sexes was emphasized.

Seats in particular coaches were upholstered in either blue, green, or beige, establishing the basic color for that car. A car with green seats, for example, had floor, walls, and ceiling of corresponding hues. Pier panels between windows and the bulkheads at the ends of the main section of the car were brown leather, with pairs of horizontal gold stripes near top and bottom. Window frames were dull chrome, and the windows had cloth

The lead cars of regular 400 consists were the versatile baggage-tavern-lunch counter-lounges. (Above) Attendants await 400 travelers behind the lunch counter, as viewed from the lounge area. (Above right) The taproom, or Rathskeller, was located behind the 12-foot baggage compartment which (right) is about to be loaded as 401 pauses at Milwaukee in 1943.

Clayton C. Tinkham

All photos, both pages, C&NW

46

(Facing page, top) Coach 3431 was a 56-seater built by Pullman-Standard for the 1946 re-equipping of the Twin Cities 400 and was typical of coaches used on pre-bilevel 400's. Even today the car would look quite modern, unlike the automobile nearby. C&NW's P-S cars were cooled by Waukesha air-conditioners (above). Stewardess Dorothy Whitt (facing page) is tending to the travel needs of customers in a 1939-built 400 coach. Every coach featured a smoking room, a nice touch considering that most designated smoking areas during this period were usually lounge cars or "smokers." (Right) Even stepboxes proclaim the name of North Western's fleet as an Omaha Road conductor (note the OMAHA embroidered on his lapel) assists a young traveler aboard the 400.

48

Diners on the 400 contained 14 tables for four persons each, and were staffed by seven waiters, each concentrating their service on only a pair of tables. The diner at left was built for the 1942 re-equipping of the Twin Cities 400. Interiors were bright and cheery.

C&NW

CHICAGO AND NORTH WESTERN LINE

The "400" Dinner $1.50

Dinner $1.00

Collection of William Stauss

The 400 dinner menu from August 1942 featured a painting of the 400's meeting at Adams, Wis. Inside, a complete Lake Michigan trout or prime rib dinner could be obtained for $1.50; cocktails, 40 cents extra. For the economy-minded, corned beef and cabbage or a fresh peach omelette was offered, complete, for $1. For the opulent, a sirloin steak dinner was available for $2. During C&NW's centennial year, 1948, 400 dining cars sported tablecloths that illustrated the road's famed 4-2-0, the Pioneer. (Right) Apparently the lovely dinner customer was pleased to discover that C&NW had the same good taste in material as she did.

C&NW

Parlor 6514 (interior) was built for general 400 service in 1947; parlor 6507 was built for the 1942 Twin Cities 400.

(Left) Train 401 approaches BA tower in Milwaukee, probably around 1940. In the eleven months ending in August 1940, trains 400 and 401 carried over 200,000 passengers, while earning a healthy profit. (Below) In its twilight years, the Twin Cities 400 is Minneapolis-bound west of Marcy Junction, Wis. Date: July 21, 1962.

Jim Scribbins

shades. Throughout the train, all windows had glass of a moderate green tint to reduce the sun's glare.

At window tops, above the leather bulkhead panels, and surrounding all archways and decorative mirrors were strips of corrugated aluminum, a treatment applied nearly everywhere throughout the train. Chrome open-style luggage racks ran the length of the car. The thicker supporting members of these structures housed incandescent lights behind magnifying lenses in white plastic rectangles—one above each seat, with switches for individual control. Larger incandescent fixtures were spaced above the aisle so each would shine on two rows of seats.

The smoking room, at the right rear of the coach, had a row of three seats at each crosswise wall and two more seats against the exterior wall. In the transverse walls, large round windows, centered on the aisle through the main section of the coach, provided an unobstructed view from the entry door at the "blind" (non-vestibule) end of the car through the smoking room into the main seating section.

There were round mirrors between those windows and the exterior wall of the room and round windows flanking the door to the aisle. Ceiling lights were of the same type used in the bar and lunch counter. The outside windows had shades and were set off with drapes. The floor of the smoking room was carpeted in the same leafy pattern used throughout the new *400*, while the remaining coach floor-coverings were marbleized rubber tiling in the color determined by the seats, with harmonized inlays.

The diners, cars 6950 and 6951, were normally operated with their kitchen ends forward, adjacent to the coaches. The car's dining room contained 14 tables for four persons each—a total capacity of 56, among the largest ever for self-contained single-unit food-service cars. Seven waiters staffed the rolling restaurants, each serving a pair of tables.

Chairs had gracefully rounded backs and aluminum frames. Sixteen were covered in green leather and the remaining 40 in red, and they were scattered about the room to achieve a mixture of color. Combinations of burgundy and coral, carried even to the carpet, made the diners sparkle. Windows were covered with peach-colored blinds and edged with rose drapes. The wall space between windows was filled with vertical rectangular mirrors. Lighting fixtures were artfully concealed behind four chrome strips which ran the full length of the dining room above the windows. They illuminated the tables and also bounced light against the ceiling, more gracefully curved than those in the coaches and parlors. Oversized mirrors, contoured at top to match the curve of the ceiling, were attached to the bulkheads. A double row of incandescent fixtures lined the ceiling above the aisle. Special china, rimmed with lines of coral and gold, was designed for the new *400* by Pullman-Standard. Dinner ambiance was further enhanced by a concert of symphonic selections, played over a special sound system, the speaker for which was over the rear door and had a "400" design in its center.

Behind the diner were three parlor cars, each decorated in a different color—blue, green, or yellow. At the forward or vestibule end were the women's toilet and powder room on the left and the baggage shelves and men's toilet on the right. The body of the car contained 22 fully rotating, reclining chairs, their upholstery a light horizontal weave. Aluminum armrests were upholstered in solid colors.

As in the coaches, window posts were covered with tooled leather. On the bulkheads were large golden-toned photo murals of outdoor scenes of the Wisconsin vacation country. Luggage racks and lighting were as in the coaches. To the rear of the main section of each parlor car was a drawing room, furnished with a sofa and an individual chair. Beyond the drawing room was a smoking room of the same type as in the coaches.

The parlor cars were carpeted throughout. Numbers 6500 and 6503 had blue as their basic color, 6501 and 6504 green, and 6502 and 6505 yellow. The main room and drawing room had window shades, the smoker shades and drapes. The drawing room and smoker were on the right side of the car.

Carrying the markers were parlor-bar-observations 7200 and 7201; without question, the most distinctive cars in *400* service, not duplicated in subsequent expansions of the fleet. Immediately behind the vestibule was a 12-seat parlor section, differing from the full parlors in that it did not contain a powder room and had a luggage rack at the rear of the section. In decorative scheme it was similar to the full parlors: two-tone blue carpet, tan walls, cream ceiling, upholstery of apricot herringbone weave, and tooled leather piers between the windows. In lieu of a powder room, a large round mirror was attached to the forward wall of the service room at the rear of the revenue accommodation area. Cabinets for air conditioning and electrical controls, normally at the car ends, and a linen locker were placed in this same area.

The car's two main rooms were separated by the bar service compartment, which had a stand-up bar—similar to those in some of the *City* trains' lounges—on its lounge side. Centered above was a radio speaker, which bore the name of the train in its grille. On each side to the rear of the bar were three lounge chairs, a booth seating four, then three more lounge chairs. All dozen lounge chairs had their backs to the windows. The extreme rear portion of the car was separated from the main lounge by waist-high solid dividers, from which five chrome bars extended to the ceiling. Seating in this tail-end solarium included a sofa for three facing its rear window, backed by a magazine rack with a table lamp.

Below the windows, the wall of the lounge was tan; above, it

was natural cork. Blinds were suntan and drapes were a dark pattern on medium tan. Carpeting was of the same two-tone blue pattern used elsewhere in the train. Directly above the rear center window was a speedometer, with figures large enough to be read from any place in the lounge. The blue ceiling of the lounge was shaped and lighted as the tavern. In both cars, buttons at each seat activated three-note chimes to summon waiters.

The exterior of the solarium was distinctly round rather than teardrop. The rear of the roof had a unique flange treatment both above the windows and at the top of its curve, a detail which appeared on no other observation cars. A rectangle below the rear window displayed the speedster's name, an illuminated recognition which the competing *Hiawathas* never boasted.

Though it was first thought that the new *400*'s would appear in the brown and yellow of the *City* Streamliners, when the lightweight versions of 400 and 401 actually emerged they wore North Western's own yellow with green trim. C&NW had used bright yellow as the basic color for its passenger equipment before the turn of the century. However, the 1896 version of the *North Western Limited* appeared in Pullman green, introducing a somber aesthetic to all the railways' passenger cars. In 1912 the *Limited* again appeared in green and yellow, and in 1928, the train once more wore the standard green livery of the giant sleeping-car operator. But by 1937 at least some of the pre-depression lightweight suburban cars had been painted in yellow with green letterboard and doors, as had the Omaha Road's *Namekagon* motor train between Ashland, Wis., and the Twin Cities. These may have been the quiet precedents for the streamlined *400*'s color scheme.

On the cars of the new *400*, roofs were black, except for the flange on the solarium, which was green. At the very top of the car sides was a thin black stripe marking the edge of the roof contour. The green letterboard, with CHICAGO AND NORTH WESTERN centered in silver, was edged at the bottom in black. Car sides were bright yellow, a shade with less red in it than the yellow used by the Union Pacific. The eminent rail historian Edward Hungerford once referred to it as "English coach yellow." Another thin black stripe separated the flanks from the skirts, which were green. A fourth black line ran slightly below the windows, approximately midway between the lower edge of the letterboard and the floor of the car. On the lower half of the car sides, in silver, were the car number over each truck and a central "400" design, which

The Twin Cities 400 *looks valiant and modern as it streaks past Canal tower in Evanston, Ill., clearly superior to the postwar automobiles in terms of speed, design and luxury.*   C&NW

Parlor-bar-observations 7200 (interior) and 7201 (exterior) remained in Twin Cities 400 service right to the end. Their unusual rooflines and bluntly rounded ends—versus the more-tapered round ends of subsequent Pullman-Standard tail cars—made them a unique set of observation cars. The interior view was photographed in 1963, well after both cars had been rebuilt into parlor-solariums.

Jim Scribbins

400

7201

CHICAGO AND NORTH WESTERN

(Below) C&NW's Chicago coach yard plays host to other notable trains and observation cars of the time. From left to right, the City of San Francisco, the original City of Los Angeles, the City of Denver and the 400. (Bottom) An early overhead view of a 400 obs indicates that the cars were delivered sans Mars lights. (Right) Car 7200 brings up the rear of 401 at Milwaukee on June 8, 1947. The rear windows and drumhead were washed regularly at Milwaukee.

Both photos, C&NW

Jim Scribbins

incorporated speed lines like those often drawn into passenger-train publicity photos. Trucks and underbody were black.

To maintain the uniform contour of the train, vestibules had foldaway steps, which in their closed position extended the skirting to the very end of the cars. Wide diaphragms between cars further assured the unbroken appearance of both livery and shape. In the yellow areas, grab irons and other protrusions from the car sides were of stainless steel; along the skirts they were green, and on the roof black. Dutch doors in all vestibules allowed the crew to inspect their train and watch train-order signals.

Graceful built-in markers were applied to the rear of observations 7200 and 7201 and to the forward end of cars 7500 and 7501, the baggage-tavern-counter lounges. The electric lamps on these lead cars were necessary because at St. Paul Union Depot the diesels would run around the train and pull it backward to Minneapolis, eliminating the need for wyeing. In steam days, the *400*'s E-2-a Pacific would be cut off, quickly turned on the Union Depot turntable, and attached to the solarium *Odin* or *Viking* to continue over the Great Northern to Minneapolis. An incidental benefit of this procedure was the elimination of a switching move in Minneapolis to line the train for its return trip to Chicago. With both steam and diesel locomotives the eastbound *400* was tail-hosed by the conductor for a back-up move between GN's Westminster Street tower and St. Paul Union Depot, resulting in its being properly pointed for the move to the Omaha connection at Westminster Street.

Much attention was paid to the streamlined *400*'s truck design. Though something of which the average traveler might not be consciously aware, it was instrumental in providing a smooth trip, thus enhancing the train's reputation. In place of the more common elliptical bolster springs, helical springs were used in combination with shock absorbers and stabilizer rods; this produced a more rapid response, greatly lessening the effect of the load variation which the shocks routinely encountered. Rubber bumpers on the bolsters softened extreme lateral motion. Diner trucks were also given stabilizing levers to maintain level bolsters on curves and thus preserve the equilibrium of the tables in the restaurant. Patrons found the *400*'s ride always smooth, but with a rather pleasant, gently rocking motion, not unlike being aboard a small boat floating on the ripples of a calm lake.

The four E3A's holding down the head end were decorated as were the *400*'s cars, though the top green stripe was wider,

Both photos, Jim Scribbins

The *Twin Cities 400 briefly interrupts the peace of the Neenah River west of Oxford, Wis., on June 3, 1961. This day's consist includes an RPO-lounge from one of the smaller 400 trainsets; 400 and 401 never had working RPO's.*

extending to the lower edge of the grilles and the side cab windows. It was edged with a thin black stripe, as were the letterboards of the cars; a similar black stripe edged the floorline of the units. Fuel and water tanks and the pilot were painted green. Trucks were black, as were the buffers immediately above the drawbars, but the anti-climb bumpers on either side were silver. The units shared a distinctive coupler housing with Seaboard Railroad E4's. A middle black stripe edged the bottom of the motor room windows, making it somewhat higher than its continuation on the passenger cars, though this was not aesthetically displeasing.

At the nose end of these stripes, on each side, was affixed the railway's emblem, which at that time read CHICAGO AND NORTH WESTERN LINE. The lower portion of the carbody sides were lettered, in silver, CHICAGO AND NORTH WESTERN. Classification lights were mounted on the side of the nose in the standard pre-World War II EMD manner, but the spaces in their housings normally used to display glass number plates were solid metal because it was a C&NW peculiarity not to display illuminated numbers on its locomotives. The huge expanse of yellow nose was artfully relieved by a wing design surrounding the headlight, with its lower outline dropped around a larger version of the railway's herald. (Though timetable art often showed a "400" embossed on each side of the E's prow, this was artistic license only and never actually appeared on the locomotives.)

Chicago & North Western engine crews took considerable pride in these diesels. To show it, they dressed in white coveralls, emphasizing the cleanliness of the new motive power, and wore small "400" pins on their cap fronts. The tradition of wearing white lingered until after World War II.

In its first month of operation, the re-equipped train made a tremendous impression. People traveled on it simply for the experience, and train-watchers by the hundreds observed its passing. As was commonly the case when new trains were introduced, two special demonstration trips to show off the streamlined *400* were operated for passenger department employees of connecting railroads. On Sunday, October 22, some 300 persons rode the new *400* consist between Chicago and St. Francis Tower in Milwaukee, where the train was wyed for the return; they also received the additional treat of a dinner in the station restaurant once back in Chicago. Aboard the special were a high-powered group of hosts: Trustee Charles M. Thompson, Chief Executive Officer R. L. Williams, Chief Traffic Officer F. G. Fitz-Patrick, General Manager H. M. Eicholtz, Traffic Manager Allen Gould and Passenger Traffic Manager Robert Thompson. Five weeks later another 450 guests enjoyed an identical trip.

Evidence of the drawing power of the re-equipped train was that in its first month, 12,186 passengers were handled to and from

Chicago, compared to 8,047 for the same time a year earlier. On November 5, Evanston was added as a stop to receive passengers on the outbound and discharge on the inbound journey; at the time the community was a focal point for the wealthy North Shore suburbs. Total C&NW passenger revenue in 1939 increased 2.1 percent over 1938, attributable in part to the new diesel streamliner.

Christmas holiday traffic boomed. Second and third sections of 400 and 401 operated on December 22 and 23, and second sections on Christmas Day. In all cases the extra sections were, of course, conventional steam-powered trains. On December 22 there would have been a fourth section of 401 originating in Milwaukee had not potential riders insisted on boarding the regular streamlined train, seats or not. One of the steam-powered "sections" was actually operating in advance of the regular train (as a passenger extra, technically), but prospective travelers in Milwaukee refused to board it. Therefore, when the streamliner—which had arrived with 477 through riders against a capacity of 503—stormed up the hill through Lake Park away from Milwaukee's Wisconsin Avenue passenger station, it was jammed with 662 patrons.

On January 28, 1941, when Burlington reduced the running time of its *Twin Zephyrs* because of track improvements through LaCrosse, Wis., and Milwaukee Road trimmed the times of three of its four *Hiawathas,* the North Western likewise improved the running time of the *400*'s by 15 minutes. Departures from Chicago, Minneapolis, and St. Paul remained 3 p.m., 2:30 p.m. and 3 p.m. respectively and arrivals at opposite terminals were earlier.

Good public relations were a continual priority. The *400* received exposure in spring 1941 when Sam Campbell, "the philosopher of the forest," presented a series of lectures in the dining room of North Western Station, and attendees were invited to inspect train 401, which was backed in early for that purpose. On another occasion, second grade pupils of Roosevelt School, River Forest, inspected 401 as part of their tour of the Chicago passenger terminal. Earlier, a group of junior-high students from Muncie, Ind., had toured the train while on a trip to Chicago—a good example of the attraction of streamlined trains during that era. On Mother's Day, all women passengers on the *400*—as on all principal C&NW trains—received roses.

As expected, the streamlined *400* continued to rack up improved passenger counts over its conventional predecessor. During the train's first four months in yellow and green, the number of riders increased by 51 percent—56 percent in January. That rate of increase rose slightly in February and again in March. During the five-month period from October 1, 1938, through February 1939, revenues totaled $301,901; for the same period a year later, under streamlined operation, they were $458,563.

Inevitably, the initial enthusiasm for the yellow-and-green speedster crested and then receded slightly, but during the 11 months ending August 1940, trains 400 and 401 carried well over 200,000 passengers, a highly respectable increase of 46 percent over that period the preceding year, with heavyweight operation. Based on earnings grossing over $1 million with a net of approximately $600,000 for the streamliner's first 12 months, C&NW estimated that the cost of the new equipment would be paid off within the next three years.

(Above) On a bitter cold February 7, 1959, the Twin Cities 400 ruffles the snow west of Butler, Wis. On another frigid day, January 26, 1943, a double-headed treat of Omaha 4-4-2 No. 365 and 4-6-2 No. 515 (above right) substitutes for E6's on 400 at Eau Claire. Temperature: 20 degrees below zero. (Right) The Twin Cities 400 slides by Great Northern's St. Anthony tower in Minneapolis in a dreary winter setting all too familiar to Midwesterners.

In this postwar scene at Chicago & North Western's lakefront station at Milwaukee, twin E7's accelerate train 401 away from a setting that reflected more peaceful times. Today, the splendid brick depot and Lincoln Memorial Drive bridge have been razed, the tracks replaced by a roadway, and the Twin Cities 400 long since dropped from the Official Guide of the Railways.

C&NW

It's 1939 and North Western's new streamlined consist for the 400 is on display at Milwaukee (above), an event attracting nearly 20,000 people. (Right) Two youngsters are treated to an impressive sight as they witness 401 accelerating upgrade out of Milwaukee on a brisk day in 1940. Much of the lakefront trackage north of the depot site today is a biking path. (Facing page, lower) On Christmas Eve day 1957, 401 departs Milwaukee with observation car 7200 bringing up the markers. (Facing page, upper) EMD E6 5006 was a regular on trains 401 and 406 (North Western Limited) during World War II and thereafter. Here, it leads a consist through the pleasant northern suburbs of Milwaukee.

Both photos, Chappie Fox

63

Mike Schafer

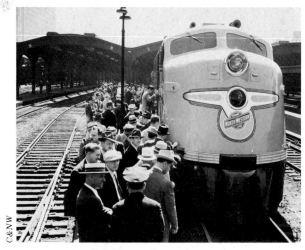

C&NW

(Top) "Home" for the 400's and their nameless descendants until the end of all C&NW intercity service on April 30, 1971, was Chicago & North Western Terminal in Chicago. In 1939, crowds eagerly waited to tour an exhibition 400 (above) on display at the terminal. Straw hats were in; obviously so were new streamliners. In Chicago, 19,965 persons toured the display 400. Years later, the train was still providing daily service from North Western Terminal (both photos, right).

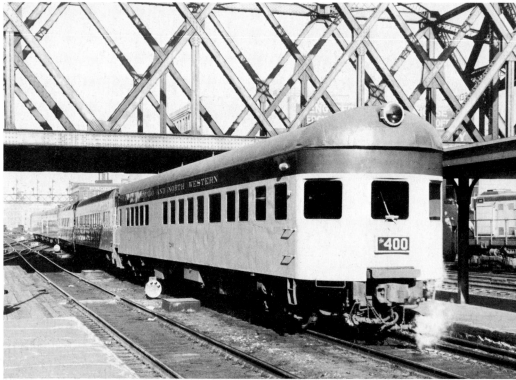

Both photos, James R. Wozniczka

In this north-by-northwest view from a Chicago skyscraper sometime during the 1950's, we see the equipment for 401 being backed through the terminal's six-track throat; just ahead of 401's locomotives is the junction between C&NW's Omaha line and the lines to Milwaukee and Madison (which split at Clybourn, beyond the perimeter of the photo). The junction is controlled by Clinton Street tower, to the right of the E units. In the foreground is the Lake Street 'L'.

C&NW

On September 24, 1940, to mark the *400*'s first year as a streamliner, a birthday cake was shown at Madison Street Station in Chicago. Passengers on the *400* received individual cakes, and a cake and ice cream party was given in Chicago for employees' sons celebrating their first birthdays that month. Christmas season 1940 saw a 13 percent increase in travel by the third week in December; the increase continued, and 16 extra sections of the *400*'s were operated between December 20 and 27.

Among both young and old, employee interest in the streamliners remained high. Wayne Norris, a young employee in the freight department in Milwaukee scratchbuilt an HO model of the streamlined *400*, which would be part of the North Western's display at the San Francisco Golden Gate Exposition. Charles E. Van Vlack, a former locomotive engineer who at age 95 was the oldest retired employee to attend the C&NW's Veterans Association annual banquet, received as part of his visit an inspection of train 401—his first time in a diesel cab.

A gracious and compassionate act on the North Western's part was to make special arrangements for 30 youngsters from Spaulding School for Crippled Children to tour 401, which was backed down a full hour earlier than usual for that purpose. Railway employees, including trained nurses, assisted the handicapped students through the train and were their hosts in the diner for an ice-cream treat. Even Trustee Charles M. Thompson was present for the occasion. Later, the children were on the platform beside the E3's to hear them dig in and to watch the *400*'s departure as the climax of their visit.

In September 1941, the American Legion national convention took place in Milwaukee, and the National Commander rode 401 to the convention city, as did many other Legionnaires. Additional tracks were constructed just outside the newly renovated lakefront station for spotting Pullmans to house delegates, and special round trips were operated each day for Chicago-area conventioneers. As part of the program, Legion Auxiliary members comprising the "400 Glee Club" won the championship for the third year. Wearing uniforms similar to those of the *400* stewardesses, they began broadcasting in December from Mankato, Rochester, and St. Paul.

On the second anniversary of the streamlined *400*, C&NW announced that during August 1941, 400 and 401 had carried more passengers than in any previous month, notching a 12 percent increase over August 1940, and that nearly a half million travelers had ridden during the two years of streamlining—58 percent higher loadings than for the last two years of standard steam operation. (Earlier that season, Independence Day traffic had been up 42 percent, mandating a second section.) As on the train's first birthday, a youngster was used to spotlight the occasion. Winston Forest Hoyt celebrated his own second

birthday as well as the train's by donning an engineer's outfit to pose—with an oil can as tall as he—seated on the pilot of 401's lead E3 before departure from Chicago.

In 1941, revenue of the *400* increased 14.8 percent over 1940, contributing to a systemwide passenger revenue increase for 1941 of $1,288,080. For the period from August 1940 through July 1941, 400 and 401 carried over 240,000 passengers, averaging 330 per trip, and yielding revenues of $3.72 per train-mile.

Then in December 1941, the attack on Pearl Harbor plunged the United States into World War II—and thereby caused all railroad passenger travel to increase tremendously. No longer was it a matter of encouraging the public to travel by rail; suddenly it became an urgent necessity to handle massive troop travel expeditiously and still find room for the unprecedented civilian ridership. At times train travel nationwide would become rather unpleasant. However, though the *400* was crowded and there were usually lines for the diner, the train operated throughout the war with no downgrading of its equipment.

In January 1942, new equipment was delivered to expand the *400* concept into a fleet of trains; some of these new coaches were placed on trains 400 and 401, which from that time on were called the *Twin Cities 400*. In the process, the consist was altered to include five coaches instead of four, while one parlor was withdrawn, thus holding the number of cars to ten. Also at this time, two new diners fresh from Pullman-Standard were traded into the consists of the flagships, 400 and 401. Soon thereafter a sixth coach was added, and 11-car trains became the norm. The displaced coaches, diners, and parlors from the 1939 *400* were distributed among the smaller *400* trains introduced with the new year. This partial re-equipping of the *Twin Cities 400* was done without publicity. The only change which might have been noticed by the habitué was the use of adjustable footrests in the newer cars instead of fixed metal bars.

In January of 1942, "Suburban Hour," a WMAQ program of some five years' standing sponsored by North Western, was renamed the "400 Hour" to honor the new fleet. This popular program, with Norman Ross or Pat Gallicchio emceeing throughout, lasted until 1955.

In the spirit of patriotism appropriate to the time, two C&NW coaches were specially painted with red roof, white upper sides, and blue sides below the windows. Coach 3420 was lettered "Fly for Navy" above its windows, with large wings below and other insignia on the side of the car. Car 3429, lettered "Be an Army Flyer," carried a painting of a Flying Fortress below its windows. After being dedicated in Chicago by military and railroad personnel, the pair entered service on 400 and 401.

On December 6, 1942, to reduce wear and tear on equipment, schedules of fast trains throughout the country were slightly lengthened on the instructions of the Office of Defense Transportation;400 and 401 suffered a 15-minute addition in running time, as did their competitiors. Departures from Chicago and Minneapolis were placed a quarter-hour earlier, and arrivals at final terminals remained unchanged.

During the war years, C&NW published a series of ads featuring its employees and emphasizing the railway's war efforts; the ads also mentioned pictured employees' sons who were in military service. One ad featured Pat Keefe, a dispatcher at Adams, and mentioned the *Twin Cities 400* meet there; a sketch showed one side's diesels beside the other's observation.

Despite the war, a substantial grade-crossing elimination project was completed in Winnetka, Ill., in 1943, where the paralleling tracks of the North Western and Chicago North Shore and Milwaukee were, for most of a 3½-mile stretch, depressed into a cut beneath overhead street bridges. Ten grade crossings were removed, taking strain off of engine crews and motorists alike.

In May 1944, growing confidence about the outcome of the war allowed Americans to begin considering postwar civilian improvements. In Chicago's North Western Station, therefore, C&NW extended its cooperation to Harvard University and seat manufacturer Heywood-Wakefield by inviting travelers to sit in a special adjustable chair used to measure occupants, as the first step in designing a coach seat that would be comfortable to 80 percent of the public. This led to the "Sleepy Hollow" seat—"the coach seat which went to college." Though C&NW never used these seats in its *400* cars, they did appear in the postwar *City Streamliners* and in three Chesapeake & Ohio coaches acquired in the 1950s by North Western, and a number of other roads acquired coaches equipped with Sleepy Hollow recliners.

On January 2, 1945, the *400* marked its 10th anniversary. Yellow roses, symbolizing the train's color, were presented to all women passengers on board that day. A brochure published for the occasion reflected on how the original heavyweight train had "set the pace for the world," how the yellow-and-green streamliner had become the talk of the nation, and how the *400* would carry on to the best of North Western's ability. The brochure's cover showed the streamliner circling the top of a birthday cake with ten candles.

Despite the pressures of too-lengthy passenger lists during the war, the crews took pride in the *400* and did their best to be helpful. A Montreal businessman appreciated how brakeman Earl Yates explained the details of the train. Steward Pete Kromy was often complimented on his cordial treatment of dinner guests.

Great Lakes Naval Training Station and Hospital straddles the C&NW main line south of Waukegan, and thousands of recruits observed the passage of the trains. Many of them traveled to and from their Wisconsin, Upper Michigan, and Minnesota homes on

the *400*'s. In the closing months of World War II, a friendly argument developed between two hospital patients concerning the color and locomotive type of the *400*, and before long the question was being debated throughout the ward. The dispute was settled when President R. L. Williams of the North Western sent a large color picture of the streamliner to be hung at the hospital.

On March 7, 1946, a small ceremony was held at lakefront station in Milwaukee. In the presence of C&NW president Williams and John Bohn, mayor of Milwaukee, Miss Ruth Vogt of the Milwaukee Association of Commerce christened the first of 20 new coaches—with a bottle of beer, naturally. The newest *400* coach was also the first passenger car delivered to any Western railroad after the end of the war. The coach entered service immediately, and as subsequent cars in the order were delivered they were placed in *Twin Cities 400* consists, enabling earlier *400* coaches to be distributed to other members of the fleet. Once again, the flagship train received a partial—and in this case final, as it would turn out—upgrading of equipment in a quiet unremarked manner. The price tag was $74,000 per coach.

In the immediate postwar era, 400 and 401 ran with their lengthiest regular consists ever, trailing 13 cars behind their twin E's. These additional coaches helped meet the increased travel demands of a public as yet unable to acquire automobiles with its new affluence but still determined to heed its growing wanderlust. The train remained an alternative for which no one needed to apologize.

With the *Twin Cities 400* whizzing along at 95 mph over the Adams Cutoff, that community among others continued to take great pride in the streamliner. In fact, the railway furnished a cut of the 400 for use on the Adams Chamber of Commerce stationery.

Prewar scheduling was reintroduced for train 401 only on June 29, 1947, with Chicago departure time remaining at 2:45 p.m. but arrival in St. Paul and Minneapolis being 15 minutes earlier, 9 p.m. and 9:30 p.m. (On this same date, incidentally, the *Olympian Hiawatha* to Seattle was introduced on the paralleling Milwaukee Road.) On December 14, train 400 also received its prewar running time of 6 hours and 45 minutes. Then, on September 26, 1948, both trains were retimed to depart from Chicago and St. Paul at the traditional 3 p.m.

At about this time, a problem arose which threatened not only the *Twin Cities 400* but all of the fast trains in Wisconsin. An unenforced, virtually forgotten law enacted in 1898 limited train speeds over street crossings in incorporated municipalities to 15 to 30 mph, depending upon circumstances. Ironically, after 14 years of extremely high-speed yet safe *400* operation, pressure built for the enforcement of this law to the letter. Speaking before the Technical Society of Madison, Frank V. Koval of North Western's public relations department indicated the damage enforcement

A. Robert Johnson

Along the route of the 400: (Above) A heavyweight business car at the head end of train 401 contrasts with the streamlined Twin Cities 400 consist pausing at Eau Claire, Wis., on August 20, 1960. (Right) An E8-E6 team eases a nine-car train 400 into Hudson, Wis., after leaving Minnesota over the St. Croix River bridge.

C&NW

would do to the schedules of 400 and 401: an addition of 2 hours and 15 minutes. Fortunately, the misguided crusade was abandoned.

On September 23, 1949, the *Twin Cities 400* began stopping at the small community of Merrillan, Wis., thanks to the work of several civic groups. The stop served not only this town, junction point with C&NW's line from Marshfield and Wausau, but also the entire surrounding area, including Neillsville and Black River Falls. Bands, Indians, and flowers greeted train 400, the first to make the stop. A floral piece approximately eight feet square—with yellow flowers forming a "400" against a background of green ferns—dominated the scene. Some 2000 people were on hand to watch the E6 on the point break a ribbon held across the track. Railway and village officials spoke, and the National Guard paraded. Guests of honor were Mr. and Mrs. John Clune. Clune at 91 was the oldest living Omaha Railway engineer; he

had retired in 1926, well before the advent of the *400*.

In time for Christmas of 1949, Varney, a now-defunct manufacturer of model railroad equipment, introduced diesel units, coaches and observation cars painted in *400* colors. Over the years, other model railroad manufacturers followed suit, and model C&NW streamline passenger cars were commercially available into the 1980s.

Effective April 30, 1950, train 400 was rescheduled to depart from Minneapolis at 12:01 p.m., St. Paul at 12:30 p.m., and Milwaukee at 5:30 p.m., arriving in Chicago at 6:45 p.m. This change provided a direct connection at Wyeville to and from train 518, which on that date became the *Dakota 400*. A subsidiary benefit was to afford a Chicago connection with the California streamliners. Number 401's times remained unchanged, except that Wyeville was discontinued as a stop since the westbound *Dakota 400*, train 519, did not operate via Wyeville anyway.

The Dakota 400 from Chicago has backed into Wyeville station and is ready to receive transfers—generally Milwaukee-originating passengers—from the Twin Cities 400, diverging from the Adams cutoff to head up the Madison-Twin Cities main. Date: March 24, 1958.

William D. Middleton

All photos, unless otherwise credited, Jim Scribb

A respectable amount of business awaits 401 as it rolls into South Beaver Dam, Wis., (left) on a sunny April 4, 1961. A pair of E7's are in charge. (Above) Railfans at a Milwaukee National Railway Historical Society convention watch a crewman on 401 snag orders at Clyman Junction on September 4, 1955. The interlocking marks the intersection of the Adams cutoff with C&NW's Fond du Lac-Janesville (Wis.) line.

R. M. Clark

A seven-car Twin Cities 400, looking clean and dignified right up to the end, rolls past Milwaukee's Juneau Park on June 22, 1963.

Train 401 slips westward over neatly manicured right-of-way at Lebanon, Wis., on April 20, 1963. During the final years of operation, after the straight parlors were dropped and the observation cars rebuilt with added parlor space, the diner was repositioned to the middle of the train.

On the Ides of March in 1959, a Chicago-bound Twin Cities 400 *provides a sparkling complement to rustic James J. Hill stone arch bridge as it rolls out of Minneapolis on Great Northern tracks.*

Three photos, William D. Middleton

73

This May 1958 scene of 401 east of Sussex, Wis., reveals two deviations from the usual operation of Twin Cities 400 consists: In the spring and summer of 1958, the road assigned a single E8 to the train until 2,250 h.p. proved inadequate to the task and double power resumed. The one-unit-powered consist includes two ex-City legrest coaches, still clad in UP colors.

In October 1951, parlor car porter Raymon Sisson, who regularly worked the *Twin Cities 400*, received the Employee's Courtesy Award from the Federation of Railway Progress. He had been cited to the Federation several times, most notably for convincing drawing-room occupants on 401 to yield their private accommodation to a heart attack victim, then arranging for medical attention. Sisson, who continued to receive compliments after this recognition, by 1955 was the only member of the original *400* crew still in service.

In March of the following year, another on-board employee distinguished himself: C. A. Brooks, lounge car attendant aboard 401, on arrival in Minneapolis found an envelope containing (ironically) $400, which he felt belonged to a passenger who had detrained in Eau Claire. Brooks turned the envelope over to the Great Northern stationmaster in Minneapolis, and the passenger and his money were soon reunited.

In compliance with an Interstate Commerce Commission order, automatic train stop was installed in 1952 between Clybourn (in Chicago) and Wyeville, enabling the existing 95 mph and 100 mph maximum authorized speeds to be maintained over more than half of the *400*'s Chicago-St. Paul route. The Omaha Road did not receive such an installation, however, so train speeds there were reduced to 79 mph. Surprisingly, no immediate schedule change resulted, though in January 1955 the time between Chicago and St. Paul was lengthened to 6½ hours.

Train 401 approaches the Brady Street footbridge on Milwaukee's East Side on January 18, 1963, the zero-degree weather having no impact on the train's schedule.

Jim Scribbins

There's a blizzard raging through Chicago as passengers head for the warm confines of train 401, but a safe and dependable trip awaits them. On the adjacent track, the Peninsula 400 from Upper Michigan has arrived in the charge of an Omaha Railway Fairbanks-Morse Erie.

C&NW

A makeup Twin Cities 400 resulting from a washout at Knapp, Wis., in October 1942 prepares to leave Eau Claire with a short and elderly consist led by Class G-3 4-4-2 No. 365.

A. Robert Johnson

75

Certainly not a cornfield meet in the traditional railroad sense, but a Midwestern cornfield does provide the setting for this meet between 401, the photographer's train, and counterpart 400 near Adams, Wis., in July 1959.

Both photos, William D. Middleton

Author's collection

A pristine 400 led by E3 set 5002A&B captivates onlookers at Milwaukee, circa 1940. Toward the end of the day, the locomotives will head back to Chicago on the overnight Minneapolis-Chicago North Western Limited.

A little 1939 folder printed in yellow and green touted the new 400 as "The Train that Set the Pace for the World." It also provided schedules for all C&NW through trains between Chicago and the Twin Cities.

Chappie Fox

While the custom of publicly marking the *400*'s birthday had long since ceased, the January 1953 *Newsliner*—the C&NW employees' magazine at that time—did comment that the *Twin Cities 400* was 18 years old and had rolled 5,511,640 miles, the equivalent of 220 trips around the world. The whimsical might have seen as a belated birthday present the new neon display sign mounted atop Madison Street Station, which included the *400*'s as one of its three changing messages. The 3000-foot-square sign consumed enough electricity to illuminate all homes in a community with a population of 1000.

In spite of these bright lights, the national outlook for the passenger train was in reality growing dim, as suggested by a report from the National Association of Railroad and Utilities Commissioners in the spring of 1953. This report claimed that passenger deficits nationwide equalled 42 percent of net freight earnings, and that freight rate increases were the most ready source to make up passenger losses. The obvious conclusions were that freight rates would be lower—and the railroads better able to make improvements in freight service—if freight earnings did not need to be used to offset passenger losses. Clearly, the simplest step to ease this problem would be to eliminate the most unprofitable trains. However, the report tempered this recommendation by suggesting that remaining passenger service be made economical and attractive enough to assure its financially successful future. Also recommended was elimination of laws—where they existed—prohibiting abandonment of the last passenger train on a given route.

The North Western was not immune to the malaise addressed by the report, and some minor changes began to occur aboard the *Twin Cities 400*. On that train and elsewhere in the fleet, lunch-counter service was quietly dropped; the cars continued to operate, but for beverages only, now referred to in the timetable as "tap-lounges" or "tavern-lounges." On October 30, 1955, another 10 minutes was added to the schedules in both directions—two minutes south and eight minutes north of Milwaukee.

With the spring 1957 edition of the timetable, 401 had its schedule advanced to a 12:15 p.m. departure from Chicago, still retaining its 7-hour timing to Minneapolis. This restored the traditional meet of 400 and 401 at Adams. (They had been passing on the double track east of Clyman Junction during the time when only train 400 had a noon start.) A conditional stop at Racine for 401 was changed to a positive one, and a positive stop was also

The war has swelled the consist of the Twin Cities 400 *to eleven cars on this April day in 1943 in Milwaukee. Even the engineer of the steam switcher in the background has focused his attention to the long streamliner.*

There's not much snow on the ground for 401 to kick up at Clyman Junction on New Years Eve day as 1960 bows out.

established there for 400. No additional running time was allotted for either. Six weeks later, the Wyeville stop was reinstated for 401, and *Dakota 400* 519 was rerouted via Wyeville instead of the Elroy-Sparta cutoff to connect there with 401.

By the fall of 1957, a remanufacturing of *400* equipment was well in progress. Both observation cars, 7200 and 7201, had been remodeled extensively; their tavern sections were replaced with parlor chairs, leaving only the small solarium areas as lounges. This meant that first-class patrons had to walk to the opposite end of the train for beverage service. Despite this alteration of their interiors, the two observations retained their original exterior appearance, though a change to a simpler livery and removal of their skirts lurked in the future.

The point of the interior conversion was to make possible the removal of one—or later both—of the straight parlors. In October 1958, parlor-car service was officially restricted to observations 7200 and 7201, which eliminated drawing rooms from the train. Actually, there had been frequent occasions during the spring and summer of that year when no full parlor was included in the consist, dropping it to seven cars in the charge of a single E8.

(Single-unit operation did not last long; even with these smallest streamlined consists ever, 2,250 h.p. proved inadequate to maintain the schedule.) Low fares introduced in 1959 were to encourage enough business for two additional coaches, putting nine cars behind an again-standard pair of E's, but the regular consist never regained its previous length.

In the train's waning years, various maverick equipment appeared in the consists: American Car & Foundry-built diners from the *City* Streamliners, surplus since Milwaukee Road replaced North Western as joint operator of the trains with UP and SP; and baggage-RPO (inactive)-tap-lunch counter or postwar baggage-cafe lounge cars in place of the 7500 and 7501. With consists shorter, and since the tavern no longer provided food service, dining cars were placed in the middle of the train, the usual arrangement being baggage-tavern, two coaches, diner, two

The overnight *North Western Limited* made its final trips between Chicago and Minneapolis on June 14, 1959. This discontinuance created a long layover and 50 percent less work for the diesels handling 400 and 401, since they had also worked the *Limited*. It also resulted in an added stop, at Menomonie Junction, for the *Twin Cities 400*'s. Though in terms of running time the trains apparently could handle the extra stop with ease, in October another 10 minutes were added to the schedule between Minneapolis and Milwaukee in both directions—plus another five minutes from Milwaukee to Chicago on train 400.

In October of 1960, 401 was rescheduled to depart Chicago 10 minutes earlier—at 12:20 p.m.—with five minutes added to Milwaukee and five more to St. Paul. In spring 1961, 400 was given five minutes additional station time in Milwaukee and a lengthened 95-minute schedule on the final subdivision into North Western Terminal, for a 7:30 p.m. arrival. These schedules remained in effect—with just seasonal adjustments to and from daylight saving time—for the duration of the *Twin Cities 400*'s career:

401		400	
Lv. Chicago	12:20 p.m.	Lv. Minneapolis	12:01 p.m.
Lv. Milwaukee	1:50 p.m.	Lv. St. Paul	12:30 p.m.
Ar. Eau Claire	5:40 p.m.	Lv. Eau Claire	1:55 p.m.
Ar. St. Paul	7:10 p.m.	Lv. Milwaukee	5:55 p.m.
Ar. Minneapolis	7:40 p.m.	Ar. Chicago	7:30 p.m.

A peaceful late afternoon sky above South Beaver Dam beckons the Twin Cities 400 *to follow the setting sun toward the Land of 10,000 Lakes.*

Clayton C. Tinkham

C&NW

Minnesota 400 and kin

Multiple monickers: Minnesota, Dakota and Rochester 400's

THE *Minnesota 400*—a Mankato, Minn., to Wyeville, Wis., service with connections for Chicago—was unveiled to the public on June 3, 1936, in a preliminary announcement which stated, incorrectly, that the new train would connect with the existing *400* at Adams, Wis. A few days later a correction set the matter straight, indicating that the trains would connect at Wyeville but speculating that Adams may have been considered initially as the eastern terminus since trains 400 and 401 did not at that time pause at Wyeville. This same news item also mentioned that the new train would be 25 minutes faster than at first contemplated, and that "when first placed in service," the train would operate only Mankato-Wyeville, where Chicago passengers would be required to make across-the-platform transfers to the *400*—an arrangement that would last far longer than this wording suggested.

Eight days in advance of the initial departure of train 418, the eastbound *Minnesota 400*, Mrs. H. I. Lillie of Rochester, Minn., made the first parlor seat reservation through to Chicago; meanwhile, a group of Rochester businessmen planned a round trip to Wyeville on the first runs. The schedule for the 370 miles between Rochester and Chicago called for 400 minutes in each direction, perhaps a coincidence but nonetheless one that could be capitalized on in view of the train's name.

The *Minnesota 400* was a completely new additional service—not an improvement or replacement of existing trains. In connection with 400 and 401, it was approximately five hours faster between Mankato and Chicago than those trains already running. Although planned as a two-car train of just a combine and cafe-lounge, it began operation with a consist which also included two coaches. Because of the train's uniquely high speed, C&NW instructed agents and other station personnel to guard grade crossings as the train hurtled through.

Heading the *Minnesota 400* between Mankato and Winona on June 14, 1936, its inaugural day, was Class D Atlantic 125, freshly painted and gleaming—as were the combine, two coaches, and cafe-lounge. At Mankato, for publicity purposes, the drumhead was taken from its customary position on the train's last car and suspended beneath the 4-4-2's headlight. An appropriately festive atmosphere surrounded the train's debut. Large wicker baskets of gladiolus adorned both sides of the locomotive's footboard above the pilot. Flanking the Atlantic were Kathryn Richter and Velzora Round, who held large bouquets of chrysanthemums, to which were attached the ceremonial ribbon. Frank J. Mahoweld, Mankato's mayor, and Vivien Chesley stood between the rails to support and later cut the ribbon. After this ritual was performed, the drumhead was removed from below the Atlantic's headlight,

Even with reconditioned equipment, C&NW made certain that train inaugurals were classy in every respect. Behold the polished consist—locomotive and all—of the first eastbound Minnesota 400 *at Mankato (above and right) on June 14, 1936. Mankato Mayor Frank Mahoweld and Vivien Chesley have the ribbon-cutting honors as a properly attired crowd looks on. For the occasion, the train's drumhead was temporarily suspended beneath the headlight.*

and the 125, a high-wheeler of turn-of-the-century design, barked out of the Minnesota River valley.

A large crowd witnessed the *Minnesota 400's* send-off from Mankato, but the throng was even greater at Rochester, where another ribbon-cutting ceremony was held while the locomotive's water supply was replenished. There the ribbon was held by Girl Scout Joanne Kingrey and Eagle Scout Richard Thorson. Chamber of commerce president Roy Kingrey and two-year-old Diane Fischer clipped the ribbon, while the Veterans of Foreign Wars junior drum corps played.

The new train made intermediate stops in Minnesota at Waseca, Owatonna, and Winona (where the steam locomotives were changed) as well as Rochester; and in Wisconsin at Onalaska (with a private bus connection to downtown La Crosse, which the C&NW main line only skimmed the outskirts of) and Sparta. These were all positive stops in both directions. The Mankato-Wyeville trip was made with a single set of equipment, departing Mankato at 12:55 p.m. and returning at 11:35 p.m., with an hour and 12 minutes turning time at Wyeville. Trains 400 and 401 had Wyeville stops inserted, with no additional allowance in running time, to provide the connections to and from the east for the *Minnesota 400*. Train 419, the westbound *Minnesota 400*, made a close connection at Mankato to train 503 for Huron and Pierre, S. Dak. Train 503 was upgraded to eliminate an after-2 a.m.

Crowds also jammed the station grounds at Rochester, Minn., as lanky Atlantic 125 led the four-car Minnesota 400 eastward for the first time on June 14, 1936. Although there apparently was less pageantry at this important stop on the route than at Mankato, the crowds were certainly no less enthusiastic about their new train. In the lower photo, note the second sleeper parked across from the depot; it is equipped with special doors for stretcher patients for Mayo Clinic.

For less than a year, from August 8, 1937, to June 26, 1938, the Minnesota 400 was extended through to Chicago. A two-color folder announced the new service, with a map and schedule inside that explained how connections could also be made with the 400 and Madison-Milwaukee trains.

change from steam cars to motor train at Tracy, Minn., and to include a through Minneapolis-Mankato-Huron sleeping car.

The trip between southern Minnesota and Chicago using the *Minnesota 400* was described in much the same terms as one aboard the original *400* to and from the Twin Cities: a pleasant afternoon and evening ride in maximum comfort on a speedy, air-conditioned train featuring modern coach and cafe-lounge accommodations.

The success of the *Minnesota 400* during its first year encouraged the North Western to begin operating it—in what turned out to be a short-lived experiment—as a completely separate through train between Mankato and Chicago. In so doing, C&NW extended the benefits of *400* service to the populus along an additional line—through Madison and Janesville, Wis. south of

the *400*'s route via Milwaukee. It was on August 8, 1937, that 418 and 419 were extended to Chicago as a completely new "limited" service south of Wyeville, with intermediate stops at Elroy and Baraboo in addition to Madison and Janesville; 419 only paused at Sharon and Clinton Junction as well, to enable passengers from Chicago to detrain.

In this process of extension, 418 received a substantially altered carding, with a 10:30 a.m.—2 hours and 25 minutes earlier—departure from Mankato, and arrival at North Western Terminal in Chicago at 7:35 p.m. Moreover, 418 bypassed Wyeville via the Elroy-Sparta cutoff (abandoned, now a famous bike trail) southwest of Wyeville, thus eschewing the CStPM&O and remaining on C&NW rails throughout the run. Train 419 departed from Chicago at 2 p.m.; unlike 418, it used the Omaha Road from

Elroy to Wyeville, where it met 401 to receive passengers from Milwaukee before heading west again on the C&NW. Since it no longer connected with 418, train 400 dropped its Wyeville stop; riders on 418 destined for Milwaukee detrained at Madison, where they boarded local No. 620 (which carried a cafe-parlor) for the Cream City. Operation of 418 via the Elroy-Sparta cutoff rather than by way of Wyeville saved running time and allowed some padding in the schedule between Elroy and Chicago. Because of the lower maximum speed—70 mph—and several severe curves (as well as a tunnel) on the southerly line via Madison, the time between Chicago and Wyeville on that route was 53 minutes longer than through Milwaukee.

The consist of the *Minnesota 400* was expanded to reflect its greater status: additional coaches, a cafe-lounge with a radio, and a full parlor. Class ES, the medium-size Pacifics then the standard passenger power for the North Western, took over from the Atlantics, which were too light for the enlarged consist. With the new year, several additional improvements subsequently were made to the service, including a change from cafe-lounge to dining-lounge. Upgrading of first-class accommodations came in April 1938 with substitution of a compartment parlor car for the regular parlor.

The January 1938 timetable gave 419 a conditional stop to entrain at Harvard, Ill., and also made Dodge Center, Minn., a conditional stop for the *Minnesota 400* in both directions. In spring 1938, Evansville, Wis., became a stop for 418 only.

On June 26, 1938, the *Minnesota 400*'s through operation to and from Chicago ceased, and the train reverted to its original Wyeville-Mankato schedule, though it did continue to make the Dodge Center flag stop added while the train was running through. The change brought about the restoration of the 12:55 Mankato departure and meant that train 400 once again stopped at Wyeville to connect. The consists of trains 418 and 419 were consequently reduced to coaches plus the dining-lounge car, and in the fall the dining-lounge car was discontinued in favor of a cafe-lounge. Finally, in January 1939, the consist reverted once again to a full complement of coaches, diner-lounge, and parlor car. In April of 1939 the schedule underwent another change: insertion of a conditional stop at St. Charles, Minn., between Winona and Rochester. Also at this time, nurse-stewardess service began.

With the streamlining of the *400* on September 24, 1939, the *Minnesota 400*'s passengers were afforded excellent connections for Milwaukee and Chicago. Then, in the spring of 1940, the new *Twin Cities 400*'s schedule was cut by 15 minutes, resulting in a slight improvement of the overall time on the *Minnesota 400* route—a five-minute net reduction between Mankato and Chicago in both directions. (Actually, trains 418 and 419 themselves had

their schedules slightly lengthened.) In terms of equipment, however, retrogression prevailed for the *Minnesota 400*. The diner-lounge was removed west of Rochester; later, beginning in February 1941, it was cut out of 419 at Winona, to be forwarded to Rochester the next morning on train 515 for breakfast service, then resume its *400* duty on 418 in the afternoon. But though food and beverage service was somewhat diminished for the time being, patrons of the *Minnesota 400* were soon assured of a more bountiful future. In March 1941, trains 418 and 419 were included among those to receive full status as yellow-and-green speedsters when streamlined *400* service was expanded.

Because of the growing concern for national defense, Wisconsin's Camp McCoy (east of Sparta) was reactivated, and on May 1, 1941, the *Minnesota 400* began stopping there with no increase in running time—only an increase in skill from the engine crew, and a bit more work from the locomotive.

In July 1941, countering a move made by the Milwaukee Road with its new Sioux Falls-Chicago *Midwest Hiawatha,* operation of C&NW's train 514, the *Minnesota and Black Hills Express,* was quickened by more than 4 hours to bring it into Mankato just in time for its passengers to transfer to 418. This large reduction in running time on the Dakota Division combined with the close connection with the *Minnesota 400* netted a time saving of 8 hours and 25 minutes, allowing one-night-out travel from the Black Hills to Chicago.

Additional evidence of the good things C&NW had in store for southern Minnesotans was the reconditioning of the passenger station at Rochester. Exterior and interior were both completely cleaned. Waiting room walls and ceiling were refinished in harmonizing colors of green, tan, and pink, with chrome striping as trim. All seats were finished in light wood color and grouped to relieve the monotony of rows of benches. Heavily barred ticket windows were replaced by an open counter, faced in green with a black top. Washrooms were renovated. Red-and-black checkerboard flooring and new doors and windows in the public portions of the building rounded out the improvements.

It was on Saturday, January 3, 1942, that the newly streamlined *Minnesota 400* was first exhibited—in La Crosse, Winona, and Rochester, perhaps providing a boost in morale for the local populus in those early days of World War II. As an expression of gratitude to North Western for the new, improved service, the Mayo Clinic in Rochester sponsored a dinner on the evening of January 3 at the Kahler Hotel for civic leaders and business people. Presiding was Frederick J. Furlow, president of the chamber of commerce. Principal remarks, complimenting the railway on its accomplishments, were delivered by Paul A. Grassle, Rochester's mayor. Representing the C&NW were F. G. Fitz-Patrick, chief traffic officer; A. R. Gould, traffic manager;

Charles Ost, collection of William A. Raia

From its stable of Pacifics, C&NW selected 4-6-2's 1620 (above) and 1617 (below) to lead the valiant new Minnesota 400's. The style of the shrouding that C&NW applied was similar to that of the North Western's Class E-4 Hudsons used between Chicago and Omaha.

C&NW

86

Pullman-Standard

Reproduction In 1978
By Herb Danneman

CHICAGO and NORTH WESTERN LINE

takes pleasure in introducing a

NEW STREAMLINED MINNESOTA "400"

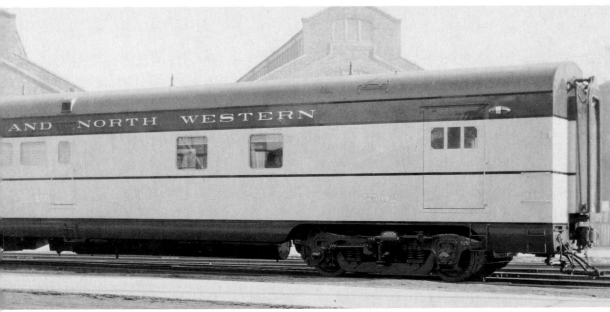

**LUXURIOUS COMFORT
SMOOTH RIDING EASE**

**BEAUTIFUL APPOINTMENTS
SPEED AND SAFETY**

The NEW MINNESOTA "400" provides the Ultimate in Travel Pleasure

The MINNESOTA "400" is a masterly achievement of interior decoration. Striking and harmonious color schemes greet the eye in every car. The lighting is as much a part of the interior decoration as any other detail. Soft, diffused illumination that rests the eyes come from lamps with special "luminator" lenses. Mirrors enhance the charm of car interiors and add to the effect of spaciousness and beauty.

A "400" feature that appeals to every traveler is the "Solex" glass windows, which reduce sun glare to a minimum. Draughtless air-conditioning through the ceilings provides an even distribution of pure air throughout the cars.

COACHES are luxuriously comfortable and tastefully decorated. Deep, rubber-cushioned seats are individually adjustable to several reclining angles. There is generous leg-room for even the tallest

person and individual reading light for each seat. Lounge-smoking room for men and women is a feature of each coach—for women, exclusively, a delightful little powder room with convenient dressing table and mirror.

The PARLOR CAR is finished in restful pastel tones and with photo-mural panels of scenes reached by "North Western." The comfortable individual chairs are adjustable to any position. An inviting Lounge-smoking room is for men and women, with a powder room exclusively for the use of women.

TAVERN-LUNCH COUNTER CAR. The Taproom section has the friendly atmosphere of a continental café. Here in comfortable facing seats, upholstered in tufted blue leather, one may while away a pleasant hour in cards or conversation. A circular bar, upholstered in red tufted leather and sparkling with chrome and "Lucite," is at your service for refreshments.

The other section of this car is an attractive lunch counter. The front of the lunch counter and the seats of the revolving chairs are upholstered in deep red leather. With its flesh-tinted mirrors and gleaming "Lucite" and chrome trim, it is a cheerful spot where inviting lunches and light meals are served quickly and at most moderate prices.

Sleekly streamlined, the new MINNESOTA "400" is a striking example of the advance in train design and construction—a scientific reduction in weight without any sacrifice of strength and sturdiness. The frames are high tensile steel alloy; the underframe center sills of a special steel with a yield strength of 40,000 pounds per square inch; sub-flooring of .051 aluminum and flooring of pressed corrugated aluminum with 1" layer of cork. Insulation of "Stonefelt" throughout.

Perfect relaxation is assured in the Coaches

Tavern-Lunch Counter Car—where food is served as well as beverages

The Parlor Car is as luxurious as it is comfortable

The MINNESOTA "400" will operate daily between Wyeville and Mankato, and provides exceptional service to Winona, Rochester, Mankato and other Southern Minnesota points. Passengers from Chicago and Milwaukee will board the Twin Cities "400", which makes close connection with the MINNESOTA "400" at Wyeville, Wisconsin.

Schedule of the NEW MINNESOTA "400"
(Passengers transfer at Wyeville)

Read Down		Read Up
3:00 PM	Lv. ..... Chicago ..... Ar.	9:15 PM
A3:12 PM	Lv. Evanston (Davis St.) Ar.	A9:00 PM
B	Lv. ..... Racine ..... Ar.	
4:15 PM	Ar. ..... Milwaukee ..... Lv.	8:00 PM
4:15 PM	Lv. ..... Milwaukee ..... Ar.	7:55 PM
5:12 PM	Lv. So. Beaver Dam ..... Ar.	
6:09 PM	Ar. ..... Adams ..... Lv.	7:00 PM
6:38 PM	Lv. ..... Wyeville ..... Lv.	6:09 PM
6:41 PM	Lv. ..... Wyeville ..... Ar.	5:37 PM
7:00 PM	Ar. Camp McCoy ..... Lv.	5:30 PM
7:12 PM	Ar. ..... Sparta ..... Lv.	5:05 PM
C7:58 PM	Ar. ..... La Crosse ..... Lv.	4:56 PM
C7:20 PM	Lv. ..... La Crosse ..... Lv. C4:05 PM
7:43 PM	Ar. ..... Onalaska ..... Ar. C4:45 PM
8:25 PM	Ar. ..... Waseca ..... Lv.	4:25 PM
8:30 PM	Lv. ..... Winona ..... Ar.	1:27 PM
D	Ar. ..... Winona ..... Lv.	3:50 PM
9:35 PM	Ar. St. Charles ..... Lv.	3:45 PM
9:35 PM	Ar. ..... Rochester ..... Lv.	2:40 PM
	Lv. ..... Rochester ..... Lv.	2:40 PM
10:25 PM	Ar. Dodge Center ..... Ar.	2:40 PM
10:45 PM	Ar. ..... Owatonna ..... Lv.	1:45 PM
11:30 PM	Ar. ..... Mankato ..... Lv.	12:45 PM

A—Will not carry passengers locally between Chicago and Evanston (Davis St.)
B—Stops to receive revenue passengers for Rochester and beyond.
C— .....service Onalaska to La Crosse and La Crosse to Onalaska is via Onalaska Trans. Co. One way fare 15 cents, round trip 25 cents. Running time 20 minutes.
D—Stops to receive revenue passengers for, or discharge from, Milwaukee and beyond.

NOW! A Fleet of "400" Streamliners

The MINNESOTA "400" is a member of "North Western's" new Fleet of "400" Streamliners, all units of which will be in operation on January 12, 1942. Included in this "400" Fleet is frequent, throughout-the-day service between Chicago and Milwaukee; also service between Chicago and Green Bay, between Chicago and Negaunee-Ishpeming and the iron and copper regions, and between Chicago and Madison; also the original "400" which operates between Chicago and St. Paul-Minneapolis.

87

A 1978 Herb Danneman reproduction, author's collection

Crisp weather greeted the westbound streamlined Minnesota 400 exhibition train at Mankato, along the Minnesota River, on the afternoon of January 4, 1942. Previous engagements that day included Waseca and Owatonna. Temperature: 25 degrees below zero—almost cold enough to turn the little yellow-and-green speedster blue!

C&NW

The lack of crowds may indicate that this scene of the westbound exhibition Minnesota 400 at Rochester was recorded on January 4, the day following debut in that city, just prior to departure to Waseca, Owatonna and Mankato. You can bet it's a cold wind making those white Extra flags flutter.

C&NW

The 1620 has 418 in tow on August 15, 1948, at Dodge Center, Minn. A rear view of 418, also at Dodge Center but in July 1948, shows the modest drumhead that adorned the parlor car for a number of years.

The railroad sometimes had to substitute or supplement streamlined 400 consists with equipment from the standard-car pool, especially during the war years. Number 418 is near Onalaska, Wis., with three heavyweights sandwiched by a streamlined coach and parlor car.

K. L. Zurn

4-6-0 223 is on the tail end of the Minnesota 400 consist at Mankato, "coming down the hill after being turned" to quote photographer Ost. Meanwhile, a Baldwin switcher awaits less prestigous assignments.

Charles Ost

Train 418 in the command of Pacific 1620 charges through the undulating Minnesota countryside near Mankato on an August midday in 1947. Even after five years of rigorous service under wartime conditions and grueling Minnesota winters, the yellow-and-green streamliner continued to be a sharp-stepping operation. (Left) Sister Pacific 1617 pauses at the rambling brick depot at Winona in August of the same year. Only the pilot and C&NW nose herald reflect the wear and tear of day-to-day service.

Both photos, Charles Ost, collection of William A. Raia

In a rare scene recorded from Minnesota 43/Wisconsin 54 state highway bridge at Winona, train 418 rolls out over the Mississippi for Wisconsin destinations and a rendezvous with the Twin Cities 400 at Wyeville.

Donald Rice

One could photograph both streamlined Pacifics when they changed engines on 418 at Winona, as in this scene in November 1942. The 1617 was on train 418 while 1620 stood on an adjacent track waiting to go to the "house."

A. Robert Johnson

and R. Thomson, passenger traffic manager. They had traveled to Rochester aboard a business car on train 515, the overnight *Rochester Minnesota Special*. Arriving on the exhibition *Minnesota 400* to be present at the banquet were H. C. Duvall, general passenger agent; N. A. Hersether, assistant general passenger agent; and division freight and passenger agent E. J. Carland. They were met at the station by a group of chamber of commerce and city officials. Also present at the Kahler Hotel were Elmer Terrill, division superintendent, and trainmaster J. S. Eva. A statement made by the railroad on this occasion explained that steam locomotives would be used on the streamlined *Minnesota 400*, since diesel power was too expensive for short-distance runs. The host, Mr. Furlow, responded that Rochester would care for the train "as though it belonged to us."

A radio program touted the new train, and in Rochester some 2000 persons braved inclement weather to wait in line to enter the baggage door of the head-end car, pass through the train, and exit through the rear diaphragm of the parlor car and down the wooden stairs placed between snow-covered rails. Throughout the public showings, the reception accorded the streamliner was as warm as the Minnesota winter was cold. At the division point of Waseca, more than 400 residents turned out in 25-degree-below-zero weather during the midday two-hour stop there on Sunday, January 4. The elements had been scarcely less bone-chilling

during an earlier display at Owatonna, nor would they moderate for an afternoon and evening presentation in Mankato.

With "a good load" out of Mankato and a group of Rochester businessmen aboard who round-tripped to Winona, streamlined 418 and 419 entered service on Monday, January 5, a full week in advance of the other new members of the *400* fleet. Indicative of its relative prestige, the *Minnesota 400* was the only new streamliner accorded a special promotional descriptive brochure. The yellow-and-green train was placed in service with four cars, and because of this small consist and the short daily mileage, was steam-powered. Two Pacifics, the 1617 and 1620, were shrouded for this service, matching the cars in livery and resembling C&NW's streamlined Class E-4 Hudsons which ran on the Chicago-Omaha line. In contour, they were also reminiscent of the artistic steam of competitor Milwaukee Road.

Streamlined Pacific 1620 striding along with a clean stack and a full Minnesota 400 *consist made for a smart-looking train in this August 1948 scene at Rochester.*

J. Konas, collection of William A. Raia

(Left) For the inaugural festivities of the new Dakato 400—the longest 400 route ever established—EMD E7 5018-A received special lettering. The 5018-A&B led a six-car exhibition train into communities that were on the Dakota 400 route extended west from Mankato. At New Ulm, Minn. (above and at right on facing page), bands played and crowds marveled at the train; streamliners were an unfamiliar sight in western Minnesota.

The first car of the train was No. 7502, the only tavern-lunch counter among the new equipment that included a small lounge section to the rear, making it virtually identical to the forward cars of the *Twin Cities 400*, cars 7500 and 7501. Since the whole *Minnesota 400* was turned at Wyeville and Mankato, the tavern-lounge was always adjacent to the engine. A regular coach, a coach with a stateroom for the nurse-stewardess, and a parlor car completed the consist. In response to increased wartime travel, another coach was soon added.

On December 6, 1942, the Office of Defense Transportation order slowing fast passenger trains nationwide gave Nos. 400 and 401 different stopping times at Wyeville. The *Minnesota 400*

schedule was adjusted without adding to its own running time (which was padded enough not to require change) to continue convenient connections with the fleet leaders. Nearly 11 months later, however, the *Minnesota*'s schedule was increased 20 minutes westbound and 25 minutes eastbound.

During holidays, the Christmas-New Year season particularly, the *Minnesota 400* was run as a through train to and from Chicago, operating as sections of 400 and 401 east of Wyeville. This meant pressing into service a train of standard heavyweight cars for the first through departure from Chicago, with the streamlined trainset coming east from Mankato. Consequently, 418 and 419 became alternately streamlined and standard until the usual connecting service was resumed. Class E-2-a Pacifics—fueled by coal after their release from duty on 400 and 401—relived their glory years by handling this special through service between Chicago and Adams.

In March 1944, 10 minutes were added to 419's timetable between Rochester and Mankato and a flag stop was established

Sleepy Eye, the oft-mentioned community with a storylike name in the popular "Little House on the Prairie" television series based in western Minnesota, was indeed a very real stop for the Dakota 400. Here in 1950, Sleepy Eye residents demonstrate their interest in the new service as they eagerly wait to walk through the train. The mayor even proclaimed that businesses and schools should close in respect to the train's honorable exhibition visit.

at Claremont, Minn. On June 29, 1947, when 401's time was reduced, 419's departure from Wyeville accordingly became 7 minutes earlier with no change in Mankato arrival, thus slowing the train a bit. In the opposite direction, however, 418's schedule was tightened so the train could arrive at Wyeville 10 minutes earlier. In September 1948, the schedules of both sides of the *Minnesota 400* were shifted to 15 minutes later throughout to correspond with the later departures of trains 400 and 401.

The North Western was the first Western railroad to receive postwar streamlined passenger equipment. It arrived in early spring of 1946, which for the *Minnesota* was none too soon. As a result of wartime and immediate postwar travel growth, the train's consist had been filled out with heavyweight equipment. Numbers 418 and 419 often ran with the tap-lunch counter-lounge and parlor being the only streamlined cars on the train, what with all coaches standard. On other trips, one of the four coaches might be streamlined.

As the new coaches arrived, they were immediately put in service on the *400* fleet, replacing both the elderly heavyweights and some coaches borrowed from the UP-SP-C&NW *Challengers;* this made the *400*'s entirely uniform again after more than four years of equipment substitutions. Furthermore, the coaches permitted *400* consists to expand to meet still booming travel requirements. The addition of the new coaches occasioned an announcement by Vice President Carl R. Gray that 1947 would see, for the first time in a decade, through operation of the *Minnesota 400* into Chicago, via Madison. Actually, this service improvement did not materialize for three years—though in the interim, ads in timetables and elsewhere continued to proclaim its advent.

At Tracy, Minn. (above left), the westbound exhibition Dakota 400 *met winter weather moving east. (Above right) Crowds await inspection at Brookings, S. Dak.*

As things turned out, through service was extended westward as well as eastward. In early 1950, after the last of the new equipment needed to complete expansion of *400* service had been received, the longest *400* route was inaugurated—Chicago to Huron, S. Dak.—when the *Minnesota 400*, trains 418 and 419, became the *Dakota 400*, trains 518 and 519. The problem that had prevented this service from being instituted earlier was the block signaling required by the Interstate Commerce Commission for high-speed operation between Wyeville and Huron. C&NW protested that the cost—$2,242,775 to install and $12,250 annually to operate, at 1948 prices—was prohibitive. The solution was to go ahead and place the *Dakota 400* in operation, but on a slower schedule.

Locomotive 5018, an E7, was specially lettered "DAKOTA 400" on its nose below the number boxes and dispatched with an exhibition train into the territory west of Mankato, where winter was lingering. On April 29, while deadheading west to begin service, the two-unit six-car train paused for public inspection at New Ulm, Sleepy Eye, and Tracy, Minn., and at Brookings, S. Dak. Sleepy Eye's municipal government made formal note of the occasion:

PROCLAMATION: Whereas Sleepy Eye has been scheduled as a stop for the *Dakota 400* luxury train, and; Whereas said train will be on exhibition from 9:10 a.m. to 9:40 a.m., April 29, 1950, and; Whereas it is fitting that the citizens of Sleepy Eye welcome this splendid addition to our railway service; I therefore as mayor of this city respectfully ask that all business and professional firms close their doors from 9:00 a.m. to 9:45 a.m., Saturday, April 29, 1950.

Forrest E. Schott, Mayor

When the inaugural 518 came through the following morning on its first revenue run, Sleepy Eye would turn out in force behind Mayor Schott to wish it well. Public and parochial high-school bands as well as the local American Legion Post state champion drum corps gave it a rousing sendoff. This celebration was in a sense a tribute not only to the train but also to Sleepy Eye resident J. R. Hauser, who had worked for extension of *400* service since 1946 and had been instrumental in persuading North Western not to bypass Sleepy Eye by running the train nonstop between New Ulm and Tracy.

On the day of the demonstration tour, a storm of near-blizzard proportions greeted the train at Tracy; in Brookings, snow

All photos, both pages, C&NW

It would have taken more than an April blizzard to keep Huron residents from seeing their new train as it rolled into town for the first time (right). Most of the inaugural celebrations took place at Huron, the train's western terminus. Miss Agnes LaCroix, National Indian Beauty Queen and a member of the Dakota Santee Sioux tribe, christened the streamliner from a specially prepared flat car.

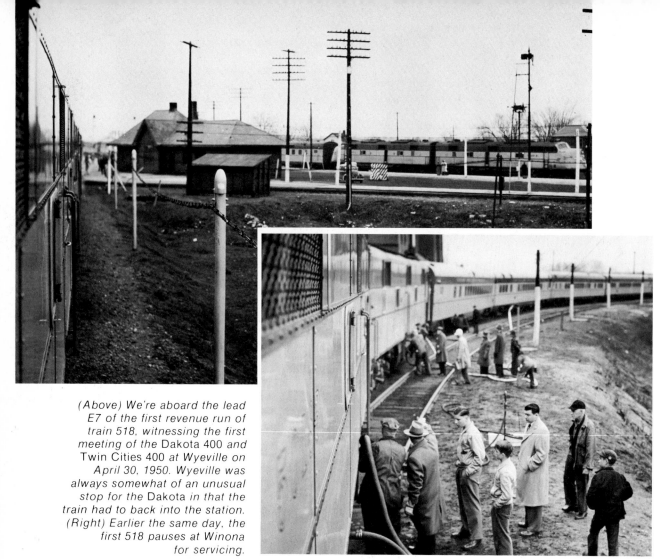

(Above) We're aboard the lead E7 of the first revenue run of train 518, witnessing the first meeting of the Dakota 400 and Twin Cities 400 at Wyeville on April 30, 1950. Wyeville was always somewhat of an unusual stop for the Dakota in that the train had to back into the station. (Right) Earlier the same day, the first 518 pauses at Winona for servicing.

Both photos, C&NW

continued to fall as Mayor Homer Diggins (a former C&NW employee) cut a symbolic first-trip ribbon. By the time the demonstration extra arrived Huron at 3:40 p.m., it looked as though it might have been a visitor from the subarctic, with icy snow clinging to its exterior protrusions and sticking to the flat surfaces of locomotive and car sides.

There, engineman Homer Classick eased his charge midway across Dakota Avenue, where a flat car was placed almost knuckle-to-knuckle with the E7. From atop the flat car, Miss Agnes LaCroix of Rapid City—a member of the Dakota Santee Sioux tribe and National Indian Beauty Queen—christened the

streamliner bearing the name of her people by smashing a bottle containing water from Lake Michigan, the James and Missouri rivers, and Rapid Creek (in the Black Hills) over the coupler of the diesel, exposed for this purpose. With Miss LaCroix were Abe Berg of the Huron chamber of commerce, who also acted as master of ceremonies for a special program over KIJV, which aired the entire proceedings; Mayor J. S. Tschetter; F. G. Fitz-Patrick, C&NW traffic vice president; and Chris Merkle of the South Dakota Public Utilities Commission.

After apologizing for the four-year delay in obtaining equipment for the $2.5 million *Dakota 400*, Fitz-Patrick expressed

The Dakota 400 *in the charge of a single E8 slides into Elroy, Wis., in September 1950 enroute to Huron, passing the author's 1950 Ford parked at the depot platform. Beyond Elroy, 519 will pass through three tunnels as it negotiates the Elroy-Sparta cutoff bypassing Wyeville.*

his hope that South Dakotans would show their appreciation for the train by patronizing it. Then the newest *400* pulled entirely across the avenue and into the passenger station for display. A sizeable crowd had been present for the ceremony, and in the four hours that followed, more than a thousand people contended with snow, slush and chilling temperatures to inspect their new link with the east.

The local press praised the North Western for this new contribution to passenger travel. The DeSmet *News* editorialized that Chicago would be as accessible by means of the new *400* as the Twin Cities were by automobile and predicted that central

The exact date is unknown, but the former C&O coach tucked into the consist of 519, as well as the RPO, suggest that this Chicago scene was recorded circa 1957; RPO service began in summer 1957.

C&NW

The Dakota 400's route was the most scenic of any 400, what with the rolling hills of western Wisconsin and eastern Minnesota, three tunnels (for 519 anyway) and close encounters with numerous bodies of water. A favorite location was the Wisconsin River crossing at Merrimac: (above) 519 on the Merrimac bridge on July 28, 1957; (left) 518 as seen from the highway 113 ferry on September 30, 1955.

South Dakotans would find Chicago the more attractive for shopping and business. The *Plainsman* of Huron reported that the North Western had gone to considerable trouble and expense to install the *Dakota 400* and urged its readers to ride it, the only train on the railway named for a state. The *Plainsman's* front-page headline on the morning of the first departure read "SD Greets New Dakota 400"; four large ads sponsored by 112 local companies and professional people, and illustrations of the train's interior urged patronage. "Travel in luxurious comfort thanks to the C&NW Railway and their new Dakota 400," a typical ad read.

That the *Dakota 400* was there to stay was indicated by the transfer of five car-department employees from Mankato to Huron and the changing of the car foreman's position at Huron from a day job to third-shift hours to allow him to supervise the cleaning and servicing of the new streamliner. High-capacity water pipes, a sewer and floodlights were all installed at the depot in Huron to facilitate washing the *400* during its layover.

The *Dakota 400* reinstated through service from Chicago via Madison, as during the early operation of the *Minnesota 400*. It also extended streamliner service over 223 new route-miles—between Mankato and Huron—making possible a westbound running time of just over 24 hours between Chicago and Rapid City, matching service that had existed eastbound only since July 1941. These timings were in connection with the rescheduled Chicago-Rapid City *Minnesota and Black Hills Express,* trains 514 and 515 (which, between Chicago and Mankato, were called the *Rochester-Minnesota Special*).

At Mankato, the *Dakota 400*'s parlor car was exchanged for an 8-section 2-compartment drawing room standard sleeper, which was handled between Huron and Rapid City on 514 and 515. Thus, the *Dakota 400* became twice unique: not just the only *400* ever to have a sleeping car in its consist but also the only one in the streamliner era regularly assigned a heavyweight car—though various heavyweights had been used frequently on a substitute basis in *400* service during World War II. In October 1958, one of these unusual characteristics was lost when a pair of *American*-series 6-roomette 6-section 4-double-bedroom streamlined cars from the Overland Route pool were placed in *Dakota 400* service, followed by two *Northern*-series 16-duplex-roomette 1-compartment 3 double-bedroom cars in the spring of 1960. These cars retained this assignment until the termination of passenger-train service in South Dakota.

West of Mankato, the *Dakota 400* in Minnesota made regular stops at New Ulm, Sleepy Eye, Springfield and Tracy, and in South Dakota at Brookings. Conditional stops were made at Lake Benton, Minn., and DeSmet, S. Dak., while Arlington, S. Dak., was made a conditional stop for 519 but positive for 518. Between Wyeville and Chicago, regular stops were made in Wisconsin at Elroy, Baraboo, Madison, Janesville, and Beloit.* Harvard, Ill. became a positive stop eastbound but a Sunday-only conditional westbound. Reedsburg, Wis., was a conditional in both directions, and Evansville a Sunday-only conditional stop for 519. Routing between Milwaukee and Wyeville was just the reverse of what it had been in steam days: 519 operated via the cutoff between Elroy and Sparta and received passengers from Milwaukee at Madison from coach-only train 601; 518 and 400 exchanged passengers at Wyeville, affording not only a Milwaukee connection from that point but a faster trip into Chicago as well, and a Twin Cities-Madison service.

The schedule called for 518 to depart from Huron at 5:10 a.m. and arrive in Chicago at 7:45 p.m., while 519 left Madison Street Terminal at 9:45 a.m., arriving at Huron at 11:59 p.m. Because of

---

*Unlike the *Minnesota 400*'s through routing to Chicago, the *Dakota 400* operated via Beloit rather than Sharon, Wis.

Both photos, Jim Scribbins

In 1955 Dakota 519 was permanently rerouted off the Elroy-Sparta cutoff and through Wyeville. For a time, Camp Douglas was the meeting place for 518 and 519. In October 1957, 518 thunders through Camp Douglas while 519 patiently waits in the siding. *(Facing page)* The westbound Dakota slows for the Milwaukee Road diamonds at Camp Douglas, some 13 miles north of Elroy, enroute to a passenger exchange with the Twin Cities 400 at Wyeville.

Trains 514 and 515 to and from Pierre and Rapid City (renumbered 518 and 519, October 1955)

HURON　　DeSmet　　Arlington　　BROOKINGS　　Lake Benton　　Tracy　　Springfield　　Sleepy Eye　　NEW ULM

SOUTH DAKOTA

the loop through Wyeville, the eastbound route at 667 miles was 14 miles longer than the westbound route via the Elroy-Sparta cutoff. The average speed for the *Dakota 400* was approximately 45 mph.

To equip the *Dakota 400*, one coach was built new with a special room similar to the existing stewardess's rooms in three coaches already in service on the *Twin Cities 400* and *Minnesota 400*. Because female attendants were not assigned to the train, the rooms were used by patients traveling to and from the Mayo Clinic in Rochester until the cars were ultimately rebuilt. The newest *400* coaches—constructed in 1947—and parlors—built in 1949—filled out the *Dakota 400* consists. Since dining aboard the *Minnesota 400* had never progressed beyond the lunch counter, C&NW assumed that type of food service to be adequate over most of 518 and 519's route, and a single 48-seat diner—No. 6955—was acquired in 1950 and placed in service between Chicago and Elroy only, making a daily round trip serving both sides of the *Dakota 400*.

Although the interior of car 6955 was virtually identical to that of the larger 56-seat *400* diners, there were some differences in the decorative scheme. Ceiling, walls and baseboard were light, medium and dark blue. Chairs were upholstered in blue, and the carpet was two-tone blue hook-loom. There was no sound system; the use of music had been discontinued without comment on the *Twin Cities 400* and had never been incorporated in the diners of the new *400*'s of 1942. From the exterior, No. 6955 was distinguishable from the other diners by its window arrangement and its two service doors instead of one.

In summary, the *Dakota 400* carried a tavern-lunch counter and coaches for its entire run, a parlor as far as Mankato, where it was exchanged for the Rapid City Pullman, and a diner and an additional parlor car and coaches south of Elroy.

One of the head-end cars was baggage-tavern-lunch counter-lounge 7502, built for the *Minnesota 400*. Because there was no railway post office service on the *Dakota 400* at this time, baggage-tavern-lunch counter car 7602, released from short-distance *400* service by the arrival of baggage-cafe lounges Nos. 7625-7628, could be used in the second consist. In their tap room or tavern sections, both cars featured murals of the South Dakota

outdoors, made from originals by Huron photographer Sid Glanzer. No. 7602 did not have a lounge section, so the *Dakota* was enhanced with additional non-revenue seating on alternate days only. During their stint on trains 518 and 519, these cars were referred to as "tavern lounges"; only infrequent mention was made of their lunch counters, although they were used for food service between Elroy and Huron.

Originally, the *Dakota 400* was powered by twin E7's, which operated on the train until the summer of 1950, when they were replaced by the more powerful E8's. The extra horsepower of the E8's (2250 per unit versus 2000 per unit on the E7's) proved adequate to propel the 8- and 9-car consists which were common between Chicago and Elroy, and more than sufficient for the five or six cars carried beyond.

In 1950 and again in 1952, the *Dakota* was used for 9-day tours between Chicago and the Black Hills, as well as weekend jaunts to the Wisconsin Dells and to Devil's Lake State Park at Baraboo. In fact, the 1951 C&NW calendar depicted train 518 traveling beside Devils Lake with two E7's and a coach directly behind them—though in reality the *Dakota 400* was then running with a single E8 and a tap-lunch counter car on the head end.

The *Dakota 400* received its share of compliments. In fall 1953, a family from Sturgis, Mich., praised the porter and conductors on 518 for the courtesy and helpfulness shown their 10-year-old daughter during her homeward journey from surgery in Rochester. Later, a Reedsburg (Wis.) couple found that Mr. Yates, a brakeman on 518, extended "much courtesy and patience, which will not soon be forgotten," in dealing with their 5-year-old son. The president of a small on-line southern Minnesota brewery received "excellent and courteous" service for his party of eight. A French passenger discovered a bilingual porter, Lafayette Gayles, whose grandfather had come to the United States from Haiti and had kept the French language alive in his family.

For seven months beginning in September 1950, the parlor car was extended to Huron—giving the *Dakota 400* two first-class cars west of Mankato, since the Black Hills Pullman was still

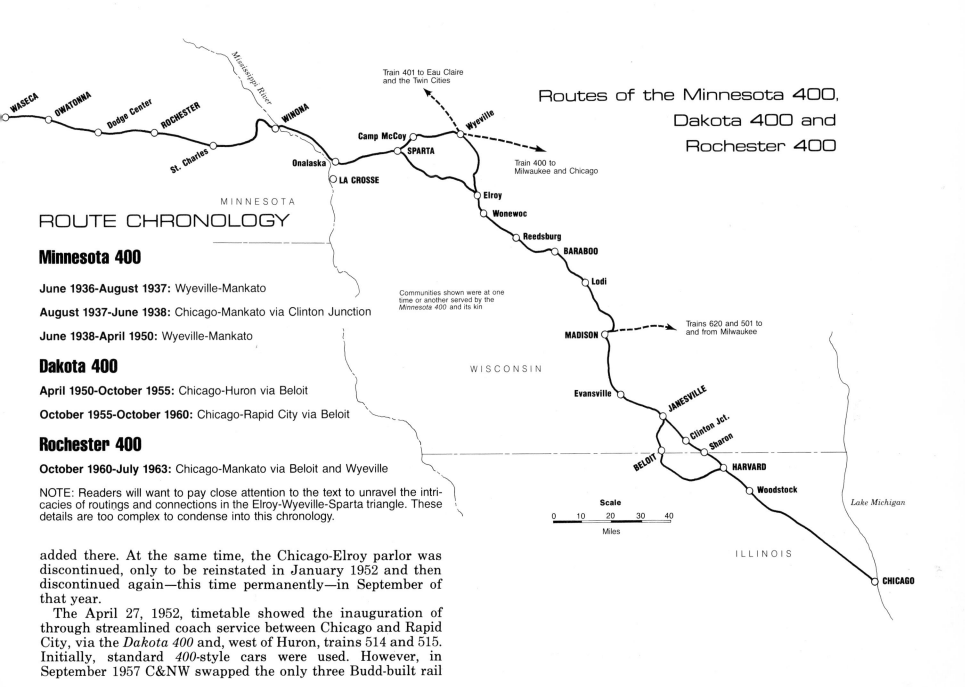

Routes of the Minnesota 400,
Dakota 400 and
Rochester 400

Train 401 to Eau Claire
and the Twin Cities

Train 400 to
Milwaukee and Chicago

Communities shown were at one
time or another served by the
Minnesota 400 and its kin

Trains 620 and 501 to
and from Milwaukee

Scale
0 10 20 30 40
Miles

ROUTE CHRONOLOGY

Minnesota 400

June 1936-August 1937: Wyeville-Mankato

August 1937-June 1938: Chicago-Mankato via Clinton Junction

June 1938-April 1950: Wyeville-Mankato

Dakota 400

April 1950-October 1955: Chicago-Huron via Beloit

October 1955-October 1960: Chicago-Rapid City via Beloit

Rochester 400

October 1960-July 1963: Chicago-Mankato via Beloit and Wyeville

NOTE: Readers will want to pay close attention to the text to unravel the intricacies of routings and connections in the Elroy-Wyeville-Sparta triangle. These details are too complex to condense into this chronology.

added there. At the same time, the Chicago-Elroy parlor was discontinued, only to be reinstated in January 1952 and then discontinued again—this time permanently—in September of that year.

The April 27, 1952, timetable showed the inauguration of through streamlined coach service between Chicago and Rapid City, via the *Dakota 400* and, west of Huron, trains 514 and 515. Initially, standard *400*-style cars were used. However, in September 1957 C&NW swapped the only three Budd-built rail

105

E8 5025-B trundles across the Mississippi River bridge into Winona with the westbound Dakota 400 *on August 23, 1958, with a consist that included a streamlined RPO and an ACF diner-lounge released from joint C&NW-UP* City *train service.*

diesel cars on its roster for a like number of Chesapeake & Ohio coaches constructed by Pullman-Standard, and these cars were placed in Chicago-Rapid City service. Their exteriors were unique on the C&NW, since they retained the C&O stainless-steel fluting below the windows, while the upper portion of the sides were the usual yellow with green letterboard. The cars' interiors were broken into two separate rooms. (These coaches eventually found their way to Southern Pacific when reductions in C&NW passenger service made them surplus.)

On October 30, 1955, dining-car service was extended through to Mankato, requiring the use of two diners—most likely American Car & Foundry-built stock released from *City*-train service when

those streamliners were moved from the North Western to the Milwaukee Road for their run between Council Bluffs and Chicago. At the same time, one-of-a-kind cafe-coach 7000 began running on the west end between Huron and Mankato in daily round-trip service. This arrangement lasted only until the following spring, when the Chicago-Elroy diner and Chicago-Huron tap-lunch counter reappeared.

A year later, the diner was once again extended to Mankato, where one or more coaches also were cut out of 519 and into 518. Now the timetable specifically mentioned the availability of meal service in the tap-lounge between Mankato and Brookings. Although the equipment listing indicated this arrangement until the fall of 1957, the tap-lounge was actually replaced four months earlier by a full diner, which operated between Mankato and Huron but served food east of Brookings only. In the summer of 1956, an ex-*City* ACF diner ran in the *Dakota 400*, along with a

tavern-lunch counter car. From then on, either those diners or ACF ex-*City* cafe-lounges were operated on the *Dakota* in preference to the *400*-type cars. By fall of 1957 the ex-transcontinental diners were newly painted in C&NW yellow and green, but Union Pacific "Streamliner" livery remained at least into summer 1958 on the cafe-lounges. With the time change in spring 1959, these cafe-lounges were redesignated "diner-lounges," since they provided complete meal service. They ran between Chicago and Mankato until the *Dakota 400*'s successor, the *Rochester 400*, was discontinued.

The ultimate elimination of the tavern-lunch counter cars occurred in the summer of 1957, apparently a result of the institution of railway post office service on the *Dakota 400* at that time. Thus heavyweight RPO-express cars became the standard head-end equipment; at least one received the *400* livery. Some trips also operated with an additional full mail storage or express

car of heavyweight construction and Pullman green exterior. The following year, streamlined RPO-express cars were used alternately with the older cars. After the addition of the RPO's, meal service in the Black Hills state consisted of breakfast stops at Brookings for 518 and Phillip for 519.

With the spring 1951 timetable, 519 began operating 15 minutes later at all stations, and its conditional stop at Harvard was changed from Sunday-only to daily. Number 518 was given an additional 5 minutes running time from Harvard to Chicago. Both trains had their Dodge Center station stop moved to the Chicago Great Western crossing, approximately half a mile east of the C&NW depot and at the north end of the platform of the CGW's modern brick station. This arrangement continued for the duration of C&NW passenger service. Arlington became a conditional stop in both directions as of July 1953, and Reedsburg, a positive stop. Fourteen months later, Arlington became a regular

Another favorite "aquatic" photo location of Dakota 400 devotees was Devils Lake, near Baraboo, Wis. (Right) The catch of the day at the lake in this scene is most certainly the pair of CStPM&O Fairbanks-Morse "Eries" on train 518. (Below) Train 519 on August 10, 1958, skirts the lake with a consist of note: two units (an E8-E7 combination), heavyweight RPO, coach, ex-C&O coach, another regular coach, ex-City train diner, parlor and two bilevel suburban cars whose destination is unknown (they were usually cut off at Madison).

Jim Scribbins

C&NW

Young picnickers in classic 1950's dress enjoy a warm spring day in 1956 at Devils Lake State Park as the westbound Dakota 400 whizzes through the popular recreation spot.

William D. Middleton

Both photos, Jim Scribt

Three fair-size lakes dominate the geography of Wisconsin's capital, Madison. Many years ago, when CMStP&P and C&NW were building their lines from Chicago into the city from the south, the lakes posed quite a challenge. The two roads met the challenge by simply building across Lake Monona, although it was necessary for the two lines to cross in mid-lake (and it is the only middle-of-the-lake interlocking known to exist in the U.S.). Here, 518 strikes out across Monona, its consist and Madison's skyline recorded from the photographer's vantage point on the Milwaukee's causeway.

(Right) An E8 and an Erie move 518 onto the Monona Lake bridge and causeway on August 2, 1955. (Center right) On June 18, 1955, 518 approaches abandoned MX tower, stilled by automation.

Both photos, William D. Middleton

stop. Spring 1955 saw the addition of Woodstock, Ill., as a positive stop for 518, and in spring 1957 conditional stops were added for both trains at Des Plaines, a suburb of Chicago.

In October 1955, No. 518's schedule was lengthened somewhat, and additions were made to 519's schedule in April 1956. Many local trains were discontinued on June 17, 1957; to fill the void this left, 519 was given positive stops at Crystal Lake, Woodstock, and Harvard in Illinois, and at Evansville, Lodi and Wonewoc in Wisconsin. The Madison-Milwaukee runs were among the trains eliminated, so 519 began to operate via Wyeville to provide a connection with train 401 for passengers traveling from Milwaukee. Madison benefited from the new routing, for the first time enjoying service to the Twin Cities via 401 from Wyeville. After rerouting from the Tunnel District (as the Elroy-Sparta cutoff was known in its latter years, because of its three tunnels), 519 stopped regularly at Camp Douglas, where it pulled ahead to do its station work after occupying the passing track to meet 518, which did not stop there. At Camp McCoy, 519 made a flag stop. These alterations increased the Chicago-to-Huron running time by 1 hour and 5 minutes, though the timing west of Mankato was 15 minutes faster.

Because of the reductions in service occuring at this time, the now-isolated remnants of 514 and 515 between Huron and Rapid City were redesignated 518 and 519—extending the *Dakota 400*

Mark Nelson

Madison was a hub of passenger activity into the 1950's. (Above left) The stately passenger station as it appeared in May 1964 when only one train remained, Madison-Chicago locals 507 and 508/510. The structure survived into the 1980's, but not as a railroad facility. (Below left) Crowds watch as a suburban bilevel is shunted in onto waiting 518 at Madison on July 20, 1957. Suburban cars often were added to Dakota consists to accommodate weekend crowds traveling between Chicago and Madison. (Bottom left) In this scene of March 28, 1955, a bilevel trails 518's consist for a different reason: It is the first (car No. 1, of course) of 16 such cars to be received by C&NW. It ran north to Madison on 519 the previous day and returned south on 518 for testing purposes. (Below) Train 519 approaches Beloit, Wis., as eastbound Madison-Chicago local 510 accelerates out of town.
Date: November 10, 1957.

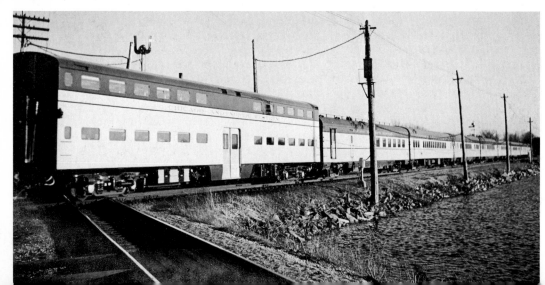

The westbound Dakota 400 cants through the reverse curves at Ableman Narrows near Rock Springs, Wis., in September 1957. It is from this location that C&NW quarries its famous "Pink Lady" ballast.

Jim Scribbins

name to the foot of the Black Hills. West of Huron, the new schedule was shortened 30 minutes by demotion of some local points to "freight service only" status. The most modern aspect of this rather unimpressive extension of *400* service was its ex-C&O coach and the diesel—sometimes an E7—on the head end. Between them was an assortment of head-end cars, and carrying the markers was the Pullman. It was not uncommon for an olive-drab baggage-express car to trail the sleeper.

In October 1957, 519's time was lengthened 15 minutes between Tracy and Huron, and 10 minutes padding was provided for 518 Madison to Chicago; the following spring, the westbound schedule was eased by one hour between Wyeville and Rapid City and the eastbound schedule stretched by half an hour before Mankato was reached. In October 1958, a conditional stop was added at Lodi, Wis., for 518, and in April 1959 an additional 10 minutes was allotted between Madison and Chicago.

On October 25, 1959, the *Dakota 400* underwent its final adjustment in running times. Although 519 departed Chicago 10 minutes later and arrived in Rapid City 25 minutes later for a net loss of 15 minutes, intermediate times varied by as much as half an hour. A 25-minute stop in Madison—unnecessarily long—helped to change the *Dakota 400*'s meet to Elroy, where train 518 now arrived at the same moment its westbound counterpart pulled away from the platform, allowing 519 a better run to its appointment with 401 at Wyeville. Time was added between Huron and Pierre and taken out between Pierre and Rapid City. Adjustments in schedule also occurred across South Dakota for 518, and the schedule between Mankato and Chicago was changed so the train arrived at North Western Terminal 10 minutes later than before.

As happened on many trains through the early 1950s, baggage-car service was gradually curtailed on the *Dakota*. As of July 1953, checked baggage was carried only to and from Chicago and stations between Winona and Mankato, plus Huron. With the extension of the *400* to Rapid City in 1957, baggage-car service was temporarily improved, as luggage could be checked between Chicago and all stations Winona and west. In the spring of 1958, however, this service was restricted to the Winona-Tracy subdivision, Huron, and stations Pierre to Rapid City. Baggage-car service was eliminated altogether in 1959.

By this time, the majority of North Western's once plentiful local trains had disappeared from the timetable, but passenger-train losses continued unabated. Management had already concluded that *North Western Limited* service was expendable and had received permission from the Interstate Commerce Commission to discontinue it in June 1959. The future of the *400*

A half mile or so after entering Wisconsin from Illinois, C&NW trains called at Beloit depot, an impressive, towered structure that unfortunately succumbed to the wrecker's ball in the late 1960's. On a frigid day in January 1961, 519 delights a couple of children. (Above) On another day, 519's smiling conductor and trainman welcome passengers.

It's just about noon on October 12, 1956, as the westbound Dakota 400 *behind a single E8 rolls off the single-track Beloit loop and into Janesville station. Already at the depot waiting for 519 to clear is Madison-Chicago 504, which on this day is powered by the 5000-A—C&NW's one-of-a-kind Baldwin DR-6-2-10 locomotive-baggage unit—and an F7B. The 5000-A was originally intended for the Sioux City section of the never-born* Corn King 400.

In a classic scene dating from 1956, the eastbound Dakota 400 *kicks the dust as it brakes for its evening station stop at Beloit on its way down from Janesville. The Beloit cutoff was principally a passenger route in later years and by 1980 had been taken out of service between Beloit Janesville.*

Jim Popson

A deep rock cut belies that this northbound Dakota 400 is practically within the city of Madison. An FM Erie and E7 and their 10-car consist have a 12:35 p.m. appointment at the Wisconsin state capital on this June day in 1950.
William D. Middleton

The westbound Dakota pauses on the southwest wye at Wyeville as an eastbound freight behind a Geep-Alco lash-up trundles off the Winona line on its way to Adams. Once the freight has cleared, 519 will pull forward onto the Winona line and back into the station (visible just ahead of the freight) for its meet with the Twin Cities 400. Date: July 25, 1959.

Jim Scribbins

William D. Middleton

(Left) Number 519 emerges from the west portal of the bore at Tunnel City, Wis., in September 1957; the tunnel has since been closed and C&NW freight traffic rerouted onto parallel Milwaukee Road tracks. (Above) The passage of 519 in the snow at Madison brings home the holiday spirit on this last day of 1954.

Jim Scribbins

117

William D. Middleton

A seven-car 519 skirts Lake Wisconsin near Merrimac in July 1959. Trailing was one of the ACF-built ex-City diner-lounges.

fleet was under close scrutiny as well, and as a result, C&NW approached the commission in May 1960 with a request to discontinue the *Dakota 400* between Mankato and Rapid City.

Reaction to the proposal was mixed, but there was enough opposition to warrant postponement of the discontinuance until hearings could be held. Southwestern Minnesota offered the least resistance to the discontinuance application. Some newspapers there editorially supported the cutback in service, arguing that the North Western could not rightfully be expected to bear continuing drains on its treasury. Ben Heineman, the C&NW chairman, said that the losses on passenger service west of Mankato totaled $1.1 million annually. Moreover, the editorial

writers felt, the quality of service had remained good; it had been the public that had deserted the railroad, not the reverse.

The number of passengers handled at Rapid City per train during 1959 ranged from 11 to 14 in coach and averaged three in the sleeper. Railway Express Agency had removed its business from the *Dakota 400* in 1959, which contributed to the loss. Undoubtedly, North Western's position was strengthened when the Post Office announced its intention to discontinue RPO service west of Huron in May 1960—an additional loss of $115,000 in annual income to C&NW. One explanation of the slump in ridership aboard the *Dakota 400* was that, as soon as the novelty of the streamliner had worn off, patronage began a never-ending

decline. The Sioux Falls *Argus Leader* suggested a more basic reason for the passenger decline: travelers' preference for their own automobiles or commercial aircraft.

The Minnesota Railroad & Warehouse Commission conducted its own investigation of the situation, presumably to bolster its testimony at the ICC hearing held in Pierre, on July 27. However, since only a handful of citizens appeared at the Minnesota state hearing in Mankato, it would seem that the Minnesota commission had a greater interest in the issue than did its constituents, who stood to be directly affected by the removal of the train.

On Friday, October 21, 1960, the Interstate Commerce Commission announced its approval of the discontinuance of the *Dakota 400* between Mankato and Rapid City. By this time, the train was down to as few as three cars on this portion of its route: head-end, coach and sleeper. The *400* made its last departures from Mankato and Rapid City on the evening of Monday, October 24, with final arrivals at the opposite terminals the following morning. Several riders on the overnight trip were there to bid the train farewell, among them Julia Tallege of Midland, S. Dak., and Roy Logan of Rapid City, both of whom had been passengers aboard the first C&NW train west of Pierre in 1907. The final 518 into Huron was powered by an E7, with Fred Lehfeldt at the throttle; rounding out the crew were Wayne Lyle, fireman, Glen Dickinson, conductor, and K. H. Sachett, brakeman.

The Huron *Plainsman* was displeased with the reduction in service and editorialized that the removal of passenger trains from the second and fourth largest cities in South Dakota—Rapid City and Huron—as well as the state capital and the state's largest educational institution—Pierre and Brookings—could hardly be termed beneficial. The paper did concede, however, that C&NW could now provide better freight service for Huron and would continue as an important element in the city's economy.

Since 518 and 519 no longer entered South Dakota, the name *Dakota 400* was obviously obsolete. Thus the train became the *Rochester 400.* Its equipment usually consisted of a single E8, two coaches, an ACF-built diner-lounge, and a parlor. A tap-cafe sometimes replaced the diner-lounge after 1961. The *Rochester 400* schedule covered the eastern portion of the former *Dakota's* route with only minor revisions.

Jim Scribbins

119

Mike Schafer

Flambeau 400

The vacationer's choice to Wisconsin's resort country

FROM the time Midwesterners became affluent enough to enjoy vacations at summer retreats, the North Western played an important role in carrying them to resorts or second homes, particularly those located among the water and wood of northern Wisconsin. It was to this end that, in the 1920s and '30s, the *Wisconsin Lakes Special* steamed between Chicago and Antigo, Wis., and points north during July and August, terminating at Watersmeet, Mich. Some years, the train included a section which continued along the main line of the Ashland Division to Ironwood, located at the extreme northwest tip of Michigan.

Encouraged by the success of the Chicago-Twin Cities *400*, the C&NW established an additional summer-season limited to capitalize on the public's new fondness for speedy passenger trains. On June 21, 1935, this new weekend service was introduced, supplementing space on the *Special*. The *Flambeau*, as the Friday northbound/Sunday southbound flyer was called, was listed in the public timetable as an "Extra Train." New employees' timetables were not issued for the three divisions—Wisconsin, Lake Shore, and Ashland—over which the *Flambeau* operated, so the train displayed the white flags and lamps of an extra. (Actually, the train may have operated as second sections of existing schedules between Chicago and Oshkosh.)

The *Flambeau* followed the route of the *Wisconsin Lakes Special* north from Oshkosh to Hortonville, Wis., over an even-then rather obscure cutoff which formed the southernmost extent of the Ashland Division. From there, the train traveled a more important subdivision of the Ashland Division through Eland, a typical railroad junction community, to reach the route used by the year-round *Ashland Limited*. At Monico, the *Flambeau* split into two sections, one destined for Watersmeet, 52 miles away at the end of the branch, and the other for Ironwood, 89 miles distant. Ironwood was not on the Ashland main line, so the *Flambeau* had to back for nearly a mile into Ironwood from the main at Hurley, Wis.

The *Flambeau*'s Friday departures from Chicago's North Western Terminal were at 1 p.m., with arrivals in Watersmeet at 9:35 p.m. and Ironwood one hour later. On Sundays, the train left Ironwood at 1:45 p.m., while its Watersmeet counterpart began rolling 55 minutes later. Arrival in the Windy City was set for 11:15 p.m. Between Chicago and Ironwood, a parlor, diner and coaches operated, while a parlor and coaches covered the Watersmeet line.

The train's name derived from the northern Wisconsin territory between Woodruff and Mercer, site of Lac du Flambeau, Flambeau flowage and the Flambeau River. Here the railway creates a steel path through the Lac du Flambeau Indian Reservation. The name "Flambeau," which means "flaming torch," was given by the French explorers to the area's native Americans, whom they found fishing at night by torchlight. Until World War II, the *Flambeau* carried a drumhead featuring a red torch on a white background.

It would seem that the *Flambeau*'s introduction was a surprise move by the North Western, because the May 5, 1935, timetable, which could have been expected to list all summer operations, did not mention the train. The new northwoods express ran without timetable mention until a revised edition appeared with a July 15 date.

After a suburban Chicago stop at Evanston, Wisconsin stops were made at Kenosha, Racine, Milwaukee, Fond du Lac, Oshkosh, Clintonville, and Antigo. Fast running was in order between Chicago and Milwaukee to achieve a 90-minute timing—which was excellent, considering the three stops en route. Although no *400*-like speeds were achieved beyond the Cream City, the schedule was kept respectable by elimination of all stops outside the most important population centers until resort country was reached.

Then, north of Antigo, operations became more leisurely and stops frequent. Pelican Lake and Monico marked the entry into the vacation area. On the Watersmeet branch, the train stopped at Three Lakes, Clearwater Lake, Eagle River, Conover and Land O' Lakes. Continuing along the main line, the Ironwood segment served Rhinelander, Lake Tomahawk, Woodruff, Ojibwa Lodge, Lac du Flambeau, Manitowish, Mercer and Hurley. Other than Rhinelander, these towns ranged from small to tiny.

For the Independence Day holiday, an additional trip was scheduled on July 3. By its fifth weekend of service, the *Flambeau* had become so well received that separate sections were operated from Chicago to and from each end-point, rather than splitting the train at Monico. One result of this was the addition of dining-car service into Watersmeet. Two-section operation continued through Labor Day; that weekend, nearly 400 passengers were aboard each of the trains that steamed into the north country, a certain indication of the passenger extra's popularity. In fact, because of its remarkable acceptance, the *Flambeau* continued to run through the month of September, rather than being terminated after Labor Day as had been contemplated originally.

On the basis of its first year's achievement, the *Flambeau* was placed in the timetable for the 1936 season as train 105 between Chicago and Ironwood, with the Monico-Watersmeet portion running as train 5. Eastbound (southbound geographically), the train numbers were 110 and 10. Beginning Memorial Day weekend, the trains were scheduled on Fridays from Chicago and Sundays returning. Then, in a major advance, operations were increased to five days per week from the end of June through mid-September. Number 105-5 departed from North Western Terminal Tuesday through Saturday, returning as No. 110-10 Wednesday through Sunday. For the final two weeks in September, Friday/Sunday operation was resumed. Only minor adjustments were made in the schedule, with 20 minutes added to train 5 and 10 minutes to 105. Additional stops were made at New London westbound and eastbound at New London Junction (the Green Bay & Western crossing) and at Elcho.

Equipment for the completely air-conditioned *Flambeau* included coaches and a parlor car to each northern terminus, plus a diner to Ironwood and a newly remodeled full buffet-lounge to Watersmeet. This heavyweight had new lighting fixtures, both suspended from the center of the ceiling (there being no clerestory) and mounted vertically above the windows; a large, colorful stand-up bar in its middle section; and individual chairs as well as booths for riders desiring a beverage or snack. In fact, the car was even more cheerfully attractive than the lounge of the *400*.

When the North Western placed stewardesses aboard the *400* during the second week of August 1936, the third girl of the trio, Ruby Williams, relieved the regulars for one day each and spent the remainder of her six-day work week making two round trips on the *Flambeau*. These improvements in *Flambeau* service, together with the train's frequent mention in the company magazine, *Timely Topics*, lent credibility to the oft-expressed opinion that 105 and 110 were exceeded in rank on the routes north of Chicago only by the *400* itself. Clearly they were considered prestige trains.

For Independence Day, two sections were operated, conveying more than 500 holiday-bound travelers. Business was even better over Labor Day, when 105 and 5 ran as individual sections both Friday and Saturday, and a special movement of 110 and 10 was provided on the holiday itself to return 700 people to Chicago.

In 1937, the *Flambeau* was scheduled daily between May 28 and September 25 northbound and May 29 through September 26 southbound. Equipment was unchanged from the previous year, but times and route were modified. Number 105-5 departed from Chicago 1 hour and 10 minutes earlier, at 12:05 p.m., to arrive Ironwood at 9:55 p.m.—a modest five-minute lengthening of the running time. Number 5 had 15 minutes added, arriving Watersmeet at 9:15 p.m. Number 110 left Ironwood at 12:48 p.m., and 10 began rolling from Watersmeet at 1:50 p.m.; the combined train reached Chicago at 10:45 p.m., the same time as the previous year.

A major change was that the *Flambeau* began serving Ashland, Wis.—the westernmost point on the division of that name—once a week. Number 105 was extended to that city on Chequamegon Bay on Friday nights, arriving at 11:15 p.m., with a Saturday return departure at 11:35 a.m. This extension was a noteworthy event, since it provided the first true daytime train service on the North Western between Chicago and Lake Superior. There was another alteration, this one in the Fox River valley: The *Flambeau*'s routing was restructured so that the train remained on the Lake Shore Division through Neenah (where a stop was made) north to Appleton Junction, also a stop and the point where the *Flambeau* now instead entered the Ashland Division. Farther north, stops were added at Nawaii and Marlands, both near Woodruff. With the July 8 timetable, another stop

Minutes out of North Western Terminal, Pacific 2905 and its heavyweight Flambeau *consist bound across the Chicago River near Fullerton and Ashland avenues circa 1940.*

was inserted, at Stronghart, between Lake Tomahawk and Woodruff. During the 1937 season, 110 once again stopped at Kenosha to detrain passengers.

Indicative of its rank, the *Flambeau* shared ads in the 1937 timetable with the *400*. At the close of the season, the railway issued a statement with the pleasing news that the northwoods train had been carrying capacity crowds throughout the summer.

The 1938 season began as usual for Memorial Day, with weekend operation; on June 17—a few weeks later than the previous year—the *Flambeau* once again became a daily train. The schedule was essentially unchanged, though the Marlands stop was eliminated while one was added at Wittenberg, south of the junction community of Eland. Ashland again had once-a-week service, but northbound operation was now Saturday and southbound Sunday. Racine and Kenosha were made regular stops for 110.

The weekend of July 9 and 10, 1938, was an important one in Green Bay. On Saturday the city lost its streetcars, but on Sunday it gained the *Flambeau*. Numbers 105 and 110 were rerouted to serve Appleton proper instead of Appleton Junction, Green Bay (the headquarters of the Lake Shore Division), Shawano and Eland where it now entered the Ashland Division. This route change required adjustments of intermediate times in both directions. Time was taken up west of Monico, allowing arrival in Ironwood only five minutes later despite the longer mileage via Green Bay. However, times on the Watersmeet Branch were 20 minutes later at all points. Eastbound departure was at 12:10 p.m. from Ironwood and at 12:45 p.m. from Watersmeet, with Chicago arrival at 10:15 p.m., a 35-minute lengthening of the schedule for train 10 and a 12-minute addition for 110. Saturday night arrival at Ashland was at 11:28 p.m., with departure at 10:57 a.m. Sunday. At this time the Marlands stop was reinstated. Number

123

The sign on the platform canopy at Green Bay depot gives plaudits to the Cloverland, *but it is the heavyweight* Flambeau *that commands the attention of station visitors and train passengers on this September 4, 1939. Proud Pacific 2911 appears to be just getting underway with train 110.*

110 was given a conditional stop at Appleton Junction to allow passengers to transfer to 109, a train for Merrilan which now originated at Manitowoc rather than Green Bay.

Both *Flambeau*s operated daily through September 3; 110 made a special trip on Labor Day—not only was it the last Ashland departure of the season, but as it would turn out it was the last Ashland departure ever until the *Flambeau 400* was born years later. Trains for both Watersmeet and Ironwood continued to operate northbound on Fridays and Saturdays and southbound on Saturdays and Sundays through September.

Through the next four summer seasons, the *Flambeau* followed the established pattern, its schedule never varying more than five or ten minutes, with service initially weekends-only and becoming daily during the warm months. Equipment remained basically the same, though in 1941 first-class accommodations were provided by a compartment-parlor to Ironwood and a parlor-

drawing room car to Watersmeet. The one major change during this period was the cancellation of the weekend extension to Ashland. Summit Lake, 4.5 miles south of Elcho, was added as a conditional stop. The Independence Day weekend of 1941 was called the busiest in a decade, and two sections of the *Flambeau* were operated in each direction.

After the summer of 1942, 105 and 110 ceased to operate for the duration of World War II, since the Office of Defense Transportation prohibited seasonal trains for vacation travel in order to conserve equipment for the war effort. Though the Association of American Railroads urged the public not to travel, limitations on the use of private automobiles through gasoline and tire rationing and the prosperity resulting from wartime full employment swelled rail passenger volume to twice what it had been in 1941 and four times that of 1939.

Moreover, the movement of armed forces personnel required

Delivered from Electro-Motive at La Grange, Ill., only a day or so earlier, twin E6's return south to Chicago with Flambeau *110 on August 16, 1941. (Above) right) On May 27, 1950, Mayor David H. Winter of Shawano, Wis., cuts the ribbon in the path of the* Flambeau 400's *first southbound trip.*

more than half the sleeping cars and one-third the coaches of all railroads—this at a time when the carriers owned approximately the same amount of equipment as in prewar years. Material was not available for construction of new passenger equipment for civilian use, though a limited number of troop sleepers of spartan design were built exclusively for the military.

Germany surrendered on May 7, 1945, and Japan followed on August 14. Sixteen days later, the Office of Defense Transportation ended its restrictions on operation of nonessential schedules. The very next day, C&NW reinstated operation of the *Flambeau.* Equipment was identical to that of prewar years, but service was provided northbound on Fridays only and southbound on Labor Day and then Sundays for the remainder of September. F. G. Fitz-Patrick, chief traffic officer, said C&NW was happy to be able to reinstate the weekend service.

For 1946, the schedules were lengthened 20 minutes in each direction. On 105 the time was added between Green Bay and the northern terminals, and on 110 south of Green Bay to Milwaukee. Lake George, east of Rhinelander, was added as a conditional stop, and Nawaii eliminated. In both 1946 and 1947, weekend service began for Memorial Day; operation was daily in July and August, then weekends-only again after Labor Day through September. While the *Flambeau* carried parlors for each destination on its few trips in 1945 as it had in prewar years, these first-class cars were discontinued for the following two seasons, though the Ironwood parlor was restored in 1948 and 1949.

Both the route and the times for the southbound *Flambeau* were changed in 1947. Departures from Ironwood and Watersmeet were moved 30 minutes earlier—to 11:30 a.m. and 12:10 noon—and arrival in Chicago was 35 minutes earlier, at 9:55 p.m., the five minutes being gained between Green Bay and Milwaukee, where the train was now routed over the Lake Shore Division, stopping at Manitowoc, Sheboygan and Port Washington. The only change in the northbound train was that—since the joint C&NW-UP *City of Portland* had been renumbered in 1946 to 105—the *Flambeau* was changed from 105 to 115. Its Monico-Watersmeet portion, however, remained No. 5 rather than becoming No. 15.

In 1948, while 115-5's schedule remained unchanged, 110 was advanced to a 45-minute earlier departure from both Ironwood (at 10:45 a.m.) and Watersmeet (at 11:25 a.m.), with Chicago arrival being 20 minutes earlier, or 9:35 p.m.—a 25-minute increase in running times resulting from the train's again being routed via the Fox River valley, stopping at Appleton, Neenah, Oshkosh and Fond du Lac. Marlands was eliminated as a stop for both trains. By this time, C&NW had received enough streamlined equipment from its postwar order that yellow-and-green coaches could accommodate usual traffic on the *Flambeau* as long as consists of the existing *400*'s did not require amplification.

An important change in *Flambeau* service occurred on July 25, 1949, when the train was combined with the existing *Shoreland 400* northbound and *Valley 400* southbound—trains 153 and 216—between Chicago and Green Bay. In effect, 115 and 110 were then independent trains north of Green Bay only, being handled as part of the *400* consists—though with their own train numbers —on the southern portion of their route. Inclusion with 153 brought the outbound *Flambeau* to the Lake Shore Division for

E7 pair 5013-B&A slide into Green Bay on July 21, 1949, with a mixed consist of heavyweights, lightweight 400 rolling stock and ex-City cars that comprised a pre-400-status southbound Flambeau.

the first time. The northbound *Shoreland 400*'s schedule was moved 50 minutes later to conform to the existing departure of 115. Even with the heavier train, the 3-hour 50-minute *400* timing was maintained through the use of twin E7's, available because of a recent delivery of new units. However, a longer stop at Green Bay offset some of the 40-minute gain this timing represented for the *Flambeau*, and it reached Watersmeet 30 minutes earlier and Ironwood only 15 minutes earlier.

Southbound, 110 departed Ironwood 30 minutes earlier, while 10 left Watersmeet 45 minutes earlier. The combined train reached Green Bay at 4:20 p.m., one hour earlier. Less time was spent attaching to the *Valley 400* than detaching from the *Shoreland 400* on the outbound trip, and with the faster schedule of train 216 *Flambeau* riders now found themselves in Chicago 55 minutes earlier than previously, when 110 operated separately. The new *400-Flambeau* combination used primarily standard cars for the northwoods train, with occasional streamlined coaches, plus a regular complement of yellow-and-green lightweight equipment for the Chicago-Green Bay *400*'s. Among adjustments to the schedules of 115 and 110 on the north end was discontinuance of the Stronghart stop.

As early as July 1946, North Western had forecast a new streamlined train to operate on a daytime schedule between Chicago and Ashland—a replacement for, and extension of, the *Flambeau*. Preliminary announcements said that it would be similar to the existing *400*'s. Faster than 115 and 110, the train would run year-round with coaches, parlors, and a tap-diner-lounge. The new train was expected to begin with the summer 1947 season, and in the fall of 1946 announcements began referring to the forthcoming streamliner as a *400*.

In late 1946 the schedule of local train 125, which ran north from Appleton Junction to Ashland, was adjusted to connect with Chicago-Green Bay train 149 at the junction, providing a daytime service from Chicago to Ashland similar to that which had existed southbound via Nos. 116-154-216 for several years. However, the promised new *400* service did not materialize until three years later; there were delays in delivery of new equipment after the war, and as cars did arrive they were used first to increase the capacity of existing *400*'s. Nevertheless, the 1950 calendar provided a hint of what was to come when it depicted a *400* with twin E7's and train passing a northwoods lake, with a girl on a raft in the foreground.

(Left) E6 5005-B and FM Erie 6002-B team up with the northbound Flambeau 400 on March 29, 1952, at Shorewood, a northern Milwaukee suburb. Only a short distance up the line, in a 1955 scene at Glendale, E7 5012-B and E8 5029-B roll 153 above the Milwaukee River in a landscape frozen by January weather.

Both photos, Jim Scribbins

The proud E's of the Shoreland 400 *(at right) and the* Flambeau 400 *await their late afternoon highballs to resume their trips to Chicago. Sunday-only 168 has come from Menominee, Mich., and will head to Milwaukee via Manitowoc and Sheboygan; 216 will take the valley route through Appleton and Fond du Lac.*

E-2-b 4-6-2 2911 subbed for diesel power on 216's trip to Chicago from Green Bay on this day, probably early in the 1950's. The northbound Flambeau, *train 153, is sitting at the Green Bay depot. The engineer is Oakman Mullen who was a fan and active in the Chicago & North Western Historical Society.*

The April 30, 1950, timetable changed the times of trains 153 and 216, the *Shoreland 400* and *Valley 400*, to agree with those that, beginning in May, would be used by the *Flambeau 400*—an extension of those trains. Number 153 was retimed 15 minutes later at all stations, with Chicago departure now 11:30 a.m. and

Green Bay arrival 3:20 p.m. Number 216 whistled off from Green Bay at 5 p.m., 30 minutes later than previously, and came to a halt at the bumping post in North Western Station at 9 p.m., also 30 minutes later. This revised schedule allowed 15 minutes more turnaround time in Green Bay.

On Friday, May 26, 1950, *400* service was extended to Ashland with the first through run of train 153. The following day the train's counterpart number, 216, became the first southbound *Flambeau 400*, all this in keeping with the *Flambeau* tradition of starting operation on Memorial Day weekend. (The 1950 holiday was particularly timely for inauguration of the new streamliner, since it was predicted that 30 million automobiles would choke the nation's highways during the weekend.) Motor trains 125 and 116, all-stop locals between Antigo and Ashland, were eliminated, replaced by the modern *400*'s.

Between Chicago and Green Bay, the *Flambeau 400*'s stops were the same the predecessor *Shoreland* and *Valley 400*'s made. North of Green Bay to Ironwood, the stops were those previously scheduled for seasonal 115 and 110. In the remaining 39 miles into Ashland, Saxon was the only stop. Number 153 had to back into Ironwood from Hurley after stopping at the latter, before proceeding west to Saxon and Ashland. Number 216 stopped at Hurley, then headed into Ironwood. After station work there, 216 backed out to Hurley Junction, then continued east along the main line.

North of Green Bay, two E units pulled a *Flambeau 400* which carried a new 7625-series baggage-diner, coaches and two parlors. Between Chicago and Green Bay, the train was filled out with an additional parlor, diner and coaches—in effect, the former *Shoreland* and *Valley 400*s. Between Antigo and Watersmeet, a unique coach-cafe lounge, No. 7000, was added to the consist. At Monico, this car, two or more coaches and one parlor were detached to become trains 15 and 16 for the round trip to Watersmeet behind—of all things—a hand-fired Class R-1 4-6-0.

There was no exhibition tour for the new *Flambeau 400*, though there had been one for the *Dakota 400* just a month earlier. The first southbound departure of the *Flambeau 400* carried as honored guests Ashland city manager Joseph A. Warren and officials of the local chamber of commerce. C&NW representatives included J. R. Brennan, assistant passenger traffic manager, and F. V. Koval, assistant to the president. Farther down the line, at Shawano, Mayor David H. Winter cut a first-trip ribbon, and a key to the city was presented to engineman H. A. Webber.

The equipment for this northern extension of *400* service continued the basic design of the first streamlined *400* of 1939 and the expanded fleet of 1942. The only noticeable difference in the coaches and parlors was the use of venetian blinds in place of shades in the new cars. In actual practice, in fact, equipment was pooled, so 1939 and 1942 cars often ran on 153 and 216. However,

The streamlined Flambeau 400 *provided inspiration for this famous North Woods lake scene used on a C&NW calendar and, as illustrated here, on a 1962-issued menu.*

Collection of William Stauss

ROUTE CHRONOLOGY

Flambeau

1935-1936: Chicago-Ironwood/Watersmeet via Oshkosh, Hortonville

1937-July 1938: Chicago-Ironwood/Watersmeet via Appleton Junction, Hortonville

1937-1938: Once-weekly operation beyond Ironwood to Ashland

July 1938-1942: Chicago-Ironwood/Watersmeet via Appleton Junction, Green Bay

July 1942-August 1945: Service suspended

August 1945-July 1949: Chicago-Ironwood/Watersmeet via Appleton Junction, Green Bay except for train 110 during 1947 operating via Manitowoc

NOTE: *Flambeau* cars handled on *Shoreland 400* northbound and *Valley 400* southbound, making 115 and 110 independent trains only between Green Bay and Ironwood/Watersmeet effective July 1949.

Flambeau 400

1950-1956: Chicago-Ashland/Watersmeet, northbound via Manitowoc, southbound via Appleton Junction

1956-May 1968: Same, but without Watersmeet section

May 1968-1971: Chicago-Green Bay via Appleton Junction; seasonal service only beyond Green Bay to Ashland after fall 1968

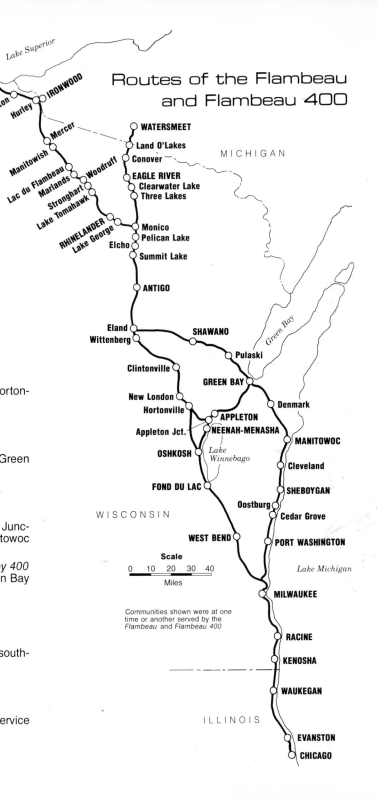

Routes of the Flambeau and Flambeau 400

Lake Superior

ASHLAND
Saxon
Hurley IRONWOOD
Mercer
WATERSMEET
Land O'Lakes
Conover
MICHIGAN
Manitowish
Lac du Flambeau
Marlands Woodruff
EAGLE RIVER
Clearwater Lake
Three Lakes
Stronghart
Lake Tomahawk
RHINELANDER
Lake George Elcho
Monico
Pelican Lake
Summit Lake
ANTIGO

Eland
Wittenberg
SHAWANO
Green Bay
Pulaski
Clintonville
GREEN BAY
New London
Hortonville
Denmark
Appleton Jct. APPLETON
NEENAH-MENASHA
OSHKOSH
Lake Winnebago
MANITOWOC
Cleveland
FOND DU LAC
SHEBOYGAN
Oostburg
Cedar Grove
WISCONSIN
WEST BEND
PORT WASHINGTON

Scale
0 10 20 30 40
Miles

Communities shown were at one time or another served by the *Flambeau* and *Flambeau 400*

Lake Michigan

MILWAUKEE

RACINE
KENOSHA
WAUKEGAN

ILLINOIS

EVANSTON
CHICAGO

Patrick Dorin collection: Pullman-Standard

Baggage-cafe-lounge 7625 and three sister cars were built in 1950 by Pullman-Standard; two were assigned to the Flambeau 400 *and two to other 400's of the fleet. Passengers could avail themselves to food service at a lunch counter or at tables set up for 2-4 seating.*

C&NW

two new types of cars introduced with the *Flambeau 400* did make its consists a little different from all the preceding yellow-and-green streamliners.

The forward car in each of the two sets of equipment was one of four brand-new baggage-cafe-lounges just received from Pullman-Standard. Behind the baggage room and kitchen—the latter only about 14 feet long but extending the full width of the car—was a lunch counter and the dining-refreshment room. With only six stools, this counter had less seating than those aboard earlier cars but was otherwise identical in arrangement and decoration. The dining room, however, was refreshingly different from any other *400* restaurant car.

It was arranged in a manner typical of Pullman-Standard diners of the postwar period. Tables for four were angled so that two diners occupied bench-type seats and had their backs partially to the windows, while their companions at each table sat in movable chairs with their backs toward the aisle. Across the car, a row of triangular tables for two pointed toward angled banquettes against the wall. An overhead strip of continuous lighting above each row of tables provided illumination. The 30-seat dining room, carpeted and draped, had small photo-murals between windows. Large photo-murals adorned the rear walls on both sides of the access door to the train, as well as the bulkheads between the dining and counter areas. At other than meal times, the dining tables were used for beverage service, and a steward was in charge of the car.

Seen from the exterior, the baggage-cafe-lounges cars showed five broad windows on each side corresponding to the location of the dining tables. The left side had two additional windows of this size in the counter area, while the right had two smaller kitchen

windows. There were access doors on both sides at the forward end of the kitchen; wide doors with windows provided the only glass area for the baggageman. Passenger access to the car was from the train only. Though operated in the trailing position Chicago-bound, cars 7625-7628 did not have the built-in markers of the earlier *400* head-end lounges.

One-of-a-kind cafe-coach 7000 also arrived from Pullman-Standard early in 1950, intended for use on the *Corn King 400,* a train which never materialized. While a group of coach-lounges converted from existing *400* coaches did not offer food service, the 7000 did. Later, when consists became less sacrosanct and cars were shuffled about freely, the 3400-series coach-lounge rebuilds did fill in on 153 and 216, running through to Ashland, not Watersmeet. But for the summer season of 1950, the 7000 made a daily round trip between Watersmeet and Antigo on trains 16-216 and 153-15, necessitating switching moves at Antigo.

Car 7000's vestibule end was identical to all the regular *400* coaches, with men's toilet and baggage shelves on one side of the entry aisle and ladies' toilet and powder room on the opposite side. There were 36 blue seats in the coach portion of the car. In the rear

The heavyweight era of the Flambeau lasted all the way through the 1940's. Service crews at Green Bay in August 1948 perform the age-old ritual of icing air-conditioned standard cars, in this case the Flambeau's diner.

(Left) Class R-1 4-6-0 No. 1331 arrives Monico, Wis., on June 27, 1951, with a six-car Watersmeet (Mich.) section of the new streamlined Flambeau 400. (Below) One-of-a-kind cafe-coach 7000 was a Pullman-Standard product of 1950 and for a time provided food service on the Watersmeet section—in fact, the only food service that run ever had.

The healthy consist for the southbound Flambeau 400 at Wrightstown, Wis., included a former City train articulated coach set immediately behind the RPO.

section, an aisle ran along the left side, passing first the kitchen and then three booths, each of which accommodated four persons in its red leather seats. Beyond the last booth, a mini lunch counter, lined with four stools of cream leather, curved across to the right side of the car. This cafe-coach and the other *Flambeau 400* cars were among the final 14 single-level cars delivered specifically for *400* service.

From the inauguration of the streamliner until September 5 northbound and September 6 southbound, the Monico-Watersmeet section of the *Flambeau 400* operated on a daily basis. After that, cars serving the branch ran from Chicago Fridays and Saturdays and from Watersmeet Saturdays and Sundays through October 1, when they were discontinued for the winter.

The *Flambeau 400* drew many favorable comments during its first months of operation. The editor of the Ashland *Daily Press,* after traveling to Rhinelander aboard the train, reported that it represented travel deluxe, with a luxurious modern snack bar and diner (actually the cafe-lounge). He commented particularly on the angular placement of the tables, the photo-murals, and the "wonderfully accommodating steward, waiter and chef," finding that the train was sheer luxury on wheels and afforded a fast, smooth ride. It was, in short, the most enjoyable and comfortable train ever encountered by the editor, who went on to offer the North Western hearty congratulations for the *Flambeau 400*.

At the time of its inauguration, the *Flambeau 400* took 90 minutes less than the fastest bus to make the run between Chicago and Ashland, and passengers were known to drive considerable distances to the depot in order to travel aboard it. They came from the Duluth-Superior area to Ashland and from Michigan's "Copper Country" to Ironwood and Rhinelander to board the *400*. However, as early as 1952 ridership out of Ashland had begun to dwindle, indicative perhaps of the future of an area which would become depressed economically.

The first change in the *Flambeau 400*'s schedule occurred in the spring of 1952, when 216 was given five additional minutes of station time in Milwaukee and the same amount more running time on its final lap into Chicago. In the fall of that year, 30 minutes were added between Ashland—where the departure time was moved back from 10 to 9:30 a.m.—and Milwaukee. Some of this time was used for a lunch stop at Antigo, necessary now because the train had become coach-only north of Green Bay. The spring 1956 folder added time at Milwaukee's lakefront station and on the run into Chicago, making arrival there five minutes later. By July 1953, the Marlands stop (between Woodruff and Lac du Flambeau) was eliminated, as was Lake George by January 1955. Meanwhile, conditional stops were added at Pulaski (between Green Bay and Shawano). Lake George was reinstated as a conditional stop for subsequent summer seasons.

Again in 1951, Monico-Watersmeet trains 15 and 16 operated on a seasonal basis, running for Memorial Day weekend, then Fridays and Saturdays northbound and Saturdays and Sundays southbound until late June, when daily operation began, continuing through Labor Day; for two weeks in September, the trains provided weekend service.

After Memorial Day operation in 1952, train 15 ran only on the last two Fridays and train 16 on the last two Sundays of June. Daily operation began for Independence Day and terminated on Labor Day, with the trains then making a single round-trip on each of the next two weekends. In 1953, the period of daily operation was somewhat longer, extending from July 1 through September 11, with additional trains southbound on September 13 and 20 and northbound on September 18. For this season, 16 was given a 25-minute-earlier departure to mesh with 216's earlier time, and 15 arrived in Watersmeet five minutes later than previously.

In 1954, for the first time since the *Flambeau*'s inception, there were no Memorial Day trains on the Watersmeet line. In 1955, operation was further curtailed, now limited to only the peak of the summer season—from Independence Day through Labor Day, with an additional southbound movement only on the Sunday after Labor Day. The steady erosion continued; in 1956, trains 15 and 16 no longer handled any through equipment, becoming a coaches-only Watersmeet-Monico round trip. The end came quietly—unrecognized, in fact, at the time it actually occurred. Though Independence Day-Labor Day service was initially contemplated for 1957, it never materialized, since 15 and 16 were among a group of passenger trains Wisconsin's Public Service Commission allowed C&NW to discontinue, effective June 16, 1957. The final runs, as it turned out, had been made the previous September.

The 1950 season—when cafe-coach 7000 was used—proved to have been the only occasion when Watersmeet-line *400*'s offered food or lounge service. The following year, a parlor car was included for Memorial Day and for the period of daily operation. During that summer, the consists of 15 and 16 typically included a heavyweight baggage car (operated only on the branch), the parlor, and four coaches. (In one of the two consists was a two-unit articulated ex-*City of Los Angeles* coach set—*Las Vegas* and *Salt Lake*—still in UP livery, along with two *400* coaches.) On the head end was a venerable Class R-1 Ten-Wheeler. All of the streamlined cars ran through to and from Chicago.

During the remaining years of through operation, the Watersmeet parlor ran north on Fridays and returned to Chicago on Sundays. In 1956, when a change of trains was required at Monico, the formal designation *Flambeau 400* was dropped for the Watersmeet operation, and these trains were identified during

Less than a month old, the new streamlined Flambeau 400 *behind E7 pair 5020-B&A rumble above the deep, cool waters of the Wolf River near Shawano on June 11, 1950.*

Brad Kniskern

their last summer on the branch by their numbers alone.

In January 1951, the *Flambeau 400* to Ashland received its first equipment change; the discontinuance of the baggage-cafe-lounge north of Green Bay. As a replacement, cafe-coach 7000 began operating Ashland-Antigo round trips, so food service was still provided at normal meal times and beverage sales eliminated only during the late afternoon hours. Another change was the reduction of the Chicago-Green Bay parlor car to a northbound-on-Friday, southbound-on-Sunday pattern. Four months later, in time for the summer season, the baggage-cafe-lounge was extended again to Ashland and the Chicago-Green Bay parlor restored to daily operation. However, first-class business was lean, and the parlor was discontinued completely in mid-July.

During the summer of 1951, a typical consist for 216 in the north country would have had a pair of E6's or E7's on the point. (Occasionally, one such unit was lashed up with a lone EMD E2, an ex-*City* diesel; originally jointly owned with UP and SP, this rare unit later was numbered 5003 when C&NW assumed sole ownership.) Following the EMD's would be a streamlined RPO-express, a parlor and coaches, with a cafe-lounge-baggage trailing and displaying oil markers. At Monico, the parlor and

coaches from Watersmeet would be cut in immediately behind the parlor from Ashland. By this time new equipment had been received for the *City* trains, so some *400*-type 3400-series coaches which had been painted for Overland Route service would show up on 153 and 216—still in their Union Pacific-style livery.

For fall and winter, the baggage-cafe-lounge was again withdrawn north of Green Bay and, along with it, the parlor. A "cafe-lounge" was used for the Ashland-Antigo turnaround, most likely cafe-coach 7000. In any event, the car was dropped from the consist after the New Year's holiday of 1952, demoting the trains to coach-only status in northern Wisconsin for the off-season, though both parlors and baggage-cafe-lounge would be back in the summer.

For approximately six weeks in the fall of 1952, no tavern car operated between Chicago and Green Bay, though one of the beverage-service cars was subsequently restored to that portion of the *Flambeau*. Later, in June of 1954, a coach-lounge, one of the 3400-series cars, was added through to Ashland, remaining in service until January 1955. This coach-lounge returned again with the spring time change, and the parlor and baggage-cafe-lounge were back once again for the summer season. Though the

133

usual post-Labor Day equipment curtailments occurred, a second parlor between Chicago and Green Bay was added at the same time.

Throughout these years, ski-resort business was often very good, expanding some *Flambeau 400* winter consists to as many as 10 coaches into the north country. On these occasions the baggage-cafe-lounge and sometimes the full diner would run to Ashland. The routine winter *Flambeau 400* on the north end, however, was an RPO-express and two coaches (or one coach and a coach-lounge). In the summer of 1956, the coach-lounge, which had been running continuously, was supplemented by not only the usual parlor but also a full diner—the first regular dining-car operation over the northern portion of the route.

At this time, an ex-*City* club-lounge was assigned to Nos. 153 and 216 instead of the usual 7625-series car. This increased the lounge space aboard the train, since the ACF-built club car had neither baggage compartment nor kitchen. The ex-*City* club-lounge continued to run in 1957 but was not extended over the northern portion of the route. That year, before the resort season was in full swing, the parlor and diner terminated in Ironwood, deadheading between there and Ashland in both directions. The spring 1958 timetable showed the coach-lounge which had operated into Ashland replaced by an ex-*City* ACF-built diner-lounge, which ran through to Ironwood between late May and mid-September, during which time parlor-car operation was again extended to Ashland. While the usual club-lounge was carried over the south end of the route, there was no full diner—probably because these cars were then being converted to electric operation to make them compatible with the bilevel *400* cars then under construction.

Beginning in the spring of 1957, the schedules of both sides of the *Flambeau 400* were lengthened. Number 153 was stretched 25 minutes in April and again 15 minutes in October; No. 216 was slowed by five minutes at that time and another 25 minutes the following spring. During the next decade there were other adjustments to the schedule, with time added or taken up over various portions of the route, in some cases reflecting changes in meets on single-track sections. Adjustments were also made in station time at Milwaukee and Green Bay. The trend throughout was toward longer overall running times. Prior to enactment of the Federal Uniform Standard Time Act in the mid-1960s, schedules were also changed, without alteration of running times, in an attempt to match train times with the various terminating dates for Daylight Savings Time in Wisconsin and Illinois. Illinois observed daylight time in October, while Wisconsin did not.

A change of substance occurred on May 6, 1968, when 153 was rerouted from the Lake Shore Division to operate via the Fox River valley. The longer route resulted in 40 minutes additional

running time between Chicago and Green Bay, where some station time was cut to allow 153 to arrive at Ashland only 35 minutes later than previously. That moved the southbound departure from Ashland 40 minutes later; cutting 15 minutes from an unneccessarily long 50-minute stop at Green Bay and reducing the schedule elsewhere allowed the 9:30 p.m. arrival in Chicago to be maintained.

On October 26, 1958, bilevel *400* equipment was put in service. To accomplish a quick round trip between Green Bay and Chicago, one bilevel consist traveled north as train 153 and returned south as train 206—newly christened the *Green Bay 400*.

Thus the northbound *Flambeau 400*, though nominally a through train, actually required a change at Green Bay for all passengers traveling north of there. The southbound *Flambeau 400*'s 3400-series coach from Ashland was joined at Green Bay by a parlor, additional coaches, and ex-*City* diner-lounge and club-lounge, all of which had come up the previous evening on train 215, the *North Woods Fisherman*. This arrangement not only inconvenienced northbound *Flambeau 400* passengers but also

Brad Kniskern

Jim Scribbins

Jim Scribbins

(Above left) It was not uncommon for single-level equipment to be mixed with bilevel equipment, as this view of 216 just out of Green Bay station on May 2, 1962, demonstrates. The Flambeau went two-story in the spring of 1959. (Above) The northbound Flambeau 400 eases across the Milwaukee Road diamond at Tavil interlocking south of Green Bay station in August 1970. (Left) The Flambeau 400 of the late 1960's often was but two cars north of Green Bay; 216 is slipping into Rhinelander on May 1, 1966. During the summer season, passengers could make bus connections here for Eagle River, Land O'Lakes and other havens for summer vacationers.

(Facing page) Ashland, Wis., the remote northern terminus for the Flambeau 400 on Lake Superior's Chequamegon Bay, was 452 rail miles from Chicago, making that 400 route the second longest (behind the Dakota 400's 653 miles). On August 21, 1960, 216 prepares for departure from Ashland's ample brick depot. (Above) Train 216 nearing Shawano on July 27, 1962, reveals a modest but noteworthy consist. The RPO-express lasted until the U.S. Post Office cancelled hundreds of such operations throughout the country in 1968; the heavyweight storage-mail cars, brought north on 215, the North Woods Fisherman, were often handled east on 216. (Left) The northbound Flambeau calls at Shawano on August 10, 1968.

All photos, unless otherwise credited, Jim Scribbins

Mike Schafer

Typical of North Western's efficient passenger operations was the quick turnaround of equipment at various terminals and stations. On a drizzly June day in 1967, we see one of the more well-known turnaround rituals being performed, that of Flambeau 400 equipment at Green Bay. In the top photo, 216 has arrived from Ashland with two units, an RPO-baggage and three coaches; 153 stands in the distance adjacent to the depot-side platforms. In the bottom photo, taken moments later, an FM switcher has just attached the diner, coach and baggage-lounge that had come up on 153, along with a deadhead single-level coach, to the rear of 216. Meanwhile, 153's power returns to its Ashland-bound cars to resume the trip north. The schedules allotted 30-45 minutes for the turnaround. (Below) On August 21, 1960, train 216, with a five-car consist that included three suburban bilevels, pauses at Antigo, Wis., to change engine crews. During the existence of the Ashland Division, the large station housed division offices.

Both photos, Jim Boyd

Jim Scribbins

138

The Flambeau *and its* 400 *descendant presented riders with a contrast of scenes, from the bustle of Chicago and Milwaukee, to glimpses of beautiful Lake Michigan shoreline, to the serenity that is the Wisconsin North Woods. East of Woodruff in May 1966, the southbound* Flambeau 400 *slips across an inlet of Lake Minocqua where perhaps decades ago native Americans fished by torchlight.*

Jim Scribbins

Milwaukee's Memorial Art Center is as modern as the bilevel Flambeau 400 passing before it. On this August 5, 1960, we note a slight deviation in the consist of the train: The diner has been placed adjacent to the baggage-lounge—normally a coach separated the two.

All photos, both pages, Jim Scribbins

Intermodal transportation made travel on the 400's even more attractive for vacationers destined for points not served directly by rail. Here at Manitowoc, for example, passengers headed for Wisconsin's famous Door County peninsula could make an across-the-platform transfer from the Flambeau 400 to Bay View Bus Lines' motor coach to Sturgeon Bay and Gills Rock. Date: September 21, 1963. Note the neon "400" sign at the end of the depot.

140

An E8-F7 lashup rolls out across the Manitowoc River in November 1967 with 153 shortly after departing Manitowoc station. (Left) The Green Bay-bound 153 of September 23, 1970, by now known only as a "Bi-Level Streamliner", pauses at Racine, Wis., with its abbreviated consist of coach and "Sip-and-Snack Car," which featured inexpensive hot sandwiches and beverages from a self-service counter.

In 1966, C&NW closed its lakefront station in Milwaukee and rerouted passenger trains to and through the new Milwaukee Road depot. In the four photos on these two pages and the two on the following page, the northbound Flambeau 400

illustrates the new pathway through the Cream City. (Above left) Train 153 is crossing from C&NW tracks to CMStP&P rails at Washington Street in March 1968. (Above) Pausing at the new depot in January 1967.

was an inefficient use of equipment, requiring two sets to protect 215 and 216, whereas one set had sufficed for 153 and 216 south of Green Bay.

The bilevel equipment was reassigned in the spring of 1959, at which time the *Flambeau 400* was designated and advertised as a bilevel train. Once again, equipment operated through from Chicago to Ashland, although most cars—a remodeled tavern-lounge (converted from a lunch-counter car), a raised-roof diner, bilevel coach-parlor 600 and additional bilevel coaches as required—turned from north to southbound *Flambeau 400*'s at Green Bay. These cars made their Green Bay turn in one day out of Chicago, thus serving the most heavily traveled portion of the *Flambeau 400*'s route. A single bilevel coach plus a regular streamlined RPO-express car was the normal consist north of Green Bay, with the head-end car often belying its name by trailing the coach. For the summer of 1959, a regular *400*-style parlor and a 7625-series baggage-diner were added, carried on the rear (since they were self-sustaining, with Waukesha motors for their air conditioning) as far as Ironwood and deadheading in and

out of Ashland from there. Additional 3400-series coaches were often handled in this same manner.

This was virtually the final operation of non-coach equipment north of Green Bay on the *Flambeau 400*. Though a regular diner served Ashland for part of the summer of 1964, it was never mentioned in the timetable. Until discontinuance in June 1964 of Nos. 215 and 212—the *North Woods Fisherman*, formerly the *Ashland Limited*—the *Flambeau* shared with that train the movement of storage mail cars north of Green Bay. The cars were handled to Antigo, Rhinelander and Ironwood on 215 and returned to Green Bay on 216.

Number 153's final run over the Lake Shore Division in May 1968 also marked the end of the baggage-tavern-lounge; thereafter, beverage service was offered in the diner. The last *Flambeau 400* via Sheboygan and Manitowoc was made up of E8 5029B, tavern-lounge 7601, coach 703, diner 6953 and coach 704. While on the CMStP&P* in North Milwaukee, the train hit an automobile

*Effective May 1966, C&NW passenger trains began using the new Milwaukee Road depot in Milwaukee, which required routing on Milwaukee Road tracks through most of that city.

(Left) West of downtown Milwaukee at Grand Avenue tower under Wisconsin Avenue bridge, 153 swings north on Milwaukee Road's line to Green Bay. The track diverging to the left is Milwaukee's main line to the Twin Cities. (Above) Looking somewhat out of place in a setting that is very much Milwaukee Road, 153 passes North Milwaukee tower and depot on January 13, 1967.

All photos, both pages, Jim Scribbins.

parked too close to the track and lost 25 minutes, but it arrived in Green Bay only 10 minutes late after an otherwise uneventful trip. The next day, the first 153 to operate on the inland route via Fond du Lac consisted of E8 5029B, two coaches and diner 6953.

In the fall of 1956, the C&NW, under the leadership of Ben Heineman, its new chairman, proposed drastic curtailments in passenger train operations, particularly in Wisconsin. Included was a request to reduce the *Flambeau 400* to a summer-only operation between Green Bay and Ashland. At a hearing in Rhinelander in December, Heineman personally testified that

C&NW faced bankruptcy if it could not halt passenger-related losses. Though 15 representatives from the railroad were present, only Heineman spoke. Supporting the other side of the question were 75 delegates from various communities. Most witnesses were called by Attorney R. W. Peterson, former chairman of the Wisconsin Public Service Commission who was now representing several on-line towns and the railway labor organizations.

The general theme of the opponents was that wintertime discontinuance of the *Flambeau 400* would not only cripple resort business and industrial development but also harm postal service, since the train then called the *Ashland Limited* (which was to be retained) was frequently late, which delayed mail by 24 hours. The opponents' arguments were successful, and 153 and 216 were the only trains in the request that C&NW was blocked from removing.

By 1968, however, things were much different. In an increasingly automobile-oriented era, patronage had continued to decline. Removal of mail by the Post Office Department resulted in a revenue loss of $60,000 for the year ending in May 1968, in

All photos, both pages, Jim Scribbins

On the far north side of Milwaukee at a CMStP&P-C&NW grade-separated intersection, trains left Milwaukee rails at Canco and utilized new connecting tracks to head either up the valley route or the Lake Shore Division from Wiscona on the C&NW. Train 153 on this December day in 1966 is just leaving Milwaukee

rails at Canco and circling up the new interchange to the shore route at Wiscona. After all passenger service to Green Bay ceased with the start of Amtrak on May 1, 1971, the connection was removed.

addition to stated passenger losses of $435,000. Since summer revenue was good—nearly $221,000 for the preceding June, July and August, more than was taken in for all the other nine months—C&NW once again proposed summer-only operation of the *Flambeau 400* north of Green Bay, but with one difference: a bus would roll along paralleling highways for the remainder of each year.

Despite protests at hearings in Rhinelander and Ashland, the railroad won its case, and the state commission authorized substitution of a Wisconsin-Michigan Coach Lines bus, with the provision that train service would resume during the Christmas, New Year, and Easter holidays. C&NW voluntarily included operation for Thanksgiving of 1968. Easter operation was modified to include only 1969. Summer operation in 1969 and 1970 would be from Memorial Day through Labor Day. At other times, the Wisconsin-Michigan bus directly served all C&NW depots except Lac du Flambeau, which was 10 miles off the bus's route along US 51. Bus times were nearly identical to the train schedules and required faster running, since the highway schedule called for a 25-minute lunch stop in Rhinelander.

On July 16, 1969, coincident with the discontinuance of the

Peninsula 400 between Green Bay and Ishpeming, the name *Flambeau 400* was quietly exchanged for the term "Bi-Level Streamliner" in timetable schedule columns, although the cover continued to tout the North Western as the "Route of the *400* Streamliners." The October 1969 folder, however, removed even that reference to the once-famous fleet. The final change in 153 and 216's equipment came in November 1969, when a bilevel "sip-and-snack" coach was substituted for the diner between Chicago and Green Bay.

Operation of 153 and 216 between Green Bay and Ashland ceased forever—without fanfare or even a certain awareness that the end was at hand—with the final holiday trips on January 4 and 5, 1971. When the snow covering the right-of-way in desolate northern Wisconsin muffled the rumble of their wheels for the last time, 153 took a full 12 hours and 216 even 20 minutes longer than that for their journeys over the route linking Lake Superior's Chequamegon Bay with the southern tip of Lake Michigan. The trains continued their daily round trips between Chicago and Green Bay for an additional four months; then the birth of Amtrak on May 1, 1971, completed the demise of the trains that had been the *Flambeau 400*.

Racing for the North Woods, the Flambeau 400 *strikes out across the Milwaukee River at Glendale in July 1967.*

C&NW

Peninsula 400

From smelt specials to Upper Michigan's last passenger train

THE *400* serving Michigan's Upper Peninsula—the detached northwestern portion of the state—began its career on January 12, 1942, in a somewhat embarrassing if record-setting manner. On its initial trip from Ishpeming, Mich., train 214—the streamlined *Peninsula 400*—came to an unexpected halt in the cold, snow-covered landscape some five miles north of Green Bay, crippled by a broken valve on one of its two diesel units. Though supervisors were unaware of the delay until the train was overdue in Green Bay, disaster was averted when a Pacific appeared in short order from the North Green Bay roundhouse. The engine forwarded the *Peninsula 400* across the Lake Shore Division, turning in the fastest time ever for a steam locomotive between Green Bay and Milwaukee to put the train back on schedule.

Every parlor seat on the inaugural train had been reserved, and coaches were crowded with delegations of businessmen, association of commerce officials and newsmen. (Since the delay received no negative comment in the press, the various VIP's aboard must have felt that North Western performed commendably in remedying the situation.) Aboard 214 as guest of honor was Mercedes Nelson, Ishpeming's Winter Sport Queen, whom photographs show peering from the distinctive cab of Alco DL109 No. 5007A, supposedly arriving in Chicago. Though the crippled diesel units may have been towed all the way from Green Bay behind the

rescuing 4-6-2, which could have been cut off after arrival in Chicago and moved beyond the photographer's range, it is as likely that Miss Nelson may actually have posed prior to the departure of 209, the northbound *Peninsula 400*.

The seeds of this new *400* service had been sown back in 1936, when trains 209 and 210 between Chicago and Menominee, Mich., received air-conditioned equipment. Number 209 was briefly designated the *Menominee* and then became the *Winnebago;* 210 came to be named the *Valley*. Both trains operated via Fond du Lac and Appleton. Passenger traffic was substantial, and two sections of these trains were often required on holidays. With the spring 1939 timetable, Ishpeming-Chicago service was improved with the introduction of the *Cloverland*, train 214, which operated via the Lake Shore Division south of Green Bay (rather than via Fond du Lac) and was timed to connect in Milwaukee with train 401 for the Twin Cities and in Chicago with the *City Streamliners* and *Challengers* for the West. There was, however, no correspondingly excellent northbound train to match 214's deluxe service with its air-conditioned coaches, parlor and cafe-lounge.

During this period, interest in passenger rail service was high on the Upper Peninsula. In Marquette, Mich., 1,200 people inspected the first sleeping car to operate to that city, on a summer-only schedule via C&NW and Duluth, South Shore &

Atlantic in 1939. On April 13, 1940, 300 members of a Chicago sportsmen's club rode a special reserved train, complete with drumhead, to the Menominee smelt run. Despite this potential, North Western's February 1941 announcement of expansion of *400* service failed to mention improvements north of Green Bay. Perhaps it was the subsequent operation of three smelt specials from Chicago to Menominee and Escanaba during the spring of that year which influenced the railway to include the Peninsula Division among its *400* routes, for the *Peninsula 400* did become a reality.

The streamliner was exhibited to the public in Menominee and Escanaba on Saturday, January 10, 1942, and in Negaunee and Ishpeming the following day. It entered service Monday, January 12, a most welcome aid to wartime travel. On the night of January 11, a banquet at Ishpeming to celebrate the new service was

(Top) The clock on the Green Bay depot tower reads 11 a.m., so E3 5001-A and Alco DL109 5007-A are performing their Peninsula 400 *duty with punctuality as 214 departs for Chicago on May 18, 1947. (Above) Moments out of Green Bay station, the Ishpeming-Chicago* Cloverland *struts across the Fox River on the bridge that later would serve as the setting for the official portrait of Cloverland's streamlined descendant. Date: October 7, 1939.*

keynoted by Alan Gould, the C&NW traffic manager. Several Upper Peninsula radio stations highlighted the *Peninsula 400*.

The new train's original schedule called for a 4 p.m. departure from Chicago and 11:20 p.m. arrival in Ishpeming for 209, while 214 departed from the north end at 7:15 a.m. and arrived Chicago at 2:40 p.m.—or 2:45 p.m. on Sunday as 240. At first, service extended to Ishpeming just six days a week; the northbound *Peninsula 400* terminated 129 miles to the south, in Menominee, on Saturday nights, and the southbound originated there Sunday mornings. On June 7, the run was lengthened to Escanaba, Mich., and on July 18 daily operation to Ishpeming began. This just reinforced the new train's title as mileage champ of the *400* fleet, since its single set of equipment now made 773-mile round trips seven days a week rather than only six. These were over 100 miles further than the next longest, the Chicago-Milwaukee-Madison-Chicago triangles made by the *Capitol 400*. (Among locomotives, however, the *Twin Cities 400*'s units exceeded even this total, since they doubled back each night with the *North Western Limited*.)

In order to fit most usefully into the overall pattern of service between Green Bay and Chicago, the north and southbound *Peninsula 400*'s followed different paths south of Green Bay. Number 209 took the route of its predecessor, the *Winnebago*, through Wisconsin's Fox River valley, where the urban concentration of Fond du Lac, Oshkosh, Neenah, Menasha (served by the Neenah stop), Appleton and Green Bay made it the most heavily traveled train on the entire C&NW and the longest *400*. Number 214 assumed the number of the *Cloverland* and its route—the Lake Shore Division, a less populated line that included the cities of Manitowoc and Sheboygan, Wis. Number 214 also had stops at Denmark and Port Washington, with a conditional Cedar Grove stop added later. Sunday-only 240 operated via the Fox River valley, however. (During the first 6½ months—until it was extended to Ishpeming—this train was identified simply as the *Streamliner 400*.) Between Milwaukee and Chicago, the trains served Racine, Kenosha and Evanston; 240 also stopped at Waukegan.

Up north on the Peninsula Division, both sides of the streamliner stopped at Negaunee, Little Lake, Escanaba, Powers, Stephenson and Menominee in Michigan, and at Marinette and Oconto in Wisconsin. Later, regular and conditional stops were added at smaller communities: Rock, Brampton and Carney, Mich., and Peshtigo, Wis. Number 209 and No. 240 stopped at

Winding down to Milwaukee's lakefront station, the southbound Peninsula 400 *of October 6, 1954, is about to duck under the photographer's Brady Street footbridge vantage point. If you stand at this location today, you will still see the North Avenue water tower in the distance, but bikers and hikers—not 400's—are now the norm for traffic under the pedestrian overpass.*

West Bend, Wis., and Appleton Junction. Number 209, paused at the junction, one of the three C&NW depots within the city of Appleton, to transfer passengers to branchline train 109, which steamed over a lengthy route through central Wisconsin—to Wausau, usually considered the domain of CMStP&P's *North Woods Hiawatha*.

Northbound at Fond du Lac, Wisconsin Division train crews from Chicago relinquished the *400* to Lake Shore Division men from Green Bay. (Engine crews, however, changed in Milwaukee; jobs were pooled among Wisconsin and Lake Shore men north of there.) Also at Fond du Lac, 209 connected with train 9, which penetrated Milwaukee Road territory at Ripon and Wisconsin Rapids before terminating at Marshfield. Locals 9 and 109 maintained these liasons until their discontinuance, though neither was dieselized or streamlined before vanishing from the timetable. Their eastbound counterparts were without *400* association, except that the Wausau train on Sundays only delivered to 240 at Appleton Junction.

Though some stations were as little as five miles apart, the *Peninsula 400* covered a maximum distance between stops of about 40 miles in one stretch. The train qualified for mention in Donald M. Steffee's Annual Speed Survey in *Trains* Magazine, between Chicago and Milwaukee where 100-mph maximums were allowed; the fastest timing of all occurred between Kenosha and Evanston. Between Milwaukee and Green Bay, average speeds hovered around 60 mph, with maximums of 80 mph permitted through the Fox River valley and 70 and 75 mph on the Lake Shore Division. On the Peninsula Division, which lacked automatic block signals, speeds were slower—though Interstate Commerce Commission regulations mandating maximum speeds for different types of signaling were still eight years away.

Ridership doubled on the *Peninsula 400* early in its career. Originally, the success of the train could be attributed to two factors: modern equipment and running times that were two hours faster southbound than the previous service and a whopping five hours and 20 minutes faster northbound. Numbers 209 and 214 had been planned as seven-car consists: RPO-baggage-tavern-lunch counter, four coaches, diner and parlor. However, they were quickly lengthened by transfer of coaches from the smaller *400*'s. Other streamlined coaches were moved from their normal *Challenger* assignment to the *Peninsula*. These *Challenger* cars—built in 1937 by Pullman-Standard—were also added to the smaller *400*'s to replace the yellow-and-green ones transferred to the popular train to Ishpeming.

Since these *Challenger* coaches—Nos. 6132 through 6147—intended for long-distance travel, they had toilets with adjoining smoking rooms at each end and, consequently, a reduced seating capacity of 48. Their interiors were light rose, with square lighting fixtures above the aisle. Alternately wide and narrow panels setting off windows in pairs made their exteriors markedly different from the *400* cars. Most distinctive was their livery of olive green with gold stripes, identical to the Class E-4 Hudsons (which, since they were limited to the Galena and Iowa Divisions, never pulled *400*'s). The name "The Challenger" in large red script was centered below the windows of the coaches. Until the delivery of postwar *400* equipment, two of these *Challenger* cars were routinely included at the Chicago end of the *Peninsula*'s consist south of Green Bay. There, they and other coaches could simply be cut off and dropped as 209 departed for the lightly settled north country. The following morning, 214's diesels would pull into the clear while the depot switcher at Green Bay replaced the coaches for the trip back to Chicago.

Though the additional cars pressed into service left No. 209 with 11 coaches and a parlor car for a seating capacity of 638, standees were the rule almost from the start. On one weekend run, an astonishing 1,800 passengers rode aboard 209. In 1943, *Peninsula 400* ridership averaged 662 passengers per trip on 209 and 468 on 214. In less than two years the *Peninsula* carried more than 674,000 passengers.

In spite of this heavy demand, North Western was usually able to run 209 and 214 with streamlined consists, though there were exceptions—primarily during the holidays—when standard coaches were used between Chicago and Green Bay. One such time was Thanksgiving 1944; then all of the Chicago-Green Bay coaches were heavyweights, because of the transfer of regularly assigned cars to the flagship *Twin Cities 400* to keep that train's consist pure streamlined yellow and green.

Through the war years, the *Peninsula* stayed busy carrying heavy crowds behind an EMD E3 or E6 lashed up with C&NW's lone "chisel-nosed" Alco DL109, which was usually the lead unit on 214. There were some minor schedule changes, such as the addition of five minutes to 209's time beyond Green Bay. Later, in March 1945, its departure from Chicago was moved from 4 p.m. to 4:10 p.m., with a corresponding adjustment of 10 minutes throughout the schedule. Toward the end of the war, so many trains were operating in and out of C&NW's Chicago passenger terminal that empty moves to and from the coach yard became impractical; thus a number of trains were serviced in the station. Either way, it was tight for the *Peninsula 400*, which had but a 95-minute layover—even with the new, slightly-later departure.

Between the summer of 1945 and February 1946, Office of Defense Transportation Order 53 cancelled all sleeping-car routes shorter than 450 miles to secure additional Pullmans for troop movements. This led to yet more patronage on 209 and 214, since Chicago-Green Bay and Chicago-Ishpeming Pullmans were among those affected.

A Powers-Iron River, Mich., round trip which had connected with the *Iron and Copper Country Express* was discontinued during World War II, a surprising move considering the gasoline and tire rationing of the war years. However, a pair of new trains were added after the war—Nos. 9 and 14—which provided connections with 209 and 214 at Powers, affording a daytime service to the CMStP&P towns of Iron Mountain and Iron River and in the process heightening competition with that road's *Chippewa*. Before this new C&NW local service was instituted, some people were driving between Iron Mountain and Powers to ride the *400*, though rationing and difficult winter weather must have discouraged such disloyalty to the Milwaukee Road trains.

After World War II, the Marinette, Wis., depot was modernized, particularly in its interior appointments. The station received a new ticket office and wood paneling, tile flooring and fluorescent lighting in the waiting room. New round windows in exterior doors as well as at the baggage counter were apparently inspired by the round windows and mirrors in *400* smoking rooms.

The *Peninsula* underwent its first major schedule change on April 27, 1947, when 20 minutes were added to 209's running time between Milwaukee and Green Bay. Two factors were responsible for the change: the frequency of stops and the substantial number of passengers handled—requiring lengthy station stops—in the Fox River valley. In October 1944 the conditional stops at Carney had been discontinued, and four years later 209 was given a provisional stop at Bark River, Mich. Number 214 had its Cedar Grove conditional stop removed in the late 1940's, and the Denmark stop had been transferred to 306, an earlier train, by 1951. Carney now was a seasonal summer stop for Chicago passengers only. In January 1951, five minutes were added to 209's card between Chicago and Milwaukee and another 15 between Green Bay and Ishpeming, for a 12:15 a.m. arrival there. Number 214's departure was advanced from 7:10 a.m. to 6:50 a.m. and the entire 20 minutes used between Ishpeming and Green Bay.

Twenty-six *400*-style postwar coaches were delivered and placed in service in October 1947, releasing the *Challenger* cars from *Peninsula* service and adding seating capacity—thus reducing if not eliminating the problem of standees. Throughout the *Peninsula 400*'s early years, 209's diner had closed at Green Bay, but it was deadheaded on to Ishpeming to be available for breakfast on 214. Effective in March 1948, however, the diner was in daily operation south of Green Bay only and was cut in and out there. Apparently C&NW thought the lunch counter sufficient for morning meal service on the Peninsula Division. Only on Saturday night did the diner deadhead to Ishpeming, to provide Sunday morning breakfast aboard the southbound *Peninsula*. In February 1950, with postwar equipment deliveries virtually complete, a second parlor car was added between Chicago and Green Bay. For the southbound run, it was switched that fall to 306, the earlier train over the Lake Shore Division; the following July, the second parlor returned to 214.

In the spring of 1954, a curious quirk appeared in the operation of the tavern-lunch counter car: it did not run from Green Bay to Ishpeming on the second and fourth Mondays of the month, nor from Ishpeming the following mornings. Then in early 1955, these cars were cut back to Green Bay on a daily basis. One parlor continued as far as Escanaba, but the 64.8 miles north of there to Ishpeming received coach service only.

At the same time the amenities were declining on the north end, they were increased on the southern half of the route with the addition of a coach-lounge car which had become available when the *City* streamliners received new lounges. In fall 1956, however, lunch-counter service in the head-end car was quietly discontinued, and these RPO-baggage-tavern-lunch counters were used thereafter only for beverage service. The previous spring, the ex-*City* coach-lounge had been replaced by a full-length club-lounge car, made surplus by transfer of the *City* trains to the Milwaukee Road. Both beverage cars were used south of Green Bay, and the *400*-type tavern was restored north of there—needed to provide checked baggage service to Escanaba. On June 17, 1957, the parlor was again extended beyond Escanaba to Ishpeming.

On January 9, 1955, the C&NW's Manitowoc-Marshfield-Merrillan trains were discontinued, eliminating the Appleton Junction stops for 209 and 240. In April, No. 214's time was advanced 30 minutes throughout for a 6:20 a.m. Ishpeming departure and a 2:05 p.m. Chicago arrival (2:25 p.m. for 240 on Sunday). That fall, both sides of the *Peninsula* were given five minutes additional station time in Green Bay and 10 minutes more running time north of there. In addition, 209 was rescheduled to leave Chicago 10 minutes earlier. To ease the confusion potential on having both 209 and the eastbound *Twin Cities 400* in the depot at Milwaukee at the same time, 209's stop there was lengthened to 15 minutes. Four minutes were added between Chicago and Milwaukee in April 1956, but 209's station time in the Cream City was dropped back down to 11 minutes, so the overall schedule showed no loss.

Then the fall 1956 timetable moved the northbound departure from Chicago to 4:10 p.m. To accommodate the insertion of Waukegan as a conditional stop, running time between Chicago and Milwaukee was lengthened to 90 minutes, effective with the new schedule. Now the train passed through Milwaukee after No. 400 had departed, relieving congestion at the lakefront passenger station there. A reduction of Green Bay station time plus a small cut in the running time on the north end maintained the 12:30 a.m. Ishpeming arrival.

In the spring of 1957, another 20 minutes were added to the time

Routes of the Peninsula 400

Scale
0 10 20 30 40
Miles

Trains 9 and 14
to and from Iron
Mountain and Iron River

Train 109 to
Wausau and Merrillan

Train 9 to
Marshfield

Communities shown were at one
time or another served by
the *Peninsula 400*

ISHPEMING
Negaunee
Little Lake
Rock
Brampton
ESCANABA
Bark River
Powers
Carney
Stephenson

MICHIGAN

MARINETTE
Peshtigo
MENOMINEE
OCONTO

Green Bay

GREEN BAY
APPLETON
Appleton Jct.
NEENAH-MENASHA
Denmark
OSHKOSH
Lake Winnebago
MANITOWOC
FOND DU LAC
SHEBOYGAN
Cedar Grove
WEST BEND
PORT WASHINGTON

Lake Michigan

MILWAUKEE

WISCONSIN

RACINE
KENOSHA
WAUKEGAN
Great Lakes
Lake Forest

ILLINOIS
EVANSTON
CHICAGO

ROUTE CHRONOLOGY

Peninsula 400

January 1942-May 1961: Chicago-Ishpeming, northbound train 209 via Fond du Lac, southbound Sunday-only train 240 via same route. Daily-except-Sunday train 214 via Manitowoc.

May 1961-July 1969: Train 240 discontinued; 214 operated daily.

July 1969-April 1971: Chicago-Green Bay only, via Fond du Lac.

The "400" Crossing Bridge Over Fox River Near Green Bay.

Although the Peninsula 400 *had long since been bileveled when this menu was printed in 1967, C&NW continued to use the publicity scene of the single-level* Peninsula *shot many years earlier.*

Collection of William Stauss

Were it not for the then-modern automobiles, this 1950 scene of train 15 arriving at Escanaba could pass for having been taken in a much earlier era. The local operated as train 14 from Iron River, Mich., to Powers, Mich., where it delivered passengers to Chicago-bound 214; it then headed north on the Ishpeming line to Escanaba. In the evening, the Class R-1 Ten-Wheeler, the express car and air-conditioned coach will run as train 10 to Powers to become train 9, the connection from 209 to Iron River.

Collection of William Stauss

The Peninsula 400's were stronghold assignments for Omaha Road's four Fairbanks-Morse Eries, although they usually operated apart from each other, paired with EMD power. Erie 6002-B and E6 5005-A are heading south through Shorewood in suburban Milwaukee in March 1952. (Below) A bilevel-era Peninsula 400 eases into Milwaukee depot in March 1965.

Both photos, Jim Scribbins

(Right) Dad and the kids are at trackside to witness Class E 4-6-2 No. 1629 steam into Milwaukee with a special headed for Chicago as an advance Peninsula 400 on July 4, 1948. Minutes later, regular 214 slides into town with a 14-car consist filled with Independence Day travelers.

Credit a C&NW photographer for this splendid scene of the southbound Peninsula 400 *skimming* across the Brown County flatlands and the East River near Green Bay in the late forties. The Fox River is in the background.

C&NW

More than any other 400, the Peninsula *tended to be the recipient of some of C&NW's more unusual diesel breeds, such as the road's lone Alco DL109, the 5007-A. At left, the Alco trails an E3 on 214 at Wilmette tower in suburban Chicago. Below, the chisel-nose unit leads a wartme* Peninsula 400 *out of Green Bay on April 7, 1945.*

C&NW

of 209 through the Fox River valley, for a 12:50 a.m. arrival at Ishpeming. Wisconsin had adopted daylight-saving time, so trains to Green Bay and the north were retimed accordingly, though the Twin Cities route was not changed. Consequently, the connection from 400 to 209 in Milwaukee was broken. Six weeks later, another five minutes were added to 209's schedule on the Peninsula Division, and with the return to standard time in October, 214's carding was lengthened by five minutes between Milwaukee and Chicago. The April 1958 time change saw another 30 minutes allotted below Green Bay—mostly in the 62 miles from Milwaukee to Fond du Lac—as well as additional station time in

Brad Kniskern

Milwaukee and Green Bay. Arrival at Ishpeming was now an inconvenient 1:25 a.m. By this time, checked baggage was accepted on 209 only for stations Milwaukee to Green Bay, though 214 continued to provide baggage service everywhere south of Escanaba.

During the summers of 1950 through 1952, the *Peninsula 400*'s were used as transportation to northern Michigan for railway-sponsored one-week tours to the "land of Hiawatha"—a promotion that, in its naming, perhaps tweaked the nose of competing Milwaukee Road. CMStP&P's *Chippewa Hiawatha*, which also served the Upper Peninsula, was not involved in any such tour operations. During the winter season of 1951-52, a "*400* ski club" was organized for persons who had used the *Peninsula 400* to various Michigan destinations for C&NW-sponsored weekend ski outings.

A railroad's humanity is surely one measure of its success as a passenger carrier, and C&NW often received high grades in that department. In one incident, which transpired in May 1952, a Finnish immigrant couple who spoke no English were aboard train 153, the *Flambeau 400*, ticketed only to Green Bay though their actual destination was Rock, Mich. A telephone inquiry from their relatives at Rock to the Green Bay ticket office alerted C&NW to the situation, and continuation of their journey was arranged. However, where one problem ended another began: how to inform the couple of their need to detrain at Green Bay and wait some five hours for 209 to continue their northward journey. A Green Bay newspaper reporter located a resident who was fluent in Finnish; then C&NW personnel, the newsman and the interpreter met the couple and explained the extension of their trip.

Another human-interest vignette occurred during a busy July 1953 trip. Number 209's delay report carried a notation regarding station time at Escanaba: A first stop was made to detrain coach passengers, a second stop to detrain parlor-car passengers, and a *third* stop to permit a woman to reboard a coach to retrieve her year-old baby, whom she had inadvertently left aboard.

In 1952, Omaha Railway's Fairbanks-Morse "Erie-builts" replaced the often-ailing Alco DL109 No. 5007A as one of the two units on the *Peninsula 400*. After 1956, the motive power was apt to be any combination of EMD E3, E6, E7 or E8 units. A pair of units was always used between Green Bay and Chicago, and generally a single diesel with the smaller Peninsula Division consists.

In the fall of 1958, the *Peninsula* underwent a striking physical change: the introduction of newly delivered Pullman-Standard-built bilevel cars. These up-to-the-minute conveyances were long-distance versions of the successful suburban coaches featured in the North Western's Chicago commuter operations. In fact, the

Decked out in their Sunday best, Green Bay residents and visitors prepare to board train 240, the Sunday-schedule Chicago-bound Peninsula 400 *on a pleasant June 17, 1951. (Bottom) On October 17, 1947, an Alco switcher has added cars to train 214's consist and is about to reattach it to the locomotives. Extra cars in the consists of the* Flambeau *and* Peninsula *between Green Bay and Chicago were the norm account of corridor traffic.*

equipment could be converted easily for inclusion in the Chicago commuter fleet in the event that long-haul passenger service disappeared completely—an important consideration at the time of the new cars' introduction.

With this new high-capacity equipment, 209 and 214 now routinely carried only a parlor car and one coach north of Green Bay, though it was not unusual for an extra coach to be added. A coach-bar lounge, diner, tavern-lounge and additional coaches were included in the train between Green Bay and Chicago, requiring a second E8 for power. Two one-of-a-kind bilevel cars were included in the consist: coach-bar lounge 903 and parlor 6400. The diner and the tavern-lounge were conventional equipment modified to be compatible with the bilevels. Below Green Bay, the *Peninsula 400*'s consist was RPO-baggage-bar lounge 7601 (on the north end of the train, its traditional location) and five or six coaches, separated by diner 6953, coach-bar lounge 903 and parlor 6400. Appropriately for North Western's most popular long-haul passenger trains, 209 and 214/240 had the substantial seating capacity of 624 in coaches (the equivalent of 11 single-level cars) plus 60 in the bilevel parlor car.

The train was electrically heated by auxiliary power generated aboard the locomotives, and this even warmth from the head end was a welcome contrast in the cold northwoods to the uncertainties of steam lines, with their leaks and occasional broken

Both photos, Brad Kniskern

connections. However, the schedule of the *Peninsula 400* was not altered by the introduction of the bilevel equipment.

Before entering regular service, this newest *400* equipment—proudly standing tall at 15 feet, 10 inches—was exhibited to the public on Friday and Saturday, October 17 and 18, in the Fox River valley; on Sunday, October 19th, along the Lake Shore Division, including Green Bay; and on Monday, October 20, at Peninsula Division stations as far north as Escanaba. In Green Bay, a newspaper ad invited the public to inspect a "new concept in travel comfort" and pointed out some of the highlights of the new equipment: greater seat space per passenger, upper- and lower-level seating, the bilevel bar-lounge, precisely controllable electric heat and easy-access center doors. During the five evening hours the train was displayed at Green Bay, 2,600 visitors accepted C&NW's hospitality.

During the first month of bilevel operation, unfortunately, there was no rush by the public to try the new equipment; the *Peninsula*'s loads just about equaled those of the previous year. With the approach of the Thanksgiving and Christmas-New Year holidays, however, passenger traffic manager J. R. Brennan hoped that some people who normally drove would be tempted by C&NW's new concept in train travel. Brennan reported that a survey taken among those who did ride indicated approval of the interior design of the bilevel cars, with the heavily tinted windows

drawing particularly favorable comment. The electric heat was said to perform satisfactorily. Even in an era of general pessimism about the passenger train, C&NW was cautiously hopeful of success in the fairly heavily populated area between Chicago and Green Bay. To stimulate ridership, the railroad ran, throughout the holiday season, attractive ads depicting the bilevel bar-lounge; large outdoor billboards promoting the bilevels appeared on C&NW buildings.

In mid-January 1959, the *Peninsula 400*'s bilevel consist was removed from service for a month (as were the cars from the *Green Bay 400*, the other new bilevel train) to enable Pullman-Standard to correct certain malfunctions—at no charge, as part of the sales agreement. The roller bearings in the trucks had caused the greatest problems, but there were also "bugs" in the automatic doors and in the heating system. Such difficulties, of course, could be expected with any new design, and when the cars' systems were refined they proved to be trustworthy—particularly the electric heating.

The month-long withdrawal of the bilevels brought about a motive-power shortage, however. Six units had been converted to Cummins auxiliary power to operate with the bilevels, and they no longer had steam generators. Thus, locomotives equipped for steam heating had to handle their own normal assignments as well as power the substitute consists running as the *Green Bay*

Jim Scribbins

Clayton C. Tinkham

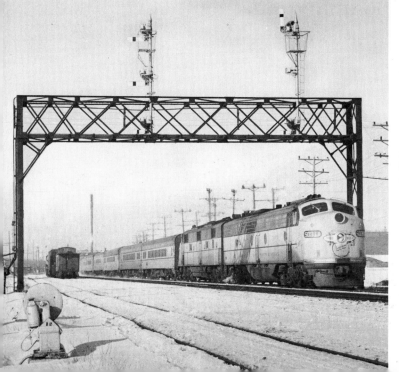

(Left) An E8 and a new-scheme coach (third car) reflect changing times for the Peninsula 400, at St. Francis tower on Milwaukee's south side in January 1958. (Above) Train 10, pausing at Ripon, Wis., on January 29, 1949, with recently upgraded rare motorcar 9915, is enroute to Fond du Lac where it will connect with 210 and, later, 209 before returning to Marshfield.

On a snowless December day in 1966, bilevel 214 slides past Grand Avenue tower on CMStP&P tracks enroute to the new Milwaukee depot.

Jim Scribbins

(Top) The fine new bilevel Peninsula 400 *passes through a familiar location in 1958. (Above) Sunday* Peninsula 400 *240 arrives at Fond du Lac's rambling brick station complex on August 2, 1959. (Right) Just a few hundred more feet to Milwaukee Road rails: 214 on January 9, 1967, eases down the new connection at Canco on Milwaukee's north side to begin its 9.1-mile trek over CMStP&P track to the new Milwaukee Road depot.*

(Right) Author Scribbins recorded 214's arrival at Milwaukee's lakefront station in August 1960 in a composition not unlike that of a C&NW publicity photo later used on menu covers; the menu dates from 1966, the year the station closed. (Below) The southbound *Peninsula 400* of October 1958 stretches beyond both portals of the train shed at Milwaukee.

Bi-Level "400" Approaching Milwaukee Passenger Station.

Both photos, Jim Scribbins

Collection of William Stauss

400 and *Peninsula 400.* Delays occurred simply because there were not enough boiler-equipped E-units to go around.

The 1959 spring timetable showed slight changes in both equipment and schedule. The parlor car no longer operated north of Green Bay on Saturday night nor back on Sunday morning, and 214 departed Ishpeming 10 minutes later, gaining time between there and Green Bay to allow operation on its previous schedule into Chicago. However, the 10 minutes were added back to the schedule with the fall time change. These changes most likely were made to allow the *Peninsula 400* to meet train 161, the *Iron Country,* east of Negaunee, when daylight time was not in effect.

October 1959 saw the end of checked baggage north of Green Bay. Six months later, 16 minutes were added to 209's schedule between Green Bay and the north end, while 214 was advanced 10 minutes across the Peninsula Division with no change in elapsed running time. This change resulted in longer weekday station stops at Green Bay, but Sunday-only 240 departed 10 minutes earlier than 214 and had its running time through the Fox River valley lengthened to reach Milwaukee and Chicago as previously scheduled. Also at this time, "tap-lounge" was restored as nomenclature for the car on the north end of the train which had of late been called the "bar-lounge." In common with other C&NW intercity trains, 209 and 214 lost their checked baggage service in April 1959. In October 1960, five minutes were added to the time of 214 and 10 minutes to 240 between Milwaukee and Chicago.

When trains 161 and 162 ceased operation on January 13, 1961, the *Peninsula 400* became the only passenger train between Green Bay and its namesake territory. (Most recently the *Iron Country,* 161 and 162 were best known as the *Iron & Copper Country Express,* a name dating from 1927 or earlier. In that year they were designated 101 and 102, and untitled trains of those numbers ran as early as 1910 on this route.) The bilevel streamliner's schedule remained the same until May 10, when the southbound's timetable was considerably altered, though the northbound's was left unchanged. For the first time in its career, the Chicago-bound *Peninsula 400* operated seven days a week via Manitowoc; gone was the Sunday routing through Fond du Lac and the Fox River valley as train 240. Number 214 now departed Ishpeming in the predawn darkness at 4:30 a.m.—one hour and 20 minutes earlier than before—and gained gradually throughout its run to arrive at Canal and Madison Streets in Chicago at 12:45 p.m.—an hour and 40 minutes ahead of its previous schedule. A Waukegan stop was inserted, positive on Sundays and conditional on weekdays.

Apparently the acceleration of 214 was not realistic, as 20 minutes were added throughout its schedule with the fall change to standard time, resulting in an even more inconvenient 4:10 a.m. departure from Ishpeming. During the same period, tap-lounge

service was modified, the car being removed from the consist of 209 on Saturdays and Sundays and of 214 on Sundays and Mondays.

The next 18 months in the life of the *Peninsula 400* were uneventful; then the April 28, 1963, folder advanced 214's schedule 10 minutes at all points, and a Lake Forest, Ill., stop was given to 209—which perhaps most benefited residents of that town returning from Chicago, rather than the long-distance travelers the train was intended to serve. Into the summer, the *Peninsula* was frequently operated with a single E8 between Chicago and Green Bay. Smaller consists brought about this reduction of units, which continued only until, as a compromise solution, E8 and F7 combinations began operating. Waukegan became a daily stop for 214 in the fall of 1963. A year later, on October 25, 1964, the *Peninsula* became a coach-only train beyond Green Bay—most often just an E8 and a lone bilevel. The following spring, 209 was given a conditional stop at Great Lakes Naval Training Station on Fridays to entrain "boots" bound for a weekend of "liberty."

On October 31, 1965, Brampton and, more importantly, Negaunee were discontinued as station stops. Residents of Negaunee were disgruntled; they persisted in appeals for reinstatement of service as late as January 1969, but were unsuccessful in regaining stops for 209 and 214—this despite the virtual impossibility of obtaining taxi service in the after-midnight hours then kept by the trains. On occasion, passengers without access to private automobiles were taken by police car from Ishpeming—the closest station—to their destinations in Negaunee.

At the end of April in 1966, 10 minutes were added to 209's schedule north of Green Bay, and 214 was retimed to start from Ishpeming 20 minutes earlier. Also on this occasion, coach-parlor 600 replaced full parlor 6400. (Within a year, No. 6400 had been converted to suburban coach 225, which could be distinguished from all others by its additional toilets, different interior wall design, and smaller seating capacity of 136.) Number 600 had a coach section seating 48 and a parlor section containing 14 rotating chairs on the lower level and 16 seats on the upper. Previously, the 600 had round-tripped daily between Chicago and Green Bay in the other bilevel trainset.

On November 1, 1967, the railway officially acknowledged that the upper-level "parlor" seats were no different from upper-level coach seats. As a remedy for this inequity, only the swivel chairs on the lower level, which were true parlor seats, were assigned to first-class passengers; the eight stationary seats in the gallery on each side were henceforth coach accommodations. Signs attached to the walls read "Reserved Parlor Chairs Lower Level," and others at the stairs to the galleries "Coach Seating Upper Level." On-board employees were given detailed instructions to insure

Jim Scribbins

On July 23, 1963, the northbound Peninsula 400 *had the dubious honor of sharing for the last time, the North Western station in Milwaukee with the* Twin Cities 400, *making its final run. The depot clock on standard time confirms train 400 to be approximately 30 minutes late. Train 209 was being held to protect the connection.*

that there were no complaints from passengers of either class concerning seating in car 600.

C&NW trains began using the Milwaukee Road's new station in Milwaukee on May 16, 1966, running over CMStP&P tracks between Washington Street, a mile south of the depot, and Canco on the Milwaukee's upper Michigan line, located on the far north side of the city, directly below the three-way junction of Wiscona on the C&NW. The new routing resulted in slightly longer running times in the Milwaukee area which, combined with increases of 22 minutes northbound and 10 minutes southbound in running time on the North Western itself, changed the terminal times at Ishpeming to a 2:15 a.m. arrival and a 3:30 a.m. departure.

Despite the forthcoming summer travel season, the single-level tap-lounge was permanently removed from the consist in June 1967, indicative of how far the one-time patronage champion of the *400* fleet had fallen—and of the great decline in railroad passenger business in general. Amenities and services continued to diminish; for one thing, by spring 1969 a parlor-car porter was no longer assigned to the *Peninsula,* and coach-bar lounge 903 was removed.

But the railroad had more major plans for discontinuance of service than dropping a single car. Shortly, the C&NW requested Interstate Commerce Commission approval to substitute Greyhound buses operated under contract to serve all points north of Green Bay except Rock and Little Lake. The buses would also call at Marquette, the largest city in the area, which supported the move since it had no direct train service. In its request, C&NW highlighted the steady decline in train travel over this northerly route. Numbers 209 and 214 were regularly operating as one-car trains over the Green Bay-Ishpeming section in question, with the northbound handling an average peak number of 48 passengers per trip in 1967, 39 per trip in 1968, and 28 per trip during the first quarter of 1969; southbound traffic dropped from 46 to 37 to 29 passengers per trip in the same span.

On-line towns—principally Marinette, Menominee and Escanaba—protested the proposed substitution, since there was no guarantee the Greyhounds would continue on a permanent basis. Though these communities requested that the ICC hold hearings on the matter, the commission approved the bus replacement on July 8, 1969, without such hearings. C&NW had agreed to contract with Greyhound on a one-year trial basis; annual evaluation and renewal would follow.

The commission felt its action justified because the trains had produced a loss on the affected portion of their route of $259,000 the previous year, and because the minimal patronage did not warrant continuation of rail service. It authorized bus service to begin on July 16. Almost immediately, C&NW and Greyhound announced that the bus would connect with earlier-running trains 153 and 216 at Green Bay, thus providing far more convenient arrival and departure times for Upper Peninsula riders. Interline rail-bus tickets would be sold, and the buses would stop at Greyhound stations except in Green Bay, where the C&NW depot would of course be used to allow transfer of passengers to and from trains 216 and 153.

This had not been C&NW's first attempt to diminish the *Peninsula 400* in the territory from which it took its name. In August 1954—an era before Interstate Commerce Commission jurisdiction over train-offs—the railway had appeared before the Michigan Public Service Commission to seek elimination of 209 and 214 beyond Escanaba. At that time, the stated annual out-of-pocket loss over the northern subdivision was more than $78,000. The state commission proposed a 10-month trial operation with a reduced consist. Proceedings continued over a long period, and by October 1956 the annual loss was being estimated at $38,000. At further hearings, conducted in January 1957, opponents of the discontinuance pointed out that C&NW's figures reflected only local revenue between Ishpeming and Escanaba and did not consider additional revenue generated by patrons traveling to or from stations south of Escanaba.

Five months later the state commission, in examining both the intrastate and interstate aspects of the case, noted that the average journey made by passengers boarding or detraining in the segment of the route to be affected was more than 300 miles, much better than C&NW's system-wide average of 92 miles, and higher even than the average for railroads in general in the United States. Finally, in July 1957, the Public Service Commission denied the request, apparently assuring operation of the yellow-and-green coaches and diesels over the north end of the Peninsula Division for some time to come.

But the Transportation Act of 1958, which gave the Interstate Commerce Commission jurisdiction over train-offs, provided a new opportunity to remove the streamliner. On February 20, 1959, C&NW posted notice under the act to remove 209 and 214 between Escanaba and Ishpeming as of March 23. Marquette County supervisors unanimously opposed this petition, calling the removal of the *400* a significant step backward in the development of the region's tourist and resort industry. The Greater Ishpeming Chamber of Commerce and the Upper Michigan Development Bureau vigorously fought the proposed cutback. Bowing to these pressures, the North Western withdrew its discontinuance request and announced that the trains would continue to operate until further notice; most likely, the alternative of substituting contract buses for the trains was already under consideration even at this early date.

It turned out to be more than a decade later when the end did finally come, however. On the night of Wednesday, July 16, 1969, a GP7 lead the farewell consist of No. 209—two 800-series low-level streamlined coaches, with 66 passengers aboard as the train departed Green Bay. The usual bilevel equipment was left behind. An era had truly come to a close, for 209 was not only the last *Peninsula 400* and the last passenger train on C&NW's former Peninsula Division (now part of the Lake Shore), it was the final passenger train operated by any railroad in Michigan's Upper Peninsula.

The startup of Amtrak was but hours away as the last northbound Peninsula 400 *remnant, Chicago-Green Bay 209, departs North Western Terminal. Three privately operated cars brought up the markers.*

Both photos, Jim Boyd

Chasing the sun toward Iowa on a summer evening in 1967, train 1 speeds under the coaling tower at Nelson, Ill., junction point with C&NW's St. Louis line. Although 1 and 2 had officially lost their Kate Shelley 400 monicker by this time, on-line residents continued to refer to the Chicago-Clinton runs as the "Kate Shelley", "Katy" or just "Kate."

Jim Boyd

Kate Shelley 400

For Iowa, a train named for a heroine

IN 1947, optimism was high within the railroad industry regarding the future of intercity passenger service. Virtually every line was announcing new streamlined trains, and the passenger-oriented North Western was no exception. Intended expansions of modern "varnish" were publicized almost as soon as the ink was dry on equipment orders, although the delivery often fell months behind the anticipated dates.

Thus far, C&NW *400*'s had operated only on the railway's northern lines. The well-known *City* streamliners of the Union Pacific ran on the western portion of the system. Although they were excellent trains, their schedules over the C&NW portion of the runs were inconvenient for local traffic, particularly to and from Omaha, which had, since the beginning of the decade, been served by high-quality trains of competitors Burlington and Milwaukee Road.

To further improve his railroad's competitive posture, C&NW president R. L. Williams had announced in July 1946 that *400* trains were coming: In 1947, a daytime streamliner would be inaugurated along the heavily-trafficked line between Lake Michigan and the Missouri River. Equipment for this Chicago-Omaha service would consist of parlor cars, diner, coaches and a tap-diner-lounge, all of postwar design. The train would, of course, be diesel-powered.

Shortly thereafter, this plan was amplified by the announcement that a new streamliner "similar in design to the *400* fleet" would operate between Sioux City and Omaha to provide direct connections with the anticipated new Chicago-Omaha train.

This connecting train, which would travel the Iowa side of the Missouri, would be composed of parlor car, cafe-coach (No. 7000, as actually delivered) and coaches, and would be powered by a 1000-h.p. diesel locomotive: lone Baldwin DR-6-2-10, delivered in 1948 as the 5000A, a unit which probably never pulled a *400*. It was used in service on secondary trains out of Sioux City and on the West Chicago-Freeport (Ill.) branch, and, later, multipled with other units on other conventional trains in Illinois and Wisconsin.

Beginning in the fall of 1946, the Sioux City connection was referred to as a *400*, and it was projected to meet the Omaha-Chicago *400* at Missouri Valley, Iowa. In personal appearances before local civic organizations, North Western officials continued to maintain that the new trains would debut in 1947 and that these first *400*'s to operate west of Chicago would contain the most modern appointments.

In reality, not much happened. Like most roads, C&NW was hampered by passenger-car deliveries that fell far behind schedule as the builders—in this case Pullman-Standard—experienced difficulties in obtaining materials in this postwar expansion period. New cars did arrive, but the first of the lot were coaches and were used to fill out the existing *400* trains; the addition of trains to the *400* fleet was postponed until the "feature" cars could be completed. The intended consist of the Nebraska-bound *400* was modified in the fall of 1947 by eliminating the dining car and redescribing the remaining feature car as cafe-tap-lounge-baggage, which became the 7625-series car.

As time went on, plans continued to be postponed and modified. Late in 1948, the trains were first referred to as the *Corn King 400*, reviving in part a name—*Corn King Limited*—used several years earlier for the overnight Chicago-Omaha limited. The title was quite appropriate, since the greatest share of the mileage would be rolled off across the undulating cornfields of Iowa. At this time, through cars between Sioux City and Chicago were planned.

In late 1948, the 5000A was delivered by Baldwin and promptly pressed into service handling local trains out of Sioux City, which is probably as close to western Iowa *400* use as it ever got. This unique example of internal combustion from the halls of Eddystone had one 1000-h.p. motor behind its cab, while the rear portion contained a baggage room where normally a second prime mover would be positioned. After a relatively brief career, the 5000A was retired in 1958.

Unfortunately, although all of C&NW's streamlined cars were delivered by the spring of 1950 and the industry-wide disillusionment with the passenger train had not yet set in, the *Corn King 400* never became a reality. There were, however, other improvements in daytime passenger transportation on C&NW through the corn belt. The westbound *Los Angeles Limited* was accelerated and rescheduled, providing convenient service for Iowans. There were similar improvements in train 14, the eastbound *Chicago Express,* though it was subsequently slowed and given an awkward 2½ hour pause in Boone.

The big travel news, however, did not occur until January 1954, when the famed *Challenger* was revived as a Chicago-Los Angeles streamliner via C&NW-UP, providing a fast westbound day train between Chicago's North Western Terminal and Union Station in Omaha. However, there was no equivalent service in the other direction because the eastbound *Challenger* traveled the territory at night.

That improvement would be short-lived. On Sunday, October 30, 1955, it and 75 years of tradition ended when the *City* streamliners as well as the *Challenger* were diverted from the level tangents of the North Western's Galena and Iowa divisions to the paralleling line of the Milwaukee Road. This move considerably reduced the number of passenger train movements on the C&NW, and the road was quick to point out that, without the heavy passenger volume, freight train performance could be considerably improved. The streamliners were money-losers—air travel, even in the pre-jet era, had deeply eroded long-distance passenger operation. North Western was quite content to concentrate on providing high quality passenger-train operation along its own route, rather than continue a joint operation.

The restructured passenger services resulted in daytime and overnight trains between Chicago and Omaha which used a mixture of C&NW-owned ex-*City* and *400* rolling stock, along with

North Western Limited sleepers. The new trains were not, however, considered to be members of the *400* fleet. Also, a Chicago-Clinton local was added to the schedule, as was an additional overnight train which operated primarily for mail and express traffic.

The final train to be added was the only *400* ever run west from Chicago, and was one of the few trains operated anywhere in North America to be named for a woman—Kate Shelley. At age 15, in 1881, she had been almost single-handedly responsible for saving the lives of two train-service employees when a bridge adjacent to her rural home west of Boone, Iowa, collapsed under the weight of a light engine in a violent rain storm. Later, she worked as agent at the small C&NW station in Moingona, Iowa.

Dixon, Ill., a city of some 15,000 residents 100 miles west of Chicago, boasted a particularly devoted clan of Kate Shelley 400 admirers. (Far left) Westbound 1 is braking for Dixon station as it glides under Galena Avenue in 1965. (Above left) Eastbound freight 252, the Rocket, struggling up Dixon hill out of the Rock River valley has just cleared the platforms as the westbound "Kate" rolls to a halt. June 1965 is the date. (Above) Eastbound Sunday-evening 12 approaches Dixon station in 1965. (Left) On another 1965 day, 12 winds up "the hill" after its pause at Dixon depot.

All photos, unless otherwise credited, Jim Boyd

169

The railway's Des Moines River bridge, constructed in 1901, was named for her in 1926.

Since Boone—the western terminus of the new *400*—was close to the Shelley homestead, it was appropriate that trains 1 and 2 be named to recognize once again Miss Shelley's act of heroism. In most respects, the schedule of the *Kate Shelley 400* was similar to that formerly run by the *City of Portland*, with added intermediate stops and a few minutes additional running time. The 340-mile trip between Chicago and Boone required six hours in either direction. Stops were made at Geneva (eastbound only), DeKalb, Rochelle, Dixon and Sterling in Illinois, and Clinton, Mount Vernon (a flag stop), Cedar Rapids, Belle Plaine, Tama, Marshalltown, Nevada (conditional only on No. 1) and Ames in Iowa before terminating at Boone. In swiftness, the schedules were comparable to those of other *400*'s, with nearly mile-a-minute overall timings. The maximum speeds were listed in the employees' timetable as 90 mph for "diesel-powered streamliners" and 80 mph for "steam-powered streamliners" although it is extremely doubtful that the Iowa *400*'s were ever propelled by anything other than an E unit.

The newspapers paid little attention to the new *400* or the other passenger trains introduced by C&NW as replacements for the *City* streamliners. Most news and editorial comment dealt with the change of route of the West Coast trains to the Milwaukee Road. Editorials found the change symptomatic of the impact of the automobile and airplane upon rail travel. Of almost equal editorial importance, it seems, was the hope that tracks could be removed from the streets in downtown Cedar Rapids, through which C&NW had a separate passenger line.

Perhaps because Boone had been born as a railroad community, the town press recognized the establishment of the new North Western passenger service, mentioning that a "new 90 mph streamliner" would operate to Chicago and adding that the city had always been "proud" of the C&NW. According to the *Boone News-Republican*, "plenty of passengers" were on hand to help trains 1 and 2 begin their life. In contrast, at Cedar Rapids, the largest intermediate city on the route, the *400* inaugural failed to merit newspaper space.

It may have been a last-minute decision to add *400* to the name of trains 1 and 2, since some early reports referred to them only as the *Kate Shelley*. These sources do not provide a certain picture of the equipment used on the train. The trade press described the new members of the *400* fleet as six-car trains composed of coaches, diner and parlor, while the railway's public time folder—

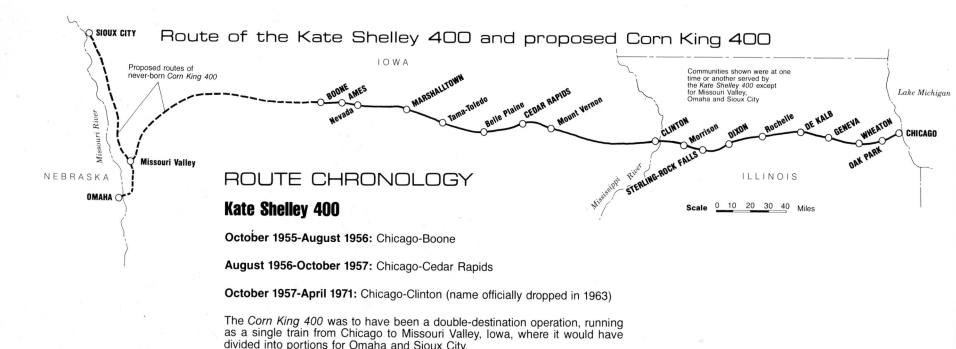

Route of the Kate Shelley 400 and proposed Corn King 400

ROUTE CHRONOLOGY

Kate Shelley 400

October 1955-August 1956: Chicago-Boone

August 1956-October 1957: Chicago-Cedar Rapids

October 1957-April 1971: Chicago-Clinton (name officially dropped in 1963)

The *Corn King 400* was to have been a double-destination operation, running as a single train from Chicago to Missouri Valley, Iowa, where it would have divided into portions for Omaha and Sioux City.

170

redesigned with an attractive yellow-and-green cover—listed parlor-lounge (a type of car C&NW did not own), diner, coach-lounge (a 3416-series car), and coaches. A North Western internal document of the time specified a consist of baggage-dormitory, coaches, diner and club-lounge. The head-end car was one of the 9300-9302 series, released from interline service with the UP and SP, as was the 7900-7902 club-lounge. Coaches and diner could have been either ACF-built ex-*City* cars, or P-S *400* equipment.

In the spring of 1956, the time of train 1 was moved ahead one hour to correspond to the change to Daylight Saving Time in Illinois, and a Sunday-only stop was inserted at Geneva. Because Iowa remained on standard time, the schedule of train 2 basically did not change, but it was altered to highball from Boone 10 minutes earlier, and the Belle Plaine stop was cancelled. Meanwhile, a stop to discharge passengers was instituted at Oak Park, Ill. The assigned equipment at this point indicated a luxury consist: drawing room parlor, club-lounge, diner, coach-lounge, and coaches—definitely a mixture of ex-*City* and *400* stock.

In mid-August, the *Kate Shelley 400* lost its tie with Miss Shelley's home territory when it was cut back to Cedar Rapids. This was part of a general belt-tightening on the western line, attributed to low ridership. The reduction in service was not reflected in print until the fall timetable was issued at the end of October.

The cutback also created an equipment change. Though parlor, club-lounge, and coaches were carried on both trains for their entire trips, the diner and coach-lounge ran only on the westbound train and only as far as Clinton. From there they returned to Chicago on an early-morning departure from Clinton—the Illinois portion of a short-lived overnight local from Omaha for which the *Corn King* name had been revived in October 1955. At this same time, the Chicago-Omaha trains lost their traditional location in Table One of the public timetable.

Spring 1957 saw the usual adjustment on train 1 to compensate for daylight time in Illinois, while 2 was advanced an hour and 25 minutes and given a 10-minute reduction in running time as well. Equipment was improved to the extent that the coach-lounge was carried to and from Cedar Rapids with only the diner returning from Clinton on morning local 10-110. Train 1's Geneva stop was expanded to include Saturday, and a Saturday-only stop was added at Wheaton, Ill.

In mid-June, at the same time several northern line trains were

(Above right) Chicago-bound 2 calls at Rochelle, Ill., in 1965. Residents of this small northern Illinois city could also catch CB&Q Zephyrs two blocks down the street. (Right) Most of the 20,000 students at Northern Illinois University in De Kalb were Chicagoans, so for many "Huskies," Kate was a natural transportation choice. Number 1 is at De Kalb depot in January 1969.

Mike McBride

Mike Schafer/Jim Boyd

Joseph Piersen

Mike Schafer

(Above) North Western Terminal is yet about
30 minutes away as train 2 swirls the snow
near C&NW's famous Proviso Yard.
An ex-City diner-lounge trails
the locomotive. (Above right) In its twilight
years, train 1 heads into West Chicago on a
pleasant spring day in 1970. (Right) Enroute
to a model railroad meeting, the
photographer intercepted Kate at Sterling
causeway along the Rock River on a
Thursday evening in the early 1960's.

Jim Boyd

discontinued, equipment for the *Kate Shelley 400* was modified, with the club-lounge and coach-lounge being replaced by the one-of-a-kind cafe-coach. The parlor was reduced to six trips a week, Saturday westbound and Sunday eastbound being eliminated. A positive aspect of this shake-up was the return of the diner on train 2 from Clinton, rather than on the local.

In the fall, the *Kate Shelley 400* was discontinued through Iowa, and terminated at the Mississippi River town of Clinton. A further reduction in equipment was effected, with the diner and parlor discontinued and car 7000 replaced by a 3416-series coach-lounge. In mid-1958, one of the 7625-series tap-cafe-lounge cars replaced the coach-lounge and operated on train 1 daily except Saturday. It journeyed eastward on early-morning local train 10, except Sunday, making the eastbound *Kate Shelley* coach-only.

A major change in the schedule took place in the spring of 1959, with train 2 moved to operate from Clinton on approximately the schedule of the now-defunct local No. 10. In this shuffle, the tap-cafe-lounge was restored to the eastbound *400*. Other changes included additional Chicago surburban stops on Sunday mornings and the termination of all checked baggage service. Within a year and a half, the Sunday Chicago suburban stops had been eliminated, and by spring 1961, an ex-*City* diner-lounge replaced the tap-cafe-lounge. On July 16, 1961, a significantly different Sunday and holiday schedule was placed in effect, with train numbers on those days showing as 11 and 12. These trains utilized the "Kate's" equipment but not the name.

As the Chicago & North Western continued to shrink its intercity passenger operations, the overwhelming bulk of attention on July 23, 1963, was given to the discontinuance of the original *Twin Cities 400*. This date is memorable for another reason, however, as it marks the last date of *400* operation across the Galena Division. The folder issued the next day made no reference to *Kate Shelley 400*, as the Chicago-Clinton trains were designated by number only. This discontinuance of the *Kate Shelley* went quite unnoticed, with no announcement, no fanfare. Diner-lounge service persisted until June, 1967, and the trains themselves remained until the coming of Amtrak in 1971. The final train 1 out of Chicago was powered by an E7 and had three 800 series coaches—but it was the *Kate Shelley 400* in memory only.

Both photos, Jim Boyd

(Above right) Accelerating away from Dixon, train 1 cants under the Rock Island Road underpass at McRoberts Crossing west of Dixon in 1964. (Right) Last run: Tomorrow there will be an Amtrak, but Kate will join its namesake heroine in history. It's April 30, 1971, and 1 has just rounded the curve at Clinton Street out of North Western Terminal.

Both photos, Jim Scribbins

The 400 fleet

The North Western knew how to run a corridor

In 1936, the country was not far removed from the depths of the Great Depression. As a consequence, most children had never been on a passenger train. More important, because of financial constraints and increasing automobile ownership, many adults had not traveled by rail in years either. Nevertheless, the original *400* had been a great success.

To gain a further share of the public's greater mobility as the economy began to improve, North Western sent an exhibition passenger train on tour through Illinois, Iowa, and Wisconsin. In a five-day trek in November through Wisconsin's Fox River valley, this "exhibition extra"—a train of conventional equipment behind a Class ES Pacific—was inspected by a total of 38,000 persons of all ages in Fond du Lac, Oshkosh, Neenah, Appleton, Kaukauna, DePere, and Green Bay. A few days later, in a single stop in Sheboygan, 12,000 citizens walked through the Pullman-green cars and stared with fascination at the cleanly wiped, lean 4-6-2 which propelled them.

During the latter 1930's, the important trains over the Lake Shore Division were 153 and 214, during much of their life named the *Shoreland*, which operated weekday afternoons between Chicago and Manitowoc. By the summer of 1937, these trains had been air-conditioned as part of a broad C&NW improvement program. In 1938, 153 was extended through to Green Bay, while 214 was transformed into an Ishpeming-Chicago train and rechristened the *Cloverland*. The Sunday equivalents of these trains were 167 and 168, an unnamed train making a Chicago-Two Rivers round trip, later cut back to Manitowoc.

Though streamlining came in September 1939 to the Chicago-Twin Cities *400*, it was unknown elsewhere on C&NW's northern lines. In early 1941, the trade press did provide a hint of the future by mentioning that C&NW was considering the purchase of a diesel-powered streamliner to run between Chicago and Green Bay. Since the railroad was in receivership, it was required to apply to the federal district court for approval to purchase equipment; in January 1941, C&NW had asked permission to expend $7,500,000 to acquire 1,700 freight cars of various types, as well as 25 passenger cars and 5 diesel locomotives. Judge John P. Barnes acted quickly, approving the outlay early in February.

The passenger equipment, said to be intended for use in Wisconsin, comprised mostly coaches, with a few parlors, diners, and baggage-tap cars. The cost of the order, placed in March with Pullman-Standard, was $1,720,000. In addition, the 2,000-h.p. diesel units—one from Alco and four from Electro-Motive—cost $175,000 each. With the new locomotives, as Chief Executive Officer R. L. Williams pointed out, North Western would own by itself or jointly with Union Pacific and Southern Pacific a total combined diesel horsepower of 67,125—considerable for that time.

The equipment, similar to that in use on the *400*, would be assigned to services averaging 60 mph start-to-stop. Inauguration of such services was planned for August or September, though C&NW acknowledged that this date might be delayed by defense requirements, since the world situation was becoming increasingly ominous due to the aggression of Germany and Japan. The new, improved, streamlined Chicago-based trains were to serve Madison-Janesville-Beloit, Manitowoc-Sheboygan-Port Washington, and Green Bay-Appleton-Neenah/Menasha-Oshkosh-Fond du Lac-West Bend. No detailed listing of intermediate stops between Chicago and Milwaukee was offered, but the projected speedsters were to be part of frequent-interval schedules between the two cities.

In spring, right-of-way improvements were launched on the routes of the new streamliners. New ballast was laid where necessary, and superelevation was increased and curves given spiraled easements to permit higher speeds. Seventeen and one-half miles of new rail were laid between Milwaukee and Green Bay. Perhaps these costs were included in the final figure for the new service: $3,500,000, approximately one-third more than originally anticipated.

In December came the annoucement that the new streamlined trains, to be introduced in January, would all bear the name *400*. To distinguish it from its new mates, the original *400* at this time became the *Twin Cities 400*; the new trains' names reflected their routes, destinations, or function: *Capitol 400*, *City of Milwaukee 400*, *Commuter 400*, *Shoreland 400* and *Valley 400*. All these names but the first two had been applied, minus the *400* appellation, at some time to other trains, but not always to the specific runs being replaced by the yellow-and-green Pullman-Standard streamliners.

As might have been expected, Green Bay was enthusiastic about the new trains. Its *Press-Gazette* reported that the sparkling equipment was used during the Christmas holidays on second sections of the *400* to Minneapolis; that the streamliners would have entered service in the fall had it not been for delays in acquiring necessary items for their construction; and that they would not carry express or storage mail (important items on most C&NW conventional trains) but would transport some letter mail and baggage. This reduction in head-end traffic would shorten times at intermediate stops. The newspaper editorialized—under the heading "Good for the North Western"—that the introduction of the *400*'s would be of value to Green Bay and, the paper hoped, profitable to the railway.

At the passenger station in Green Bay, special water and fuel facilities were installed, with electric pumps that would "fill the locomotive tanks at several thousand gallons a minute," according to the newspaper account. Extensive right-of-way work was done both north and south of Green Bay in preparation for the high-speed operation. On the Lake Shore Division between Green Bay and Chicago, running time would be reduced by one hour and ten minutes northbound and one hour southbound.

Through the Fox River valley, new trains 149 (from Milwaukee in the morning) and 154 (from Green Bay in the afternoon) were added, primarily to handle mail and express as well as local passengers. Their addition allowed other conventional runs to be speeded up.

Unfortunately, the festive inauguration of the *400* fleet was dampened considerably by the fact that the United States had entered World War II just a month earlier. Nevertheless, two new *400* display trains set out on tours on Wednesday, January 7, 1942. One train made stops of 2½ to 4 hours in Kenosha, Racine and Fond du Lac, while the other made longer stops in Sheboygan and Manitowoc. The next day, one set returned to Milwaukee, where 2000 reviewers gave it their approval between 9 a.m. and 10 p.m.; the other made stops of three to five hours in Oshkosh, Neenah and Appleton.

One train, EMD-powered, went from Milwaukee to Madison for a twelve-hour stint there on Friday, January 9, followed by visits to Janesville and Beloit on Saturday. The other set, behind "chisel-nose" Alco DL109 5007A, hosted 2000 persons at the depot on the west shore of the Fox River in Green Bay. There, after a week of sub-zero weather, the thermometer obligingly rose to nine degrees above zero when the train was opened at 8 a.m., only to slide to minus four degrees by departure time at 1 p.m. The Alco-powered exhibition train then continued on to Oconto and Marinette presentations in ten-below-zero crispness. With this train was A. R. Gould, traffic manager—sales, and Harry C. Duvall, general passenger agent.

For the occasion, the Oshkosh B'Gosh Overall Company took a quarter-page ad, which featured a close-up of enginemen Tom F. Powers and fireman Joe Demille beneath the headlight of the Alco DL109; both men, naturally, were garbed in the product. The headline read, "North Western's Super Train—The New *400* Streamliner—Salute and Welcome." Not to be outdone, Lee Overalls followed with an advertisement of its own, also with the 5007A as backdrop. "The Men on the New *400* Streamliner Prefer Lee Overalls," the ad proclaimed. "Roy Empey and Ted Black pictured above on the first trip of the new *400* are equipped 100% with Lee overalls." (The demonstration train with the Alco had proceeded on to Upper Michigan showings, and then inaugurated the *Peninsula 400*; therefore, if the ad photo was truly the first trip of a *400* fleet member, it must have shown that train.)

Publicity released in connection with the exhibition tours noted that the cars were constructed of tensile steel, welded throughout and insulated against noise and shock. Their specially developed spring suspension and hydraulic shock absorbers would make them smooth riding. Features continued from the original streamlined *400* of 1939 included Solex tinted windows, draftless air-conditioning through many tiny vents in the ceilings, deep rubber-cushioned reclining seats with ample leg room, and individual reading lights.

Thanks to the basic soundness of the 1939 design, which was

(Below) It debuted as a diesel-powered streamliner nearly three years before this scene was recorded on April 7, 1945, but the Shoreland 400 on this day carried a mix of streamlined equipment (including Challenger cars) and heavyweights, in tow behind Pacific 2911—a graphic demonstration of how the war years affected operations. (Right) Alco DL109 5007A awaits highball at Milwaukee with the Shoreland 400 in December 1942.

repeated in their newest equipment, there was a uniform excellence of appointments aboard all of the *400* trains. In fact, the equipment for the new *400* trains was virtually identical to the highly successful design of the 1939 train, with only minor changes in interior decoration. Among them were the use of rose-and-gold drapes in the bar, and blue leather upholstery for the lunch-counter stools. The 16 new coaches were separated into groups of four, determined by the keynote color of their interiors: brown, blue, green or yellow. The diners continued the use of chairs in two different colors; instead of mixing them throughout the car, however, green chairs were placed at tables at the ends of the car and red at the tables in the center. Blinds, mirrors and drapes were flesh-colored.

The single major design change was the elimination—except aboard the *Minnesota 400*—of the lounge portion of the tavern-lunch counter, the space gained being used for either an RPO section or a larger baggage room. None of the additional *400* trains were given solariums, thus cars 7200 and 7201 remained the only *400* observations.

The *400* fleet entered operation from Chicago on Monday, January 12, 1942, enabling North Western to increase the number of streamliner departures from Canal and Madison from 19 to 58 per week. During the first days of expanded *400* operation, C&NW published passing times of the streamliners through the North Shore suburban area of Chicago. Times were given for Wilmette, Kenilworth, Winnetka, Glencoe, Highland Park and Lake Forest, none of which were stopping points, in lists appearing in suburban newspapers. The public was invited to become train-watchers. (Ironically, railroads would before long consider railfans lingering along any right-of-way to be possible enemy agents account of the war.)

The official first departure for a new member of the *400* fleet was that of the *City of Milwaukee 400*, train 151, from Chicago at 9:45 a.m. R. L. Williams, chief executive officer of the railway and—reflecting the close cooperation with the armed services—Col. Edward Roth, Jr., chief of staff of the United States Army Sixth Corps Area, gave the highball to engineman Oscar Hendrickson at the throttle of unit 5001B, which was one of the four E3's from the 1939 *400*. (Its number appeared on the side as simply "5001." The "B," though fairly large, was located separately just above the builder's plate, typical of the time when many roads thought in terms of two units making up one not-to-be-divided locomotive.)

Earlier, at 9 a.m., southbound train 156, also named *City of Milwaukee 400*, made its first departure from its namesake city with a send-off by Jolin A. Seranuir, assistant to the mayor, and John L. Bohn, president of the Common Council. In reality, the first scheduled movement of one of the fleet was 214's departure from Ishpeming at 7:15 a.m., followed closely by the *Commuter 400*'s: 152 from Milwaukee at 7:25 a.m. and 149 from Chicago at 7:30 a.m. (The purist might cite the departure of the *Minnesota 400* on January 5, but that was a re-equipping of a train already designated a *400*.)

Two of the four sets of equipment delivered at this time went to cover the new *Peninsula 400* and the newly-streamlined *Minnesota 400*. For maximum utilization, the other two trainsets worked a weekday pattern that began with Chicago-Milwaukee service, and then extended deeper into Wisconsin during the afternoon and evening. One consist, which spent the night in Chicago, departed from there at 7:30 a.m. on a 75-minute dash to Milwaukee, where it attempted (seldom sucessfully) to turn in 15 minutes to retrace its route as equally-speedy train 156. Again from Chicago, it left as 153, the *Shoreland 400*, with stops north of Milwaukee at Port Washinton, Sheboygan, Cleveland, Manitowoc and Denmark, arriving Green Bay at 2:50 p.m. As *Valley 400*, No. 216, it returned at 4:20 p.m., stopping at Appleton, Neenah, Oshkosh, Fond du Lac and West Bend, then running on through Milwaukee to conclude its day with an 8:05 p.m. arrival at North Western Terminal. Throughout the day, this set carried the RPO-baggage-tavern-lunch counter, a parlor, and two coaches; for the Green Bay round trip, a diner and one coach (two on Friday and Saturday) were added.

The second consist, based in Milwaukee, began its day as train 152, with a 7:25 a.m. departure. Since it ran through the Chicago suburban area during the morning rush hour, it was the only intercity train which did not stop at Davis Street station in Evanston. After an hour's wait, the consist made a round trip to Milwaukee (with a 25-minute layover there) as 151 and 158. Next for this equipment came the *Capitol 400* assignment, which could serve as a prototype for a model railroad not having point-to-point operation: The train operated in a triangle, from Chicago to Madison via Milwaukee, returning from Madison via Janesville, Wis., and Harvard, Ill. The consist's day finished as train 163, except Saturday.

As 155, the *Capitol 400* dashed to Milwaukee in 75 minutes. There, since C&NW's Madison Subdivision diverged from the main line at National Avenue one mile south (east by timetable) from the lakefront station, the railroad allowed 15 minutes to turn the train (in the same manner as Chicago-Milwaukee round trips) to become 609 destined for the state capital. Though the track and

station arrangement in Madison allowed through running without turnaround, the Chicago-bound *Capitol 400* paused at Madison's attractive depot, virtually in the shadow of the imposing legislative building, twice as long as it had in Milwaukee. As train 500, it then returned to Chicago via Janesville, Beloit and Harvard, thus providing all stations along the Milwaukee-Madison Chicago route once-a-day *400* service in one direction only—quite an unusual situation.

The initial morning trip in each direction between Chicago and Milwaukee, then, was designated the *Commuter 400*, while all other runs linking just those two cities were titled *City of Milwaukee 400*. All the trains stopped at Kenosha and Racine, while the *Shoreland 400* and *Valley 400*, trains 153 and 216, also called at Waukegan. Though outbound trains paused at Evanston only to accept riders, commuters could use Chicago-bound trains from there to the Loop. Trains halting at only Kenosha and Racine were timed at 75 or 80 minutes between Milwaukee and Chicago, with those stopping also in Waukegan allowed five minutes additional.

Fast work (reminiscent of engine changes in steam years on the *400*) characterized the turnarounds in Milwaukee, particularly those of only 15-minute duration. As soon as a "little *400*" halted, carmen zeroed in from both sides to break the connections between the E3 or E6 and the baggage-tap. The unit immediately pulled ahead through the crossovers, then backed down a runaround track to the Erie Street roundhouse, approximately two-thirds of a mile from the depot. As passengers detrained from one end of each car, cleaners entered at the other and swung the seats to face the new direction of travel. On 155-609, the *Capitol 400*, this procedure was complicated because through passengers to Waukesha, Jefferson Junction, and Madison remained aboard.

If all went smoothly, the parlor car and locomotive clasped knuckles at the other end as boarding passengers streamed to the train. (Often passengers had to be held back at the vestibules by the brakemen as the coupling was made and stretched.) Then came a last-minute mating of air, steam and communication lines and the standing brake test, followed by departure.

On Saturday evening, when the consist usually based in Milwaukee arrived in Chicago as train 500 from Madison, it remained in Chicago for less hectic Sunday assignments, along with the Chicago-based consist, for the two short-haul *400*'s. The Chicago-based trainset departed Sunday morning at 9:30 a.m. as 239, bound for the Fox River valley and Menominee, Mich., where it terminated at 2:35 p.m. After a 95-minute layover it returned via the same route, as train 220, arriving back at Chicago at 8:45 p.m. Because there was neither wye nor turntable at Menominee, this round trip used two diesel units back-to-back. Regular stops in both directions were Evanston, Kenosha,

With its power turned for the trip to Madison, train 609, the Capitol 400, *pulls away from Milwaukee depot in October 1948 behind FM Erie-built 6001-B. A heavyweight has been substituted for the streamlined parlor car. Next stop, Waukesha, Wis.*

Racine, Milwaukee, West Bend, Fond du Lac, Oshkosh, Neenah, Appleton, Green Bay, Oconto, Peshtigo and Marinette.

The Milwaukee-based consist which stayed in Chicago on Saturday evening became Sunday-only Chicago-Green Bay round trip 167/168, operating via the Lake Shore Division in both directions. Departing at 8 a.m., it made regular stops at Evanston, Waukegan, Kenosha, Racine, Milwaukee, Port Washington, Sheboygan and Manitowoc, as well as conditionals to discharge only at Cedar Grove, Cleveland, and Denmark. The return trip from Green Bay left at 4 p.m. and stopped at all of these stations except Denmark, arriving in Chicago at 7:40 p.m., in time to resume duties as train 163. Both trainsets carried the full complement of tavern-lunch counter, diner, parlor, and coaches for their Sunday assignments, which were referred to simply as *Streamliner 400*.

The seven weekday *400*'s northbound and six southbound between Chicago and Milwaukee were claimed by the North Western to be the "world's finest intercity service." Competitor Milwaukee Road countered by adjusting seven trains in each direction between Chicago and Milwaukee to 75-minute timings.

As when the first *400* was introduced back in 1935, the

Steam power reigns on this day in 1946 as an otherwise all-streamlined Capitol 400 *rolls away from the National Avenue station near downtown Milwaukee.*

expansion of the *400* fleet did not occasion a new public timetable—perhaps because of uncertainty about the start-up date. The February 1, 1942, system folder was the first to carry schedules for the new speedsters.

Thanks to fast running between Chicago and Milwaukee, the

(Below) Train 500 Capitol 400 passes beneath the U.S. 12-18 viaduct on the outskirts of Madison in August 1949 enroute to Janesville, Beloit and Chicago. (Right) On another August day in 1949, the Capitol 400 has just arrived in Madison from Milwaukee as Pacific 2907 looks on. (Facing page) At a glance, this view in Madison could pass for the Dakota 400 rolling out for Chicago, but the September 1948 date confirms that this is the Capitol 400 clattering over the Milwaukee diamond at tower MX.

Three photos, William D. Middleton

overall average speed during a day's work for the equipment making the weekday Green Bay round trip was 582 miles in 590 minutes. The *Capitol 400* set did equally well, with a daily mileage of 649 in 655 minutes. Averages on Sunday, when a higher proportion of the running was on the more moderate (speed-wise) track north of Milwaukee, were 527 miles in 570 minutes for the Menominee train and 484 miles in 525 minutes for the Green Bay service over the Lake Shore Division.

Between Chicago and Milwaukee, average speeds were approximately 68 mph for the 75-minute trains, 63 mph for the 80-minute, and 60 mph for those making the run in "even" time: 85 minutes for the 85 miles. Because of 80 mph and 70 mph limits north of Milwaukee, Chicago-Green Bay averages were 52 mph via the

Shore Line and 57 mph through the Fox River valley. The *Capitol 400* averaged 55 mph between Milwaukee and Madison and 57 mph on to Chicago. (All these are start-to-stop average speeds. Cruising speeds once clear of terminal areas were close to the timetable-authorized maximums.)

During the first six months that the fleet was in service, the final *400* of the day Sunday through Friday was train 163—a *City of Milwaukee 400*—which left Chicago at 8:15 p.m. and arrived Milwaukee at 9:35 p.m. With the June folder, it was rescheduled to leave Chicago at 10:00 p.m., making no fewer than one conditional and seven regular stops on a very hot 95-minute run to Milwaukee. This was Monday through Friday; on Sunday the train operated as 165 with virtually the same timings, but one and

one-quarter hour earlier. This train, which also made the *Capitol 400* "circle," had its equipment altered. The diner was operated on all of its Chicago-Milwaukee trips: *Commuter 400* 152, and *City of Milwaukee 400's* 151, 158, and 163 (165 on Sunday).

While most accounts state that the trainset which made the weekday Green Bay trip also made the Sunday Menominee run, and the *Capitol 400* set made the Sunday shore line journey, one source suggests the opposite and also implies the equipment was alternated on a weekly basis between the Madison and the Shoreland/Valley assignments. This could have been easily accomplished by exchanging the RPO-tap and baggage-tap cars when both trains were in Chicago on Saturday evenings.

The *Green Bay Press-Gazette* forecast plentiful use of the new *400's* because of restrictions that would soon curtail automobile travel. The paper also called attention to heavyweight trains 149 and 154, schedule additions which would benefit travelers to and from the smaller communities between Green Bay and Milwaukee. By April, C&NW officially pronounced the new *400's* "heartily received" and "well patronized." After six months' operation, the enlarged *400* fleet had carried more than a quarter-million passengers and was averaging more than 3,200 miles daily, having run up a total of nearly 600,000 miles since the January 12 inauguration.

The new trains not only provided additional service for wartime America through better equipment utilization but also released conventional cars for use elsewhere. Typical of the attempts made by all railroads to increase passenger-carrying capacity, North Western converted 11 parlor and cafe-lounge cars (approximately half of those it owned) into coaches. The Office of Defense Transportation suggested that civilians ride midweek to make room for servicemen, war production workers and others concerned with the war effort who had to travel on weekends.

The deceleration of fast passenger trains required by the federal government effective December 6, 1942, did not affect the shorter-distance *400's*; nevertheless, in the new timetable issued on that occasion, the *Shoreland 400*, No. 153, was moved 15 minutes later throughout. This allowed extra time in Chicago to cut in the diner and extra coaches after this set of equipment arrived as train 156, the *City of Milwaukee 400*. The Sunday afternoon return from Menominee to Chicago as train 220 was retimed in the same manner.

In September 1943, the name *Valley 400* was applied to trains 239 and 220 for their Sunday-only trips between Chicago and Menominee, and Sunday trains 167 and 168 via Manitowoc to and from Green Bay were titled *Shoreland 400*. Number 220's schedule was lengthened 15 minutes through additional station time in Green Bay and added running time in the Fox River valley. By September of the next year, further minor changes had been made: *Commuter 400* No. 149 became an 80-minute train, consequently setting back by five minutes the departure of train 156, the *City of Milwaukee 400*. For the *Capitol 400*, Waukesha was made a positive stop while Jefferson Junction became conditional, and a new stop was added at Lake Mills. No. 216, the *Valley 400*, had five minutes added between Fond du Lac and West Bend, bringing about an earlier Green Bay departure. In spring of 1945, the Sunday *Valley 400*, train 220, was changed to depart Menominee 25 minutes later (at 4:25 p.m.) and arrive at North Western Terminal 30 minutes later (at 9:30 p.m.). In September of that year, *Commuter 400* No. 152 was changed to a 20-minutes-later 7:45 a.m. departure from Milwaukee with Chicago arrival at 9:05 a.m., a schedule identical to parallel Milwaukee Road's *Traveler*.

During these capacity years, heavyweight cars were sometimes found in the consists of the *400*'s serving eastern Wisconsin. Even more common were the dark-green, gold-lined streamlined *Challenger* coaches, built in 1937 for long-distance service to the West Coast. In fact, both the *Shoreland/Valley* and *Capitol* trains routinely carried a pair of those Pullman-Standard 6132-series cars in their consists, with conventional cars added holidays and weekends.

The Sunday *Valley 400* between Menominee and Chicago, for example, was averaging over 800 riders per trip. The train was often so crowded leaving Milwaukee that crews could scarcely make their way through the aisles, so passengers boarding in Racine or Kenosha would have their tickets collected in the vestibule as they entered. This was often the case as well with 216, the weekday *Valley 400*, particularly on Friday nights. There were times, too, when the trains grew longer than single 2000-h.p. units could handle. Numbers 239 and 220 routinely drew two units because of the lack of turning facilities at Menominee, so they stayed entirely in the hands of internal combustion; but other trains would find a Class ES medium-sized Pacific coupled ahead of their diesel's Mars light. Engines were changed in Milwaukee, and water stops were necessary between Milwaukee and Green Bay.

Fall of 1945 also saw Waukegan stops inserted into the schedules of 149 and 239 northbound and 152, 156 and 220 southbound. This was done without additional allotment of running time, in the case of 156 producing the extraordinarily interesting time of 11 minutes for the 15.66 miles from Kenosha, or 85.4 mph start to stop—a new record for speed on the North Western. This run garnered for the *City of Milwaukee 400* the title of World's Fastest Train in Donald M. Steffee's annual speed survey in *Railroad Magazine*. The *400* narrowly edged Burlington's *Morning Twin Zephyr*, train 21, which had an 84.6-mph sprint between East Dubuque, Ill., and Prairie du Chien, Wis.

A. C. Kalmbach, writing in the December 1945 *Trains*, reported that examination of the dispatcher's trains sheets showed the little *400* to indeed be "setting the pace for the world" without difficulty. Train sheets do not detail time to the second, however, and students of rail speed will agree they are not an accurate basis for judgment, particularly for so short a distance. In any event, it was very likely the fastest time ever carded for so short a distance. Certainly the overall 75-minute Milwaukee-Chicago schedule requiring four intermediate stops over 85 miles was itself notable.

A year and one-half later, the time from Kenosha to Waukegan was changed from 11 to 12 minutes as the schedule of 156 was eased to 80 minutes overall and that of 149 to 85 minutes, in the process moving the departure of the *City of Milwaukee 400* down to 9:10 a.m. The Sunday round trips of the small trainsets were increased at this time as well: 239 by 15 minutes, 220 by ten minutes and 167 and 168 each by 30 minutes.

In July 1944, the Office of Defense Transportation and the ICC ordered railroads to give first priority to moving invalid servicemen. To accomplish this, they were authorized to divert equipment from regular passenger service, to cancel service in order to secure equipment to move the military injured, and to refuse permission to any passengers other than disabled servicemen to board regular passenger trains. Though this meant that reservations could be cancelled without notice, the *400*'s were apparently little affected in general, though civilians may often have lost drawing-room space in the parlor cars.

In common with the crews aboard the *Twin Cities 400*, the men who operated the short-distance *400*'s received many compliments, even in the harried wartime and postwar days. The *Capitol 400*, for one, made friends along its route between Milwaukee and Madison. The regular engine crew threw off tightly rolled and tied newspapers to farmers and dispensed cloth-wrapped candy to children who acknowledged their passing. These gifts were paid for by the engineer and fireman, who preferred to remain anonymous.

In December 1947, Sunday-evening-only *400* No. 165 was replaced by 163, previously a Monday-Friday train, which now once again became daily except Saturday. In 1949 its schedule was advanced to 9 p.m. during the summer—perhaps because Daylight Saving Time was in effect in Chicago—but restored to 10 p.m. in the fall. This proved to be the last major schedule change for these two trainsets while they remained on their original assignments.

Before World War II had ended but after it had become evident that the Allies would triumph, American railroads began to publicize their intention to greatly expand existing streamliner passenger fleets. In 1944, before the Interstate Commerce Commission, C&NW president R. L. Williams testified that the carriers would need to be largely re-equipped with new passenger cars. He stated his conviction that railroads could not profitably participate in the movement of people without modernizing both rolling stock and fixed facilities.

North Western became the first Western railroad to receive postwar passenger cars when, between March 1 and April 16, 1946, it took delivery on 20 *400*-type coaches from Pullman-Standard. The most apparent difference between these and earlier cars was the use of blinds rather than shades on the windows. Unnoticed by the general public was the fact that these coaches had welded frames, six times stronger than riveted ones.

The first postwar passenger cars anywhere in the country had arrived on the New York Central beginning approximately two weeks before delivery of the first of the C&NW cars; Central's order was larger, however, and was still being delivered after all the new *400* cars had arrived on the property, so C&NW became the first line to receive a complete order of postwar equipment. Final delivery occurred just 85 days after the laydown of the first car.

As rapidly as the cars were received, they entered *400* service, replacing the older *Challenger* streamlined coaches as well as the heavyweight stock often used in overflow service on many of the yellow-and-green streamliners. For publicity purposes, C&NW took official delivery of the first coach in Milwaukee—an attempt to enhance its position relative to CMStP&P, strongly entrenched in its home town. While dignitaries looked on, Miss Ruth Vogt, of the Association of Commerce, baptized the coach with a bottle of the beverage which made the Beer City famous.

New trains and routes did not come until April 30, 1950, when the *Dakota 400* was inaugurated as a replacement and extension of train 500, the Madison-Chicago leg of the *Capitol 400*. Effective the same day, the Milwaukee-Madison portion of the *Capitol*, which had operated as train 609, was quietly discontinued. Train 155 from Chicago retained the *Capitol 400* name, even though it now terminated in Milwaukee. The equipment returned to Chicago as train 160, which meant yellow-and-green equipment and diesel power, though not the *400* appellation. This consist concluded its day by returning to Milwaukee as train 121—sometimes designated *City of Milwaukee 400*. This too was an assignment of streamlined cars to an existing schedule which included several intermediate stops, and the running time thus remained at two hours. Also on April 30, Chicago-Milwaukee train 163 was discontinued.

The Chicago-based vest-pocket *400* consist continued for the time being to operate essentially as it had since 1942, but its Chicago-Green Bay Sunday round trip was rescheduled by making 153 and 216 daily trains, and 216's time was revised to make ready for the forthcoming extension of *400* service to Ashland, Wis. Green Bay departure became 45 minutes later and Chicago arrival 55 minutes later. The procedure of holding the Milwaukee-based equipment in Chicago on Saturday night (when 121 operated with other equipment) went on as before, and this consist made a Sunday morning trip to Menominee as 239, the *Valley 400*, then returned to Chicago over a new route with a new number—as 168, the *Shoreland 400*. On May 26 northbound and May 27 southbound, 153 and 216 were redesignated the *Flambeau 400* and extended through to Ashland.

By this time, all postwar *400* cars had been delivered: 27 coaches, 9 parlors, 4 baggage-tap-cafe lounges, 1 cafe-coach, 1 diner, and 4 head-end cars. In 1947, when most of the coaches were delivered, their cost had been $80,851 each, but by September 1948, when the last of them arrived, the price had risen to $85,000. Inflation pushed the differential for the specialty cars such as cafe-lounges even higher.

Along with the *400* cars came 20 of assorted types as C&NW's contribution to the re-equipping of the *City* streamliners, and 16 diesel units for use on all trains—so C&NW's expenditures for passenger-train equipment were substantial. Spring 1950 also marked the completion of North Western's right-of-way upgrading in preparation for high-speed operation. The most recent project had involved 130 miles of 115-pound rail and 222 miles of out-of-face ballasting, not to mention other improvements to roadway, structures, and equipment—all to improve safety and increase efficiency.

There was one more true expansion of *400* service on the northern lines, and that was an additional daily Green Bay-Chicago round trip, operated as an improved version of existing train 206 on the southward journey but as a completely new service northward as train 215. These were known as the *Valley 400* and *Shoreland 400*, taking the names of the trains the *Flambeau 400* had replaced. Subsequent expansion of *400* service north from Chicago involved only assigning streamlined equipment to trains already operating.

For many years, 206 had provided convenient morning service between Green Bay and Chicago on a moderate schedule, with stops at some of the smaller communities en route. As new cars arrived after the war, this train benefitted from the reassignment of the older lightweight *Challenger* coaches, often having a brace of them—by this time painted in the gray applied to the more important limiteds between Chicago and the West Coast.

In early June of 1950, news broke of a new streamliner service to be established between Green Bay and Chicago. The *Green Bay Press-Gazette* reported that the new train—not referred to as a *400*—would include a parlor and one of the new 7625-series diner-lounges like those recently introduced on the *Flambeau 400*. Soon C&NW ads appeared announcing the new streamliner as the *Shoreland 400* and *Valley 400*, but giving incorrect starting dates for the service.

Train 215 actually began service on Sunday evening, June 11, leaving Chicago at 6 p.m., which for many years had been the departure time for 211, the *Ashland Limited*. On this date the *Ashland Limited* was combined with the *Iron & Copper Country Express* to Milwaukee on that train's slightly later schedule. The new *Shoreland 400* hurried on an 80-minute timing from Chicago to Milwaukee, with pauses at Evanston, Kenosha and Racine; then hustled along the Lake Shore Division on a 2-hour 15-minute schedule with positive stops at Port Washington, Sheboygan and Manitowoc, and conditionals (to discharge passengers from

An E7 and its seven-car Green Bay 400 consist (five coaches, diner, ex-City lounge) meets morning passengers at Neenah-Menasha on August 1, 1959.

The operator at St. Francis tower on the south side of Milwaukee waves 206, the Valley 400, on to Chicago on August 30, 1955. St. Francis marks the junction of C&NW's freight line from Chicago and the Milwaukee freight belt with the passenger line.

Milwaukee and beyond) at Cedar Grove, Oostburg and Denmark. (In September, the *Shoreland 400* would begin leaving Chicago at 6:25 p.m. and arriving Green Bay at 10 p.m. The train gained a Waukegan conditional stop to receive for beyond Milwaukee and lost its Oostburg stop.)

Number 206 became the *Valley 400* on Monday morning, June 12, highballing from Green Bay at 7 a.m., 10 minutes earlier than it had as a standard train, but reaching Canal & Madison 1 hour and 14 minutes earlier, an achievment resulting primarily from elimination of stops at DePere, Kaukauna, Appleton Junction, Winnebago, Campbellsport and Kewaskum on the single track to Milwaukee. Time was taken up in the final 85 miles by elimination of two Sunday-only stops and fast running.

This round trip was handled with a single E unit and six or seven cars: coaches, a parlor and one of the new baggage-cafe-lounges. These cars, also used on the *Flambeau 400* and additional Chicago-Milwaukee *400's*, were decorated with two-tone-blue hook carpeting, seats in crimson leather, and drapes of two-tone gold. The frieze panel above their windows was washable blue and silver textron, while the ceiling was light yellow, and the table tops were pearlescent formica. The lunch-counter section was finished in gold, blue, yellow and gray. Perhaps because there was no separate tavern section in these cars, the area behind the lunch counter resembled a back bar, unlike in the

tavern-counter cars of prewar design. Throughout the car, all metal trim was of satin-finished aluminum. The murals on the bulkheads and between the windows were hand-colored blue tone.

With the institution of the new *Shoreland/Valley 400* came some associated schedule changes. As mentioned, trains 211—the *Ashland Limited*—and 161—the *Iron & Copper Country Express*—were consolidated between Chicago and Milwaukee, and the *Ashland Limited* received a 25-minute-faster schedule between Milwaukee and Green Bay, since its smaller intermediate stops were assigned to 215. To provide a fourth eastbound weekday train on the Lake Shore Division, train 306, which had **previously originated in Manitowoc, was extended north to start** from Green Bay. It retained its convenient Manitowoc departure time and fed into streamliner 206 in Milwaukee. When it had made up in Manitowoc, 306 had received some of its equipment from Ashland Division 116, which terminated in Manitowoc the previous afternoons, but on June 10 that train was discontinued east of Appleton Junction. After that, 306's equipment came entirely from cars moving from Chicago to Green Bay on other conventional trains.

When the *Flambeau 400* extended service into Ashland, that train relieved the Chicago-based "little *400*" consist of its afternoon duties, leaving for it only a morning Chicago-Milwaukee round trip as train 149—on a 90-minute schedule with a Winnetka

ROUTE CHRONOLOGY

1942-1950

Capitol 400: Chicago-Milwaukee-Madison-Chicago via Beloit (trains 155-609-500)

City of Milwaukee 400: Chicago-Milwaukee (trains 151, 156, 158 daily; train 163 daily except Sunday; train 165 Sunday only)

Commuter 400: Chicago-Milwaukee (trains 149, 152 daily except Sunday)

Shoreland 400: Chicago-Green Bay via Manitowoc (train 153, daily except Sunday; trains 167, 168 Sunday only)

Valley 400: Chicago-Green Bay-Menominee via Fond du Lac (train 216 Green Bay-Chicago only, daily except Sunday; trains 239, 220 Sunday only, Chicago-Menominee)

1950-1971

City of Milwaukee 400: Virtually same service as listed above, except that train 151 was extended to Green Bay in 1957. Train name was dropped altogether in 1959

Commuter 400: Virtually same service as listed above, except that train 149 was extended to Green Bay in 1959. Names dropped in 1968

Shoreland 400: Chicago-Green Bay-Menominee via Manitowoc (train 215 daily Chicago-Green Bay only, 1950-1958; train 239 Chicago-Menominee Sunday only, 1968-1971; train 168 Menominee-Chicago Sunday only, 1950-1971)

Valley 400: Chicago-Green Bay-Menominee via Fond du Lac (train 206 Green Bay-Chicago only, 1950-1968; renamed *Green Bay 400* in October 1958; train 239 Chicago-Menominee only on Sundays 1950-1968)

Streamliner 400/400 Streamliner: Chicago-Milwaukee with various train numbers through the years (155, 156, 160, 121, 127); name was "reversed" in 1962; train 121 extended to Green Bay as 121X 1964-1970

NOTES: The above is only a synopsis of the Chicago-Milwaukee-Green Bay-Menominee corridor. The reader should refer to the main text for a complete description of the operating complexities of each train, particularly the *Streamliner 400.* Refer also to the *Flambeau 400* and *Peninsula 400* chapters for additional information on Chicago-Green Bay service involving those trains. All names were officially dropped in 1968.

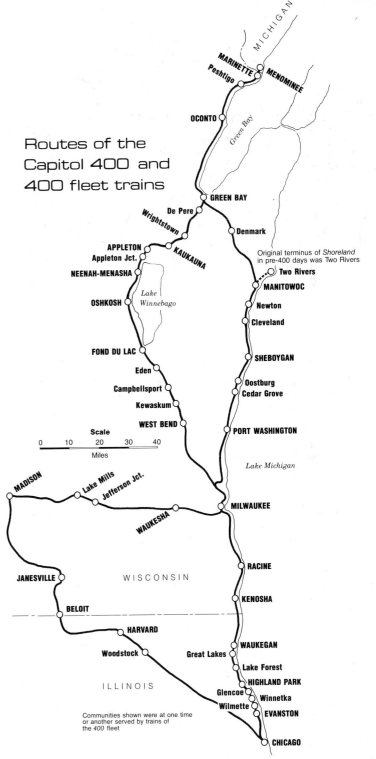

Routes of the
Capitol 400 and
400 fleet trains

Original terminus of *Shoreland* in pre-400 days was Two Rivers

Lake Michigan

Communities shown were at one time or another served by trains of the *400* fleet

185

Jim Scribbins

Mike Schafer

Jim Scribbins

(Above) By now nameless, train 239, most recently the Shoreland 400, *coasts along Milwaukee Road tracks at 16th Street west of downtown Milwaukee on March 21, 1971. (Above right) The* Commuter 400 *exits the Bush train sheds of North Western Terminal in Chicago at the start of its 212-mile sprint to Green Bay in November 1965. (Right) In April 1966, the Chicago-bound* Green Bay 400 *passes Erie Street engine terminal in Milwaukee.*

stop added—and 156. Since the new *Valley 400* passed through Milwaukee at 9:25 a.m., train 156 was rescheduled to depart Milwaukee at 10:30 a.m. for an 80-minute 4-stop run to North Western Terminal in Chicago. With these changes, trains 155 and 156 lost their *Capitol* and *City of Milwaukee* designations, both being known thereafter simply as *Streamliner 400*. (These schedule changes were not published until a new timetable was issued on July 9.) Effective with the entry of *400* service into Ashland, this Chicago-based consist replaced the Milwaukee-based one on the Sunday-only Chicago-Menominee round trip of *400*'s 239 and 168, which retained their titles of *Valley 400* and *Shoreland 400*.

In 1950, postwar automobile production was beginning to boom, with manufacturers introducing totally new stylings, rather than updated versions of their 1941 and 1942 designs. For this reason and others, the peak crowds of the late 1940's were beginning to drop away from the railroads, despite the many new streamliners. Consequently, some *400* consists began to shrink, albeit only slightly. This allowed C&NW to assign lightweight *400* equipment to certain previously heavyweight, steam-powered trains. Milwaukee-Green Bay train 151 was the first to receive this upgrading. Along with train 149, it had been listed since January 1942 in the public folder as "streamliner to Milwaukee, steam beyond." Through passengers had made a cross-platform transfer at the "Wisconsin Street passenger station" in Milwaukee. Then, late in the summer of 1950, No. 151 became basically a through Chicago-Green Bay run, with coaches and a parlor being switched from the *400* to the steam train during the pause at Milwaukee.

This equipment returned on other non-*400* trains to Milwaukee, where the parlor remained overnight before running to Chicago the next morning on *Commuter 400* No. 152. Train 121 lost its *400* label—appropriately, since it made several purely suburban stops in the Chicago area, although it did include in its consist streamlined coaches and the baggage-cafe-lounge car for the next morning's 152. The parlor which arrived in Chicago on 160, the afternoon train from Milwaukee now designated *Streamliner 400*, departed for Green Bay on 151 the next morning.

With the fall 1950 schedule change, *Commuter 400* No. 152 ran one-half hour later, departing Milwaukee at 7:45 a.m.; a 7625-

Three photos, Jim Scribbins

(Top and middle) Coming and going at Wiscona tower on Milwaukee's north side in April 1966 is the southbound Green Bay 400, *train 206. The going-away photo reveals construction progress on the new connection to Canco, designed to carry trains from C&NW's valley line to Milwaukee Road tracks to reach the new Milwaukee Road station. (Bottom) The connection is now in place in this scene dating from September 1967 as the former* Commuter 400, *train 149, plies the new trackage to return to home rails.*

187

An E7-powered *Commuter 400* with a consist of heavyweight RPO, streamlined parlor and three coaches halts at Appleton station (formerly Appleton Junction) during its northbound trek on September 21, 1963.

series car replaced the tavern-lunch counter aboard 239 and 168, the Sunday-only Menominee round trip. Following years saw minor schedule changes. In April 1951, train 158, the *City of Milwaukee 400*, was changed to depart its namesake city 10 minutes later; in fall of that year, 168 was retimed to operate 55 minutes later on its Sunday Menominee-Chicago trip. In spring of 1952 came the end of the South Milwaukee stop for 160—by then identified as *Streamliner 400*—together with a 15-minute reduction in its running time, bringing it down to a respectable 90 minutes with four positive and two conditional stops in its 85-mile journey.

In July 1953, *Streamliner 400* train 155 had stops added at Glencoe, Highland Park and Lake Forest, with its schedule being changed to a very hot—under the circumstances—95 minutes. At the same time, restrictions were removed on local ridership between downtown Chicago and Davis Street, Evanston. Not long afterward, the timing was reduced to 90 minutes by removing the Glencoe and Lake Forest stops.

In May 1954, for the opening of the second season of Braves baseball in their new Milwaukee home, *Commuter 400* No. 149 was used to haul six sleeping cars of players, team officials, sports writers and photographers to Milwaukee. Though delayed in Chicago to await the Pullmans from a connecting line, the *400* arrived in Milwaukee on time.

In spring of 1955, train 155 again was given its Glencoe and Lake Forest stops, as well as a conditional stop at Winnetka on holidays, and its running time once more became 95 minutes.

There were some equipment modifications at that time, too. The train arriving in Milwaukee as 149 at 9 a.m. lingered longer to operate back as 158, giving that 11:40 a.m. departure a lunch counter instead of a cafe-lounge. No. 156 became coach-only, though still called *Streamliner 400*. With the October 1955 release of streamlined equipment from the West Coast service, there were "domino effect" adjustments to the smaller *400*'s consists, one of which was to place a baggage-cafe-lounge on *Commuter 400* No. 149 for the first time, thereby returning a 7625-series car to *City of Milwaukee 400* No. 158.

A year later, in spring of 1956, the former *City* streamlined equipment began to be assigned directly to short-distance *400* trains, as well as to the longer hauls. One of the diner-lounges which had been used for coach passengers on the West Coast trains began making a Milwaukee-Chicago round trip on 152 and 151, and one of the regular *400* coaches which had been remodeled into a coach-lounge for the transcontinental trains was assigned to 155 and 160. All these cars replaced 7625-series cafe-lounges. The diner-lounge also worked the Sunday Menominee *Valley 400/Shoreland 400* turn. Since it was built to *City* design, its interior was considerably different from any of the *400* food service cars or lounges. The exterior featured larger windows, a squarer body and what could be termed a "heavier" look. In the fall, the diner-lounge on 239 and 168 was replaced by a 7625-series cafe-lounge, and one of the 3400-series coach-lounges was added to the consist.

Also in spring of 1956, C&NW made the first of several attempts to reconcile, at least partially, train schedules with the variances between Wisconsin's Standard and Illinois' Daylight Saving Time—an exercise eventually made unnecessary by the federal Uniform Standard Time law. Generally speaking, C&NW tended to conform with the observance periods of "advance" time in Illinois. Sometimes, however, a train departing from Chicago was run in accordance with Illinois time, while a train traveling toward there would follow Wisconsin time. Effective in 1957, when Wisconsin did adopt Daylight Saving Time, the train schedules were generally advanced in both directions, but the summer schedule would remain in effect during October when Wisconsin had returned to standard time and its southern neighbor had not.

Steam power had disappeared from regular operation over two years previous, so the "streamliner to Milwaukee, steam beyond" column heading was no longer applicable, and for 149 and 151 this was changed simply to "streamliner to Milwaukee," with no specific mention of the usual Geep north of there. By spring 1957, Milwaukee-Green Bay local trains 149 and 210 were discontinued, and train 151 officially became the *City of Milwaukee 400* for the entire distance to Green Bay operating as a through train from Chicago with parlor and diner-lounge. This equipment returned to Milwaukee as nameless Lake Shore Division local 120, laid over there, and ran as *Commuter 400* No. 152 the next morning in order to be in Chicago for its assignment as 151. The *City of Milwaukee* was a *400* in name and equipment north of Milwaukee—but not in speed, since it continued to be essentially a local train, requiring nearly four hours for that portion of the trip. At this time, *Valley 400/Shoreland 400* trains 206 and 215 were also strengthened with one of the 3416-series coach-lounges.

On June 16, 1957, North Western removed several trains from service, primarily in Wisconsin, among them Chicago-Milwaukee *400*'s 158 and 155. After that, equipment rolling to Milwaukee as 149 returned as *Streamliner 400* No. 156—giving it, for the first time in two years, tap-cafe and first-class service. An equipment cutback did occur, however: the elimination of the parlor car from trains 149 and 160 on Saturdays.

Though several of the short-distance *400*'s had time added—usually five minutes—between Chicago and Milwaukee, most fall 1957 timetable changes were merely in equipment. Train 156 lost its parlor, while *Valley/Shoreland 400*, Nos. 206 and 215, received an ex-*City* diner-lounge in place of its 7625-series tap-cafe lounge. In April of 1958, however, there was a realignment of passenger train schedules, with the evening Chicago-Green Bay *Shoreland 400* disappearing as a name, though not as a service. What happened was that the *Ashland Limited* and the *Iron & Copper Country Express*—the two traditional overnight trains between Chicago and the north country, which had been combined in recent years via the Fox River valley from Chicago to Green Bay—were again separated and retimed.

The Ishpeming overnighter was renamed the *Iron Country* and routed via the Lake Shore Division, with a schedule identical to that of the *Shoreland 400*, except for additional stops—and, consequently, slower running time—for the first 85 miles. It handled the *400* equipment to Green Bay for return as the *Valley 400*, No. 206, in addition to the through cars to the Upper Peninsula. *Iron Country-Valley 400* equipment was also modified by substitution of a full diner for the ex-*City* diner-lounge and replacement of the coach-lounge with a club-lounge. On the return journey, the two overnighters continued their combined existence from Green Bay to Chicago, via Fond du Lac. During winter 1957-58, the Appleton depot was closed and all passenger stops were made at Appleton Junction, which was within the city; that

Jim Scribbins

(Left) Train 160 Streamliner 400 rolls out across the Milwaukee River in April 1966 as it embarks on its dash to Chicago. (Below) Judging by the clock on the depot, 149 Commuter 400 has arrived Milwaukee just a bit ahead of schedule in this scene from the 1950's.

A. Robert Johnson

depot was thus renamed Appleton.

That spring also saw more juggling of equipment, with an ex-*City* diner-lounge being handled on 149 to Milwaukee, thence 151 to Green Bay, returning to Milwaukee for the night on local Lake Shore Division train 120 and ending the circuit with a morning trip on 152 into Chicago in breakfast service. At this time 152 lost its parlor car. The same equipment operated the Sunday-only Chicago-Menominee *400* round trip, Nos. 239 and 168. The diner-lounge was dropped from 168's consist in Milwaukee to be available for *Commuter 400* No. 152 Monday morning. A later modification had only coaches running north of Green Bay. Beginning in fall 1958, on national holidays 168 operated between Green Bay and Chicago only. This was a faster train than 120, and, like that local, it was the return working of the equipment which moved north on *City of Milwaukee 400* No. 151.

Train 160 lost its *400* designation in the schedule column in fall 1958, although equipment listings continued to show it as the *Streamliner 400*; train 156 also became nameless, but retained its 85-minute schedule, which was faster than many titled runs between Milwaukee and Chicago. Conversely, 121, a practically local schedule which had been unnamed since 1950, again came to be called a *400*. No. 215 again became a combination of both overnight trains to the north and took the name *North Woods Fisherman*; the appellation was at the same time applied to what had been the *Ashland Limited*. It no longer carried a parlor, the first class car for 206 now being the one which traveled north on 151.

To emphasize its new equipment, train 206 was designated the *Green Bay 400* when it began running with bilevel cars on October 26, 1958. The new train departed from Green Bay at 6:45 a.m., 15 minutes earlier than previously, and arrived in Chicago 10:55 a.m., 25 minutes earlier. This change allowed a little more turnaround time in Chicago, because the sparkling new cars—which had come from Pullman-Standard's Worcester (Mass.) plant—headed back to Green Bay as the *Flambeau 400* just 35 minutes after arrival. Now used on 206 were a converted and remodeled dining car, a baggage-tap car which had had its lunch counter replaced by additional lounge facilities when its roof was raised to conform to the bilevel height, bilevel car 600 (which had a parlor section to one end of its center entrance and coach accommodations to the other), and whatever number of bilevel coaches were considered necessary on any given day.

The last brochure for any *400* train was published to introduce the bilevels, a new concept in long-distance train comfort. The brochure—and the advertising in the timetable and newspapers as well—referred to the new trains as the *Green Bay 400*. In the schedule pages of the folder, however, train 153 continued to be called the *Flambeau 400*, even though it was actually two separate trains: Chicago-Green Bay and Green Bay-Ashland. This awkward situation for travelers to northern Wisconsin existed only until the spring 1959 time change, when the *Green Bay 400* consist began to spend the night in Chicago and operate on the *Flambeau 400* in both directions. This meant that train 206 once again received the equipment which operated north on 215. (During the winter it had been returning the next afternoon on the regularly constituted *Flambeau 400*, train 216.)

As summer commenced, the 3416-series coach-lounge on 121 and 160 was replaced by one of the more deluxe ex-transcontinental 7900-series club-lounges. (The same car worked the Sunday Menominee *400* round trip as well.) To protect this Chicago-Green Bay round trip, the car was withheld from 121 on Saturday and Sunday evenings, as had been done with the coach-lounge.

In late September 1959, additional discontinuance of train service was authorized, and train 156 (using *400* coaches) was no more, along with train 151, which ended the use of *City of Milwaukee 400* as a train name. Local service between Milwaukee, Fond du Lac and Green Bay was continued by the extension of train 149, the *Commuter 400*, which was retimed to leave Chicago at 8 a.m. Arrival at Green Bay at 2 p.m. (after stops at all communities en route except Granville, Vandyne and Little Chute) still allowed the operation of the coaches and diner-lounge to Milwaukee as Lake Shore Division 120, while the parlor remained in Green Bay to be the first-class accommodation on *Green Bay 400* No. 206 the next morning—which, along with the *North Woods Fisherman*, lost the club-lounge.

For the next few years changes were minimal in both equipment and scheduling. Spring 1960 saw the diner-lounge removed from 149 and 120 and used instead for a Milwaukee-Chicago round trip on *Commuter 400* No. 152 and *Streamliner 400* No. 121, thereby improving the quality of early-evening service afforded to Milwaukeeans returning from Chicago. Though it lost its food and beverage service, the northbound *Commuter 400* was quickened by 20 minutes between Fond du Lac and Green Bay. That fall, the club lounge was not operated on Sunday trains 239/168, allowing it to be part of 121 on Saturday evening instead.

In May 1961, train 214, the *Peninsula 400*, was placed in daily operation via the Lake Shore Division—possibly because train 106 (formerly 306) on that line was discontinued—instead of operating Sundays as train 240 via Fond du Lac. To compensate for this loss of late-Sunday-morning service via the Fox River valley, *Green Bay 400* No. 206 operated 90 minutes later on Sunday morning only and took the number 208. In fall of 1961, *Streamliner 400* No. 121 was given five minutes additional time, resulting in an even two-hour Chicago-Milwaukee run, terminating at 8:30 p.m.

April 29, 1962, saw a new *400* inaugurated: Sunday-only 127, a 15-minutes-faster version of 121, now weekdays-only. It lasted for one year, after which 121 resumed daily operation. The folder announcing 127 also contained a slight change in terminology for 121, 127 and 160, the minor members of the fleet. Each became a *400 Streamliner* rather than *Streamliner 400*. Spring 1963 saw *400 Streamliner* 160's Winnetka and Wilmette stops changed to positive, so once again a *400* was performing off-peak Chicago inbound suburban service. Also, the *Valley 400* and the *Green Bay 400* operated 15 minutes earlier between all stations, *Green Bay 400* No. 206 began operating 15 minutes earlier and fall saw a reduction in running time of 10 minutes between Fond du Lac and Green Bay for 149, the *Commuter 400*.

On June 22, 1964, there were changes in both equipment and schedule. The *North Woods Fisherman*, the overnight Chicago-Ashland train, was discontinued. To provide evening service as far as Green Bay, *400 Streamliner* 121 was extended from Milwaukee to Green Bay as 121X, the "X" denoting that it was operated on a temporary and experimental basis. No. 121 departed Chicago 45 minutes earlier than had the *North Woods Fisherman*. Though it took 15 minutes longer to Milwaukee, the total elapsed time to Green Bay was 25 minutes less, since there was a shorter stop in Milwaukee and a faster carding over the Lake Shore Division. Milwaukee-Chicago *400* No. 160 was changed to operate Monday through Friday only, its Saturday trip being handled by train 162X, which replaced local 120 out of Green Bay to Chicago and passed Milwaukee six days a week at 5:08 p.m.

Between Chicago and Milwaukee, 121 was quite a luxurious *400* for the era, carrying a diner-lounge (which actually was deadheading to Green Bay for use on 206 the next morning) as well as a club-lounge, which had run to Chicago on 160, and a second diner-lounge, which had served breakfast on 152 en route to the Windy City.

Morning *400* No. 149 lost its parlor car, as did *Green Bay 400* No. 206–208, which also had its diner replaced by a 7800-series diner-lounge that deadheaded from Milwaukee to Green Bay on 121 each evening. Beginning in the fall, lounge seats in this car could be reserved as a substitute for parlor seats, a practice which continued for the duration of the car's assignment to that run. A first-class ticket was required, but there was no seat charge.

Spring 1965 found trains 239 and 168 running without a parlor for their Sunday-only Menominee duty, and the diner-lounge was cut out of 168 in Milwaukee for use on 152 Monday morning. At this same time, those *400*'s which departed from North Western Terminal on the half-hour—Nos. 239, 153 and 121—began leaving at 31 minutes after the hour, since suburban trains on their memory-scheduled time-interval basis left on the even half-hour.

No. 121 began stopping at North Chicago on Friday nights only (149 had been stopping Saturday mornings for some time) to receive "boots" heading off on their weekend liberty from Great Lakes Naval Training Station. There were also special trains on Saturdays and Sundays for the sailors. In October 1955, 206 again became a daily schedule with discontinuance of Sunday-only 208.

On May 16, 1966, North Western passenger trains moved from their lakefront station in Milwaukee and began using the new Milwaukee Road station there. C&NW trains from Chicago gained CMStP&P rails at Washington Street, alongside National Avenue on the C&NW. Return to the Fox River valley and Lake Shore lines occurred at a new connection on the Milwaukee at Canco, directly below Wiscona, an important three-way C&NW junction. This partially single-track route was more circuitous than the C&NW's delightful passage along the lakefront and the Milwaukee River, so passenger trains to and from Green Bay were given two minutes additional running time on the Milwaukee Road between Washington Street and the depot, and an extra 10 minutes between Milwaukee and West Bend or Port Washington.

Though it would have been possible for *Commuter 400* No. 152 and CMStP&P's No. 24 to maintain their identical 7:45 a.m. departures to Chicago, the C&NW schedule was advanced to 7:40 a.m., while the host railroad's train left at 7:50 a.m. A similar problem in late afternoon had already been resolved by C&NW 160's being retimed in April to 4:10 p.m., so CMStP&P 46 could highball at 4 p.m. as always.

Curtailment of the food beverage service continued to typify the changes affecting the *400*'s. On Friday, January 12, 1968, came the final operation of ACF-built club-lounge 7900 on train 160, which thus became coaches-only, and on 121, between Chicago and Milwaukee. The next morning saw the end of dining-lounge service on *Commuter 400* No. 152. The only breakfast customers that day aboard car 7800 on the E7-powered train from Milwaukee were four railfans traveling specifically for the occasion. Nos. 239 and 168 also became coaches-only that weekend.

Saturday, May 4, 1968, was the final operation of *Commuter 400* train 149 north of Milwaukee; the final consist into Green Bay was five rebuilt *400* coaches—now designated in the 800 series—behind E7 No. 5018A. *400 Streamliner* 160 began running on Saturdays once again, since train 162X between Green Bay and Chicago was also discontinued.

Another change that weekend was the rerouting of *Flambeau 400* No. 153 via Fond du Lac. Also, *400 Streamliner* 121X had the letter removed from its designation and was thereafter considered a regular train between Milwaukee and Green Bay. Its diner-lounge, which previously had been closing on arrival in Mil-

(Above) The southbound Green Bay 400 is on CMStP&P rails at Milwaukee, passing Milwaukee Road's 35th Street shop and terminal complex. After C&NW's lakefront depot and Erie Street roundhouse closed, C&NW passenger power was serviced here. (Above right) Train 149 on this frigid January day in 1967 at the new Milwaukee Road station was delegated two units, probably to fight off subzero temperatures. (Right) In later years, Geeps supplemented E's on some little 400's; a Geep on the former Shoreland 400 in 1970 permitted fast turnaround at Menominee, Mich.

The fine reputation established by C&NW's fleet of 400's became almost as much a part of Wisconsin culture as the state's brewing industry; in some ways, the two intertwined. To this day, a number of Midwestern taverns, mostly in Wisconsin, carry the "400" monicker in their names. In one case, a beer brewed in Waukesha, Wis., until the early 1960's capitalized (no pun intended) on the Capitol 400. Fox Head "400" Beer was produced at the Fox Head brewery located across the tracks from the C&NW depot in Waukesha. Needless to say, Fox Head "400" beeriana became much sought after by railfans.

waukee, continued serving through to the conclusion of the run. These changes left one train in each direction—121 and 214—on the Lake Shore Division instead of two. There was an additional round trip on Sundays, Train 239 routed via Manitowoc for the first time in its career.

On February 3, 1969, trains 121 and 206 were assigned bilevel cars. Car 225 (formerly full-parlor 6400, rebuilt as a suburban coach with walkover seats) was used along with one or more 700-series reclining seat cars, and tap-lounge 7602, which was described as a "snack and beverage car" on the *400 Streamliner* and a "Continental breakfast car" on the *Green Bay 400*. This change of equipment was shown for the first time in the May 12 folder, wherein the equipment listing referred to the trains only as "Bi-Level Streamliners," although their *400* names continued to appear in the schedule column.

After the *Peninsula 400* made its last trip north of Green Bay on July 16, 1969, its Chicago-Green Bay schedule remained unchanged. Trains 121-206 were reduced to coaches-only status. The new timetable designated trains so equipped as "Bi-Level Streamliners" or, if they carried conventional coaches, simply "streamliners." (This included train 125 between Chicago and Milwaukee, which had never been designated a *400*.) The only appearance of the haughty number was in its traditional position on the cover, beneath the emblem, with the proclamation "Route of the *400*'s."

Finally, on the October 8, 1969, timetable, even the cover was changed to read "Route of the Streamliners." Nowhere was there any reference to the once-proud, sophisticated *400* fleet. A tradition that had started on January 2, 1935, in a brilliant burst of optimism and enlarged to become a fine example of modern passenger-train operation was no more.

Though the *400* banner was furled, the yellow-and-green trains continued to roll for a time. A spartan "Sip and Snack" dining-car service was instituted in November 1969, substituting a variety of pastry, sandwiches, cold drinks, coffee, tea and alcoholic beverages for complete meal service. At first this was provided in the regular diners; by early February 1970, however, parlor-coach 600 had had its parlor section converted to a food-service area with tables and had been assigned to 153 and 216, while the more easily remodeled coach-bar 903 was used on 209 and 214.

Service was whittled down even further on June 22, 1970, when more trains made their final runs: Chicago-Milwaukee 125, an E7

hauling 800-series conventional coaches; and Milwaukee-Green Bay 121 and Green Bay-Chicago 214, both bilevel trains. No. 214's equipment then was assigned to 206, giving that train food service again—of the "Sip and Snack" sort—and the service was re-scheduled one hour later to partially compensate for the termination of 214. No. 121's bilevel cars now returned to Chicago as train 152.

One result of this final cutback in train mileage was that the Lake Shore Division was left with just one round trip per week: Sunday trains 239 and 168, which, with Chicago-Milwaukee trains 149 and 160, were the last on C&NW's northern lines to be operated with single-level equipment and E7 locomotives. Then in November 1970, Nos. 239 and 168 received bilevel equipment—including a suburban control coach, which enabled the train to be pushed by the locomotive on the return journey to Chicago, exactly as were (and are) the suburban trains. Soon trains 149 and 160—the last northern trains to use 800-series low-level coaches and E7 steam-generator locomotives—also became bilevel push-pulls. By this time, the trains generally consisted of just two bilevel coaches, or a bilevel coach and a bilevel snack coach.

Then came Friday, April 30, 1971—the final day of private long-distance passenger-train operation by the Chicago & North Western. Train 121 arrived in Milwaukee on time at 8:30 p.m. and departed as an equipment extra east at 8:49 p.m. to St. Francis, where it spent the night waiting to be combined with 209's equipment, which deadheaded back from Green Bay via the freight belt line around Milwaukee on the morning of May 1.

Good friends were gone forever.

An ex-City diner-lounge brings up the markers of Chicago-bound 206, the Green Bay 400, in April 1966 as the train eases over the Milwaukee River bridge. The clock on the Allen Bradley watch factory in the distance reads about 9:02 a.m. which means that C&NW can report another on-time performance on its Green Bay-Chicago corridor.

Jim Scribbins

Jim Scribbins

194

The bilevel era

Gallery cars and head-end power revolutionize carbuilding

DURING 1954, in anticipation of the introduction of American Car & Foundry dome cars on the Western *Cities* streamliners, the Busch trainshed roof of North Western Terminal was raised approximately one foot to accommodate the superb new cars. Unknowingly, C&NW was making it possible for its passenger service to spin off in an entirely new direction, a move which was to eventually influence passenger train operations far beyond the geographical area of the *400*'s.

In 1955, C&NW was facing the inevitable necessity of replacing its entire Chicago surburban equipment fleet—cars and locomotives—so that it could continue to operate at adequate standards of service. The carrier had flirted with a trio of Budd Rail Diesel Cars somewhat earlier, but did not feel RDC's to be the answer. In the meantime, the Budd Company and Burlington introduced the double-deck coach, referred to as a gallery car, to the Chicago-Aurora commuter service. The North Western decided to go the same route with the Galena, Wisconsin, and Milwaukee division local traffic, and the first sixteen cars, designated as bilevels, rolled out of the St. Louis Car Company.

They made a fine impression and strongly influenced the railway when it ordered sufficient equipment to replace two existing trains as required under an order from the Public Service Commission of Wisconsin, which then permitted discontinuance of several secondary passenger trains in the Badger State. At this particular time, several variations of ultralight weight trains were being tested by some railroads: ACF's Talgo, New York Central's *Xplorer*, and the General Motors Aerotrains. Santa Fe had developed its Hi-level coaches, combining the luxury of full-size streamlined equipment with the additional seating capacity made possible by the use of cars the height of CB&Q and C&NW surburban vehicles.

In June 1957, when the intent to purchase new trains was announced, the management stated it was considering both the lightweight (including, presumably, the Pullman-Standard design campaigned for by Chesapeake & Ohio some years earlier, and which ultimately appeared shortly prior to Amtrak as the United Aircraft Turbo) and high-capacity coaches combining the desirable qualities of the AT&SF long-distance *El Capitan* cars and North Western's own bilevels. C&NW personnel rode the lightweights actually in operation before making their final decision.

In fall, the news was out that the new trains would be a pair of bilevel streamliners, and while some summertime speculation had seen them as replacements for the *Twin Cities 400*, the announcement of the two-tier design stated the equipment, when delivered, would go into Chicago-Green Bay-Upper Michigan service. This was logical, since eastern Wisconsin was the railway's most lucrative passenger travel area if, indeed, that term could still be justified in describing the passenger business. Pullman-Standard would construct ten coaches, a parlor, one coach-parlor and one coach-lounge to exterior dimensions identical to those of the new suburban cars, while two diners and two tap-lunch counters would be modified both externally and internally to conform to the new design. A major consideration in going bilevel was the fact the high capacity would result in shorter train-lengths. Some outside observers voiced the negative thought that such equipment would be easily convertible to suburban use when there was no longer any need for intercity rail passenger service.

Another first—at least in North American railroading— would be the use of head-end-powered electric heating and air-conditioning in a locomotive-propelled train. To accomplish this, existing locomotives would have their steam boilers replaced by diesel-generator sets.

Most of the cost of the new streamliners would be realized from the savings gained from the discontinuance of the fourteen red-ink "varnish" runs primarily within America's Dairyland, and were intended as evidence to the state of Wisconsin that the railway, even though it had lost faith completely in the future of the long-haul passenger train, would continue to provide a high quality form of that service where its need was justified by use. One-third of the system's passenger deficit was rolled up in Wisconsin alone; in fact, passenger losses in that state where C&NW was the major railroad were large enough to completely erase all revenue there. So Chairman Heineman and President Fitzpatrick, when they requested elimination of 21 trains in a single petition, promised the PSC they would use the anticipated $2 million annual savings to finance the new trains. Wisconsin let two-thirds of the trains disappear, and in return received some highly individualistic new trains. A noticeable side effect was the reassignment of the replaced single-level *400* cars to what conventional trains still operated, thus removing the last heavy-weight standard-era passenger carrying cars from service.

Construction of the 15-foot 10-inch tall streamliners began in April 1958 at the Worcester, Mass., facility of Pullman-Standard. The four dining and tap cars of conventional streamlined design were upgraded for use on the tall trains at the builder's Chicago plant. Most sources gave the total cost of the new passenger cars as $2,500,000, though one item of information published some two years after their delivery stated $2,250,000 had been put on the line to bolster a segment of transportation C&NW felt quite pessimistic about.

In midsummer, Mr. Heineman, Mr. Fitzpatrick and other top personnel journeyed to Worcester to view firsthand the work of the streamliners which were then well under way. In mid-October Chairman Heineman hosted a press trip between Chicago and Milwaukee as a first showing of the innovative conveyance; just a few days later he expressed a view before an Eastern audience that there was, at best, a five to seven-year future for through passenger business over his railway.

The first showing of the bilevel *400* equipment was in Chicago with a composite train made up of both baggage-tap cars, a coach, parlor 6400, diner and coach-bar 903. A Chicago-Milwaukee round-trip press run October 14 featured a train comprised of RPO-baggage-tap 7601, coach, the coach-bar, diner and the full parlor. In both instances, the two units of the 5022 provided the energy to move, heat and illuminate the train. Public exhibitions of the innovative additions to the *400* fleet were held in Chicago the 15th; Milwaukee the 16th; Kenosha, Racine, West Bend and Fond du Lac the 17th; Oshkosh, Neenah and Appleton the 18th;

Sheboygan, Manitowoc and Green Bay the 19th; and Oconto, Peshtigo, Marinette, Menominee, Stephenson and Escanaba on the 20th. Showings varied from 55 minutes in West Bend to 10 hours in Milwaukee.

The reaction of the press was reservedly optimistic. Enthusiasm was evident over the fact that new equipment was coming on the scene in a phase of the industry which outsiders, at least, considered hopelessly negative. This was perhaps more so in Wisconsin where purely local trains had persisted so much longer than on a national level, and several C&NW secondary trains had been removed—not without local opposition—in the months preceding the construction of the bilevels. The reporters dutifully columnized the center doors, increased height, electric heating, single coach seats and other fresh aspects built into the simplified yellow-and-green cars; but one can wonder just how much it all meant to a public which continued to embrace larger and increasingly luxurious automobiles on an expanding Interstate Highway system. Some editorial hope was expressed that maybe, just perhaps, the two-story streamliners could reverse the spiraling descent of passenger train ridership which, in 1958, for all railroads sunk to its lowest point in nearly seven decades. Nor had apprehension been lessened by the release in September of ICC Examiner Howard Hosmer's report anticipating the end of intercity rail passenger service in the United States by 1970.

The equipment entered service Sunday, October 26, as the *Peninsula 400*; and as the *Green Bay 400* which on its trip to Chicago was the new version of the *Valley 400*. This set immediately returned as a substitute for the Lake Shore portion of the *Flambeau 400*. The working assignments for the bilevel cars are described in detail in those chapters pertaining to their respective trains.

Chairman Heineman took issue with critics, stating that most railroad men got a terrific "kick" out of operating fine passenger trains, and that introduction of the bilevels was positive indication of that sentiment. He pointed out that the "bumped" single-level streamlined coaches would upgrade remaining non-*400* trains, bringing about a system-wide improvement in service. President Fitzpatrick stressed that while the new equipment contained several features which would help reduce maintenance, they also had a high degree of passenger comfort designed into them, and voiced the opinion that if the bilevels did not succeed, there would be no use in attempting any other improvements in the passenger situation. President J. W. Scallan of Pullman-Standard pointed out the new trains completely broke with tradition and were the result of thorough study and cooperation between the builder and the railway. Some newspaper editorial comment described the double-deckers as a desperate final attempt to gain profitability, and prophesized they would be the

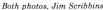

(Right) Upper-level gallery at the stairwell end of a bilevel coach, showing the individual reclining seats. (Far right) Lower level of coach side of coach-parlor 600 on the Flambeau 400. Smoking was permitted in galleries only.

Both photos, Jim Scribbins

last long-distance passenger trains built. The trade press concentrated on the fact the trains' design reduced considerably the cost of maintaining them. Interestingly, the bilevel streamliners rated one of the few promotional leaflets ever produced for the *400* trains, indicative of the esteem in which they were held.

The concept making the bilevel possible was the increase in height which, together with lowering the floors except at the car ends, resulted in a vehicle that was nearly two floors tall. It could be described as the coach equivalent of Pennsylvania Railroad's duplex single-room sleeping cars in which the same principle generated an increased number of rooms per car. Because the raised roof/lowered floor combination did not result in sufficient vertical space to permit full headroom throughout the car, the gallery design was adopted. It permits full head room in the center aisle on the lower level of the car. Upper-level balconies, or galleries, run the length of the car above and parallel to the lower-level aisle and are the same width as the lower-level coach seats. The gallery floors are approximately at shoulder height of a person standing in the lower-level aisle, and in turn they form a somewhat restricted-headroom ceiling above the lower-level seats. Above the main aisle are luggage racks which appear to be supporting the galleries; actually they provide an adequate alternative to the conventional wall-mounted (impossible in these coaches) luggage racks.

Access to the bilevel is by means of a center entry-way approximately three times the width of the customary vestibule on a single-level car. Though equipped with sliding doors (as are the commuter cars) passengers enter or exit only through the center third of each door area, the outer thirds—unlike commuter gallery cars—being utilized by four luggage shelves. This arrangement makes it possible for riders to enter the seating com-

partments with a minimum of hand baggage. The center entrance divides the cars into two compartments or seating areas. When the bilevels were introduced, quite a bit of attention was given to this diversion from the usual "tunnel" look of coach interiors.

As delivered to C&NW, the bilevel coaches each had eight rows of seats, top and bottom, in each "half" of a bilevel, totaling 96 per coach. Four toilet compartments, two near each end of the car, were equipped with something not previously found on rail cars: illuminated signs visible from the seating area indicating "vacant" or "occupied". Initially these were unisex "waterclosets," but eventually they were labeled "men" and "women" to comply with Wisconsin law.

The entry-way end of each passenger compartment has curving staircases to each of the upper levels, which consist of single seats accessible from a narrow walkway. The walkway has a knee-height wall on which is mounted a stainless-steel railing. Alternate vertical members of this railing continue to the ceiling and support, at shoulder level, a continuous solid-floor luggage shelf above the lower level luggage racks and aisle. The ceiling curves in from the walls immediately above the windows in the upper level, but permits somewhat more head room than that allowed for the double seats downstairs.

Continuous fluorescent lighting is mounted directly above the windows in the lower level and at the inner edge of the curving portion of the ceiling in the upper, providing effective illumination throughout. As delivered, bulkheads of both levels had a

Jim Scribbins

Looking toward the center of the car in the parlor section of coach-parlor 600. The stairwells to the upper-level coach seats are behind the mirrored bulkheads. Parlor sections featured carpeting.

weave or a fine line design worked into them, and pier panels between the windows on both levels had an embossed block pattern. Window frames are angled, reducing their capacity as dust-catchers. Although appearing to be leatherette or fabric, all interior walls are plastic, making them relatively dust-free and easily cleaned. When the cars were built, the windows were tinted green.

Unlike the commuter bilevels, the *400* gallery cars as built had reclining seats, each with a diamond-shaped weave pattern and a rather distinctive armrest unlike that on any other *400* equipment. The single seats on the upper level featured wing-contoured headrests, suggesting some of the luxury of parlor seats. The upper level seats also had small ash trays built into their armrests since the upper seats comprised the smoking areas of the coaches. The double seats on the first floor were done in yellow gold; ceilings above these seats as well as the side walls were shaded in dove gray. Gallery level seats had the same cloth pattern, but in blue. The single upper-level seats were a bonus for coach passengers traveling alone in that they gave a considerable degree of privacy, when such was desired. All seats had transparent plastic pullover headrest covers.

The ceiling across the car above the upper level was a lighter blue, while the stair areas were teal blue. Bulkheads at both ends of the seating rooms were entirely in walnut with vertical and horizontal lines across the surface. Marbled tile flooring on both levels was white flecked with blue, with outer edges in charcoal on the main floor, and cross strips of that color on the balconies. On the lower floor the basic white was set off with cross strips of dove gray.

Full parlor car 6400, and the parlor half of car 600, differed from the coaches in that their floors had dark tan carpeting with intermingled aqua-blue lines, and bulkheads were multi-colored, and those adjacent to the entry-way had small mirrors. Other decorations and lighting were the same as in the coaches. The lower level featured standard first-class parlor seating: reclining, rotating and somewhat larger in individual area than coach seats. Upper seating, because of the limited width of the galleries, was identical to the single coach seats. All parlor seats had ash trays, and smoking was permitted throughout the parlor areas. Originally, the parlor seats were protected with cloth head covers emblazoned with "The 400" emblem, but eventually the transparent plastic pullovers were substituted. There were no above-aisle luggage racks in the main floor of the parlors though they did have the continuous luggage shelf at the upper level. A nicety, in car 6400 only, was the addition of a storage area to hang coats— a particularly welcome convenience in winter. Parlor 6400 seated eight persons on each side of the aisle in the upper levels and seven on each side of the aisle on its main floor, a total of sixty in the car. Car 600 combined coach and parlor halves for a total of 78 passengers.

The interior design of the lounge section of car 903 took on a different approach: there were no luggage racks at all, making for a two-story-high ceiling. This and the placement of many of the lower-level lounge seats parallel to the train rather than cross-wise created an atmosphere of exceptional spaciousness. The tile flooring had alternating sections of rose and white separated by bands of charcoal. Bulkheads were of the lined walnut pattern used in the coaches, and the same scheme was used on the pier panels between the windows, as well as on the table tops. There was a table for four on one side of the aisle adjacent to the service area, and another on the opposite side just inside from the center vestibule. The other side at the service end had a magazine rack/table with a lamp. The balance of space on the lower level was taken up with modern tubular sofas for two and individual chairs of the same design, all facing the aisle. These had receptacles for beverage glasses conveniently attached to their frames, obviating the need for the usual ashtray-type drink stands which usually hampered one's progress through such cars (particularly if the patron had partaken too heavily of the liquid

(Above) Car 7601, on the tail end of 214 in 1965, and sister 7602 were built in 1941 for service on various 400's (7602 was built for the Capitol 400). *The coating of snow on the car's end plainly shows the raised roof area. When modified for bilevel service, the lunch-counter area was replaced with lounge seating.*

that made Milwaukee famous). Attached to the sides of the galleries were small gold plates depicting items of early-era railroading, such as long-necked oil cans, vest pocket watch chains, bells and whistles. Wall finishes were the same as in the coaches, but the high ceiling was of bamboo color.

The upper level contained three booths for two persons on each side. Because of the stairway from the service area and the attendant's access walk parallel to the outer bulkhead, the booths did not match up with the windows; for the same reason, the upper window nearest the end of the car was shorter than all of the other windows in bilevel cars. The booths had spring-loaded fold-up theater-type seats. For passengers, access to the upper level was by stairs immediately inside the vestibule, as in the coaches and parlors. Unlike all other bilevel cars which contained four upper-level and four lower-level windows in each half on both sides of the car, the upper-level bar section of the lounge half of car 903 had two large and one small (outer end) windows, while only the side which contained the service area bypass aisle had four windows on the lower level. Car 903 was assigned permanently to the *Peninsula 400*. The coach half of 903 had seating arrangement identical to coach sections of all other bilevel coaches. With a lounge section that accommodated 32 imbibers, the dual-purpose 903 had a capacity of 80.

In later years, suburban bilevel cab-control cars teamed up with long-distance bilevel coaches on the Chicago-Milwaukee run to obviate the need for train turnaround. "Cab-forward" train 160 departs Milwaukee on March 20, 1971.

All photos, Jim Scribbins

Beverage service on the *Green Bay 400* (whose equipment later became the *Flambeau 400*) was accommodated in one of the two modified tap-lunch counter cars (the other rolled along on the north end of the *Peninsula*). Cars 7601 and 7602 had their lunch counters replaced with lounge areas containing nine chairs on each side facing the aisle. The furniture was similar, but not identical to, that in the lounge of car 903. Seats were contoured somewhat differently, and appeared to have more padding as well as thicker armrests. Their frames were stainless and thicker than the black metal ones in the bilevel car, and since they did not have the built-in glass receptacles, standard tray stands were provided.

Diners 6953 and 6954 were constructed for the 1941 Twin Cities 400. For bilevel service, they also received false roofs and simplified but cheery interiors. Ironically, one of the "bilevel" diners became part of a restaurant complex in Lake Geneva, Wis.

Both photos, Jim Scribbins

New continuous fluorescent tubes replaced the older overhead lights, and the forward wall of the lounge area received metal decorations of the same type as in the 903. What had been the exterior wall behind the lunch counter received two large photo murals to compensate for its lack of windows.

The bar areas in these two cars were changed only in that they were somewhat spartanized. The leather upholstering on the curving side of the bars was removed as were the padded booth seats which were replaced by surplus movable dining-car chairs. The decorative mirrors between the windows were removed as were the drapes and blinds, and window panes were replaced with dark green tinted glass. Gone, too, were the photo murals which had been above the windows.

Dining cars 6953 and 6954 had their interior decorations removed as with the 7601 and 7602 tap-rooms. At times these diners were operated as 48-seat (12-table) restaurants with the pair of tables farthest from the kitchen replaced by a trio of lounge chairs on each side of the aisle. Toward the end of their service, they again became 56-seat 14-table conveyances.

The simplifying of these four cars set the style for the revamping of the regular 400 coaches when they were heavily shopped and renumbered from 3400's into 800's. Mechanically, these four holdovers from the 1942 trains were modified with electric heating, lighting, and air-conditioning systems that recieved power from the locomotive. The cars were also given false roofs so that they matched the bilevels. In any event, the modest

program was a forerunner of Amtrak's highly successful head-end power car rebuild program of the 1970s and early 1980s.

The exteriors of the bilevel 400 equipment introduced the only change in streamline livery experienced by the fleet. The tops of the cars, including the roofs, were green. The green extended down the sides to a point that matched the bottom of the letterboard of single-level cars. The lettering was changed to yellow from silver, and the black stripes on both edges of the letterboard and below the windows and above the skirts were removed. It would not have been practical to continue the window striping on the bilevels since their windows did not line up with those of the conventional cars. The visual effect of a tap or diner coupled to a bilevel was something akin to a trilevel home: three distinct window heights. The 400 emblem was also missing. Since there was only a modest amount of skirting near the vestibules of the bilevels, skirting was removed from the four modified food and beverage cars, and by the same token, since the tall cars did not have wide diaphragms, such were also dismantled from the 7600's and 6900's. All of these exterior changes were applied to the coaches which were subsequently remanufactured in the years immediately following introduction of the final 400 equipment.

Throughout the bilevels and their accompanying lounge and dining cars, much use was made of plastic and vinyl as an aid to cleaning and in retaining their like-new appearance.

An aspect of the bilevels which was not continued on the conventional streamlined coaches when they were remanufac-

200

tured was the provision for head-end-powered electric heating, air-conditioning and lighting. This was done in some specific instances: A diner was rebuilt to serve as a substitute, and some RPO cars were rebuilt to operate with the bilevels. It was possible to operate conventional coaches on the rear of a bilevel train in the summer since they had self-contained air conditioning activated by Waukesha motors.

Two pairs of E8's (5021AB and 5022AB) were converted for "electric" operation of the bilevel *400* trains, and a pair of F7 units 4081A and 4081C (F units had been originally acquired in three-unit combinations, and to maintain a uniform numbering scheme, two-unit locomotives with both units containing cabs were given the A and C suffix), were removed from freight service and equipped as standbys. Ultimately all E8 and F7 units used in passenger operation were re-equipped to supply electricity to their train. This involved removing the steam generators, and in their position at the rear of each unit installing a Cummins 575-h.p. diesel motor and a Marathon 480-volt alternator, both skid-mounted to enable easy removal for repairs. Alternating current was desirable because its higher voltage reduced transmission losses and permitted use of commercial items such as water coolers and heaters and other appliances. The constant roar of the Cummins motors, even when the locomotives were standing, led to the application of sound-deadening equipment.

The bilevel cars had no underbody equipment. Two eight-ton air-conditioning units were mounted at upper-level height in available space above their center entrances. Despite the increased size of the cars and their greater weight on a per-car basis as compared to conventional streamlined cars, the greater seating capacity of each car actually represented a considerable saving in weight when figured on a per-seat basis. In a bilevel coach (96 seats) the weight per seat was 1,302 pounds, while in a conventional coach seating 56 it was 1,827 pounds.

Electric heating eliminated the problems of steam loss due to leaks in bitter winter weather and produced a much more uniform degree of heating quality throughout the train.

The bilevel *400*s made their last runs on April 30, 1971, the day prior to Amtrak startup. But commencing in June 1973, bilevel *400* equipment acquired by Amtrak was pressed into Chicago-Milwaukee service over the rails of the Milwaukee Road. Shortly thereafter, bilevel *400* equipment showed up on other Amtrak trains such as the *Illinois Zephyr* (Chicago-West Quincy, Mo.), the *Black Hawk* (Chicago-Dubuque, Ia.), and the *Illini* (Chicago-Champaign, Ill.). As of 1981 the equipment had been assigned to Amtrak Chicago-Valparaiso (Ind.) service on the *Calumet* and *Indiana Connection.*

Apparently Amtrak was greatly influenced by North Western's application of head-end electric power plants (HEP) to supply train heating, lighting and air-conditioning. In the early Seventies, Amtrak took its first step toward establishing a total HEP passenger-car fleet when it placed its first order of Amfleet cars with the Budd Company. Although Amtrak's new SDP40F locomotives, delivered in 1973 and 1974, were equipped with steam generators, they were designed for ready conversion to Cummins HEP power plants. Later, Amtrak took delivery of F40PH's, which came equipped for head-end power. In the later half of the 1970s, Amtrak began converting its steam-heated cars to HEP.

As Amtrak entered the 1980s, its single-level Amfleet and rebuilt "Heritage Fleet" cars and new Pullman-Standard bilevel Superliners continued the *400*-pioneered method of modern train heating, lighting and air-conditioning. North Western's bilevel achievement cannot be underestimated, and it could likely be as significant a contribution to the art of railroading as was the introduction of the original *400* in 1935.

Jim Scribbins

John H. Kuehl

(Above) Not a C&NW bilevel *400* detouring over the Burlington, but Amtrak's West Quincy (Mo.)-Chicago Illinois Zephyr hurrying east through Clarendon Hills in BN suburban territory just outside of Chicago in September 1973. (Left) The inaugural run of Amtrak's Decatur-Chicago Illini arrives Homewood, Ill., on ICG tracks in July 2, 1981. Amtrak added control cabs on the ex-C&NW bilevels for push-pull operation. On the rear is privately owned Mount Ranier, formerly a Milwaukee Road business car.

Jim Scribbins

Protesters and empty seats

Minnesota loses its 400's

IN June 1959, at the same time the *North Western Limited* was discontinued, C&NW reduced fares for long-distance passengers on the *Twin Cities 400,* the only remaining train on the route. This brought coach fares to the level of buses, and notably lower than on Burlington or Milwaukee Road. Parlor seats could be purchased by holders of the new reduced-fare coach tickets, and dining-car prices were cut to a remarkable $1.25 for a full lunch or dinner.

Though originally intended to terminate in the fall, the experimental coach fares on the *Twin Cities 400* had met with enough success—initially increasing patronage about 50 percent—that they were extended into the winter to see what effect they would have on off-season travel. Though a decline in patronage would set in before long, dashing initial high hopes, the fare reduction was extended six times before finally being dropped in July 1961. The $1.25 dining car meal remained as long as the train operated. Furthermore, even after the discount fares ended, C&NW was priced 10 percent below the competition, having declined to take an increase allowed during the period of the experiment.

In 1961 the *Twin Cities 400* would lose $1,187,240 or $3.59 per mile. The 1960 loss had been over $1 million. The railroad's patience ran out. On October 31, 1961, the North Western petitioned the Interstate Commerce Commission for permission to discontinue on December 1, 1961, the *Twin Cities 400*—the train that once "set the pace for the world"—claiming that two years of lowered fares had failed to improve the flagship's financial situation. Despite an initially good start to the reduced-fare experi-

ment, passenger volume on 400 and 401 had declined 22 percent since 1959, and matters were even worse for the *Rochester 400.* (Since they were thought to complement one another, the *Twin Cities 400* and *Rochester 400* were treated jointly by both the railroad and the commission.) C&NW asserted that passenger losses were more than consuming the entire net operating income from freight service, and that it was no longer practical to raise freight rates to pay for passenger deficits.

From the time of the application onward, the city of Eau Claire was the staunchest opponent of the discontinuance of the *Twin Cities 400*—understandably, since the move would end passenger train service to that city. Joining Eau Claire in protest were several other communities, the Minnesota and Wisconsin state commissions, schools, business firms, railway labor organizations, and individuals. In response to these protests and others involving the *Rochester 400,* the ICC ordered a four-month extension of operations so hearings could be held. Meanwhile, the railway had placed newspaper ads explaining its position, enumerating the losses and detailing the abundance of alternative public transportation available—principally air.

In January 1962, hearings concerning the *Twin Cities 400* were conducted in St. Paul and Eau Claire. Additional inquiries concerned primarily with the *Rochester 400* took place in Rochester and Madison.

Testifying against discontinuance were 129 individuals, including the mayors of Minneapolis, St. Paul, and Racine, as well as those from Chippewa Falls, Chetek, and Spooner, towns located

If passenger crowds had always been this healthy at Rochester and other cities along the route of the Rochester 400 *(nee,* Dakota 400*), perhaps the train would have survived a few more years. The last 518 is arriving from Mankato on July 23, 1963.*

along the Duluth line of C&NW, which extended north from Eau Claire. Protesters represented all walks of life, some coming from several hundred miles off the *400* route to voice their need for the train.

The *Rochester 400* had its supporters too, and efforts to boost patronage of that train were hastily contrived in hopes of keeping it in operation. In November, for example, when the Rochester chamber of commerce held a large meeting attended by members of various chambers in the area, delegates were urged to travel via the *400*. Thirty persons from Waseca, 15 from Owatonna, seven from Kasson (where a special stop was made), and 16 from Dodge Center traveled together on 518.

At the ICC hearing held in Rochester, charges and counter-charges were exchanged, with the Mayo Clinic and neighboring hospitals insisting that the train was needed by their clients, though acknowledging that only 25 to 35 percent of those from distant points arrived by train. When the clinic's total patronage, including Iowa and Minnesota residents, was considered, the figure dropped to 16 percent. Though there were the usual allegations of downgrading of service from some quarters, representatives of the Mayo Clinic were satisfied with the quality of the *Rochester 400*. Precise medical explanations were advanced explaining that certain afflictions or handicaps made only train travel practical, an argument the railway did not attempt to rebut.

On March 23, 1962, the commission announced its decision to require operation of the *Twin Cities 400* and *Rochester 400* for another year, maintaining that a legitimate need for the trains existed and that their use might increase. That discontinuance would terminate all passenger train service on their routes and that substitute transportation by other modes would be inadequate weighed heavily. In the case of the *Rochester 400*, concern for patients traveling to and from the Mayo Clinic was a factor.

Much was made of the North Western's lowering fares rather than increasing them to meet rising costs; the implication was that the railway should have taken the 10 percent fare increase its competitors obtained during the discount experiment. Rather than praising C&NW for encouraging use of the trains by low fares, the ICC scolded the carrier for not charging the maximum allowable. However, the commission did reject claims that the railway was deliberately downgrading its service to discourage patronage.

Shortly after the announcement of the ICC order, the *Eau Claire Leader* commented that the fight to save the *Twin Cities 400* had just begun, that it was important to travel on the train, and that if ridership failed to increase and the train was discontinued, the public would have only itself to blame. The chambers of commerce of Eau Claire and Chippewa Falls promoted use of the streamliner. The Chippewa Falls chamber's newsletter featured a photo of the train, with the slogan "Use It or Lose It" in large print. The Eau Claire chamber estimated that 40 member firms used postage meters which could print a slogan urging patronage of the *400*; 18 companies actually did promulgate the message for approximately three months.

On January 16, 1963, the railway again petitioned the ICC to discontinue the *Twin Cities 400* and the *Rochester 400*, as of March 24, renewing its assertion that losses run up by passenger trains shouldn't be allowed to sap the road's financial strength to the detriment of its freight customers. C&NW claimed further that to require operation of the trains without real public need constituted a confiscatory incursion upon the railway, in violation of its rights under the United States Constitution.

Though management, under chairman Ben Heineman, had moved to improve the North Western and had modernized Chicago suburban service, the railroad's financial situation was precarious. There had been deficits in four of the six years ending December 1961, the cash or cash-equivalent situation had decreased 90 percent since 1947, and working capital was dangerously scarce. Common stockholders had not received a dividend for a dozen years. Thus it was impossible to acquire new freight cars as rapidly as outmoded ones were retired. Furthermore, C&NW had a high percentage of "bad order" freight cars and a substantial amount of deferred right-of-way maintenance. The red ink generated by trains 400, 401, 518, and 519 was by implication responsible for this deterioration.

In its first attempt to discontinue the *Twin Cities 400*, North

Camera-carrying onlookers join luggage-toting passengers at Eau Claire as the last eastbound *Twin Cities 400* thunders into town behind twin E7's. Thankfully, the parlor-solariums provided their extra touch of class right up to the end. (Below) Final 519 at Janesville on the same day.

Two photos, Eau Claire Leader-Telegram

Western had in effect been rebuked for not charging the higher fares permitted by the commission, and the railway had responded that if rates were increased patronage would continue to spiral downward. Acting according to ICC suggestion, C&NW did increase its fares in November 1962; its position was vindicated, since travel on the *Twin Cities 400* declined after the bus-equivalent experiment ended and dropped again with the new fare increase. This, coupled with the continuing rise in operating expenses, swelled the *Twin Cities 400*'s losses from $3,009 per day in 1960 to $3,253 the next year and $3,583 in 1962. In January 1963, when North Western filed its second petition, daily riderships for No. 400 was averaging 123 and for No. 401, 116; over three years, ridership had decreased 26 percent. The low point occurred one day when just 35 persons were aboard.*

For the most part, though, travelers had deserted the trains for their own automobiles, encouraged by ever-increasing expenditures of tax money to finance road-building—in Minnesota, for instance, a six-fold increase from 1940 to 1960. Interstate highways then under construction in Wisconsin would virtually parallel the route of the *Twin Cities 400*. In counties served by that

*Ridership on 518 and 519, the *Rochester 400*, averaged just 50 and 54 passengers per day, sometimes falling to only 13 passengers per trip. In 1962, losses averaged $3,000 daily.

Mike Nelson

train and the *Rochester 400*, according to the motor vehicle departments of the three states in which they operated, there was an automobile for every three persons.

Some opponents of discontinuance recommended cutting costs by reducing the *Twin Cities 400*'s consist to three coaches, a diner, and parlor-observation, with an additional coach and the tavern-lounge added on weekends and other busy times. Elimination of the $1.25 meal price, also suggested at first, was eventually rejected when the commission showed that C&NW's dining-car losses were favorable when compared to those of its competitors. (An opposite stance was taken by protestants who claimed that the railroad had deliberately downgraded equipment to discourage patronage. The commission would disagree, concluding that C&NW had maintained the train adequately.)

Some of the C&NW's opponents who had sought the hearings failed to attend them. Not a single representative from the Chicago area appeared. In Minneapolis, Mayor Naftalin was the sole protester. In St. Paul, the only opposition of substance was expressed by Mayor Vavoulis. It was at Eau Claire that the ICC examiner heard the most substantial opposition to the discontinuance. At Milwaukee, the city's port director contended that cross-Lake Michigan ship travelers would use the *400* to continue to Chicago. In Madison, the number of protesters was exceeded only by turnouts in Eau Claire and Rochester.

The railroad's argument was primarily this: For Nos. 518 and 519, the losses on an out-of-pocket basis had been $696,949 in 1961. For the first eight months of 1962, they totaled $451,989. On the fully-allocated basis—the often-questioned official method of passenger-train accounting required by the ICC—the amounts were much greater: $1,123,967 for 1961 and $728,960 through August 1962.

The four-month extension of service which had been ordered by the ICC so hearings could be held was scheduled to expire July 23. At virtually the last moment—July 22, to be exact—word came from Washington: The trains which had occasioned the hearings could be removed from the timetable. The commission found that they were not required by public convenience or necessity, and that their continued operation would be an undue burden on interstate commerce. Action followed swiftly. The *Twin Cities 400* and *Rochester 400* made their final trips the next day, Tuesday, July 23, 1963.

The last westbound *Rochester 400* departed behind an E7, with engineman S. J. Switalski at the throttle for the first 142 miles. At Madison, A. D. Harnish took over for the run to Winona. The fireman was A. L. Hergenrother, and the trainman Peter Polus. Leo H. Wettstein, the conductor, was retiring, at age 68, with his train. At Reedsburg, Wis., a chamber of commerce delegation met 519 and presented the crew with a farewell memorial wreath.

An E8 was on the point of 518, with engineman M. T. Fitzsimmons handling the train eastbound through Minnesota. The final ticket sold at Rochester—where more than 40 people boarded the funeral run, making it the busiest stop en route—was issued by ticket agent John Liebe to Theodore Hanson of La Crosse. Heading down the home stretch that evening was a crew composed entirely of Madisonians: R. J. Reinhold, conductor; Frank M. Chalfant, trainman; J. B. Guess, engineman; and E. L. Currie, fireman.

Displeasure over the suddenness of the train's removal was most pronounced in Rochester. Though some attempt was made to persuade the Minnesota Railroad and Warehouse Commission to appeal through the courts to have the *Rochester 400* reinstated, that enterprise never gained much momentum. In fact, the general public was quite apathetic and uninterested. That the typical layman was not keenly aware of what had happened was suggested by the headline in the Rochester *Post-Bulletin*: "400 *Puffs* Its Last Today."

Newspaper accounts of the *Twin Cities 400*'s end typically focused on quotes from passengers suddenly faced with an adjustment to other modes of transportation. Resignation rather than rancor prevailed. However, taking down the markers on "the train that set the pace for the world" was an understandably bitter pill for Eau Claire, since that city of 38,000 was left with no rail passenger service. Area spokesmen felt the notice of discontinuance abrupt and the defeat of their efforts greatly disappointing.

Steve Timbers of Eau Claire had been a *400* conductor for 20 years. For him, the final highball of No. 400 from Great Northern Station in Minneapolis meant the close of a career; he had held off an anticipated June retirement to see what would happen to the train. The *Minneapolis Star* gave him headlines and a photo, while the *St. Paul Pioneer Press* featured a photo of Timbers and engineman Clarence H. Johnson receiving their final orders. The *Pioneer Press* mentioned that a small cluster of railroad employees came down to see the *400* off, on time, and reminisced about the inauguration of the train, which it called "a great lady."

The last eastbound *Twin Cities 400* was the victim of pranksters who placed a crowbar over the rails, causing a shorted-out signal and consequent 30-minute delay in northwestern Wisconsin. Two extra coaches in the consist accommodated the train's friends who wished to say good-bye by taking a ride. Number 400's consist was two E7's, a 7625-series tap-cafe, six coaches, an ACF ex-*City* diner, and parlor-solarium 7200. It was a sparkling train, hardly appearing to be headed down its last mile.

Number 401 had troubles too, arriving in the Twin Cities an hour late. E7 5012B and F7 4052A led the seven-car pure *400* consist, modified only in that an extra coach replaced the head-end tavern-lounge. For the final lap over Great Northern rails, the units ran around their train, putting the F7 on the point.

Steward Pete Kromy of Minneapolis came from vacation to the GN depot to witness the last arrival. "She's still a pretty train," he said.

Jim Scribbins

The 400 Story

Discontinuance is less than two weeks away as E7 5015-B and a sister unit lead train 401 onto the Adams cutoff at Wiscona interlocking on Milwaukee's North side. Date: July 12, 1963.

Locomotives

WHEN in the fall of 1923 twelve heavy Pacifics emerged from the Schenectady works of the American Locomotive Company as North Western's 2900-series Class E-2, no one who participated in their design, construction and early years of operation could have forecast that a quartet of them would have great impact in the brilliant passenger train revival which commenced with the middle of the next decade. For eleven years, the dozen husky 4-6-2's wheeled West coast limiteds between Chicago and the Missouri River, as well as the *North Western Limited*. Then during autumn of 1934, four of them entered the Chicago shops.

As built, the 12 coal-burners had 75-inch drive wheels and 210-pound boiler pressure. But, upgraded into Class E-2-a, 2902, 2903, 2907, and 2908 boasted drivers increased to 79-inch diameter through application of Boxpok type A wheels. Boiler pressure was increased to 225 pounds, and tractive force was increased from 45,000 to 45,800 pounds. Also, they were converted to burn oil to avoid fuel stops and ash pan cleaning.

By lengthening the existing tenders through addition of a 6-foot center section, tender capacity was increased to accommodate 5000 gallons of black gold and 15,000 gallons of water. The tender body was remounted on a one-piece cast-steel frame carried on six-wheel trucks. The top of the tank was gracefully contoured and the tender contributed quite a bit to the esthetic grace of the four race horses assigned to maintain the hot schedule of what would become the fastest train in North America behind any form of motive power.

Because of the increase in steam pressure and the resulting added piston thrust, the diameter of the piston rods was increased a quarter inch. High-tensile steel was used to manufacture new piston rods, crank pins and main driving axles. The main driving wheels were carefully cross-counter-balanced to assure smooth running at high speeds with a minimum of stress to track and roadbed.

Steam locomotives

Class designation	Number built	Road numbers in 400 service	Assignment	Wheel arrangement	Cylinders (in.)	Boiler pressure (lbs.)	Tractive effort (lbs.)	Grate area (sq. feet)	Superheater heating surface (sq. ft.)	Drive wheel diameter (in.)	Total engine weight (lbs.)
D	91	125, 126 and very likely one or two others	Used briefly on *Minnesota 400*	4-4-2	20 x 26	200	21,800	46.3	438.5	81	Stephenson valve gear: 159,500 Walschaert valve gear: 181,500
R-1[1]		1331 and perhaps others	*Flambeau 400* Watersmeet section	4-6-0	21 x 26	200	30,900	47.2	476	63	Stephenson: 167,500 Walschaert: 186,000
E-2-a[2] (oil)	4	2902, 2903, 2907, 2908	Original *400*	4-6-2	26 x 28	225	45,800	63.1	882	79	295,000
E-2-b[4]		2901, 2904-2906, 2909-2912	Chicago-Green Bay on *Flambeau,* and on *Minnesota 400* Chicago-Adams and very likely Chicago-Elroy	4-6-2	26 x 28	225	45,800	63.1	882	79	295,000
ES[5]		1617, 1620[3]	*Minnesota 400*	4-6-2	25 x 28	200	39,600	53	691	75	279,000

[1]Specifications as rebuilt later in their careers.

[2]As upgraded for *400* service, not as built.

[3]To avoid conflict with diesel numbers, became 617 and 620 after service was completed on trains 418-419

[4]Class E-2-b had Franklin C-2-S booster.

[5]Non-shrouded class ES were basically the same, except somewhat lighter and with a tractive effort of 36,700 pounds.

Special appliances for the *400's* steeds included duplex valve and piston packing, blow-off cock muffler, low-water alarm and radial friction buffer. Combined heating surface of the boiler, firebox, combustion chamber, flues, tubes and thermic siphons, was 3,235.2 square feet. The weight on the drivers was 178,500 pounds; total engine weight was 295,000 pounds, with engine and tender together (loaded) weighing in at 529,000 pounds. Cost of the rebuild job was $14,000 per Pacific.

There were two reasons for the traditional locomotive change in Milwaukee. The more or less obvious reason was the lack of a water facility at the depot, but the other involved the intricacies of the running gear. The E-2-a's had hollow main pins, solid main-rod stubs and floating bushings in the main-rod crank pins, which were filled with nine pounds of hard grease (in addition to that in the back end of the rod). The engines ran hard and fast, and the pins ran warm, but so long as they held grease the pins would not become hot, and no damage would result. The grease would not hold up for the entire Chicago-Minneapolis run, but it would last between Milwaukee and Minneapolis, so power was changed at the lakefront passenger station. The locomotives could almost complete a Chicago-Minneapolis round trip without replenishing oil since, with a six-car train, an E-2-a burned about 2,700 gallons of fuel in one direction (not to mention a drink of about 32,000 gallons of water). In practice, of course, the 2900's departed Chicago, Milwaukee and Minneapolis with oil bunkers filled to capacity. Water was topped off at Adams and Eau Claire, both of which had station platform water penstocks.

The exchange of locomotion in Milwaukee could be done in as little as three minutes. The relief engine was positioned out beyond the end of the depot on the main track. The instant 400 or 401 stopped, car men would duck between the tender and combine, knock the steam connection apart, break the air hoses and close the angle-cocks—all in 25 or 30 seconds. Then the locomotive

Weight on drivers (lbs.)	Tender capacity (coal/water)	Builder	Date built	Scrapped
92,500	10 tons/7,500 gal.	American-Schenectady	1900-1908	
97,500				
130,000	10 tons/7,500 gal.	Alco-Schenectady and Baldwin	1901-1908	
139,000				
178,500	5,000 gal. (oil) 15,000 gal. (water)	American-Schenectady	1923	2902/1955 2903/1954 2907/1955 2908/1956
178,500	16 tons/10,000 gal.	American-Schenectady	1923	2901, 2904/ 1955 2905, 2906/ 1956 2910/1957 2911, 2912/ 1956 2909/
179,000	14 tons/8,275 gal.	American-Schenectady	1917	1617, 1620/ 1956

would move away from the train through the crossover and out of the way. Immediately the switch tender would line the switch and the fresh engine would back on to the train. The car men would make the coupling, connect the steam and air, and open the valves. Up would go a car inspector's hand and the engineer would make the brake test.

A knowledgeable spokesman of C&NW matters commented that the quartet took an unmerciful beating, particularly beginning each trip out of Milwaukee while the cylinders were cold.

Oil firing presented at least one problem in winters. Fires sometimes were accidentally extinguished when hitting snow at high speed. When this happened, the engineer had to shut off the throttle and coast so that the fireman could flash his fire anew against the incandescent brick arch in the firebox.

The quartet served faultlessly until dieselization in 1939, after which they were reconverted to coal. If nothing else, their appearance was thus further enhanced by heightening the sides of the coal bunker. Despite smaller tenders and boosters in the other members of the series (which had been designated E-2-b in 1935), the "a" and "b" sub-classifications were eventually

dropped from all Pacifics after the removal of oil firing. The 2902 was cut up in 1955; 2903 met the torch in 1954; 2907 was scrapped in 1955, and 2908 in 1956.

Initially the tenders of the E-2's carried the normal-size C&NW emblem on their flanks, but later—and apparently at differing dates for each engine—they received much larger heralds befitting the physical size of their tanks and the importance of their train. The king-size trademarks remained until the locomotives ended their careers.

Other small modifications to their external appearance were made from time to time. Initial *400* departures were behind locomotives lacking air horns or nickeled cylinder heads, and only 401's engine out of Chicago carried a small "THE 400" sign beneath its headlight number plate. By summer 1935 the headlight sign was relettered with a larger "400" and identical identification was attached to the cab immediately below the cab windows. By the following summer, the 2908, at least, boasted a large triangular "400" sign supported on special brackets from the smokebox door, twin air horns on each side of the stack, and the unique warning light positioned at a 45-degree angle immediately ahead of the stack. This forerunner of the Mars gyrating headlight served the double duty of warning motorists of the impending approach of the train and calling public attention to its passage. At night it was possible to stand on Lincoln Memorial Bridge adjacent to the C&NW station in Milwaukee and watch train 400's progress most of the 5 miles to Cudahy by following the beam from this skyward-aimed light.* This highest numbered E-2-a also boasted larger name signs, attached beneath the running boards directly ahead of the cab. These were apparently installed prior to the application of the triangular blue front-end illuminated sign.

At least one engine had nickeled cylinder heads by mid-January 1935: The 2902 had them only on its valve chamber head covers by that summer and received them on the cylinder head covers later. The 2907 had a complete set of nickeled covers as did the 2908. The 2902, apparently, never received a front-end warning light, large sign nor air horns.

In spring 1937, the original—on any railway—of the familiar Mars figure-eight gyrating warning light was installed on an E-2-a for testing purposes. Its strength was 3 million candlepower, and its beam was visible for three miles. Actually, the light itself didn't actually move, rather, a motor oscillated the reflector causing the beam to swing out and ahead in spectacular arcs 800 feet in diameter at a distance of 1000 feet, and the beam cut a

---

*The early UP streamliners, of which two were in service prior to inauguration of the *400*, as well as Illinois Central's *Green Diamond*, had a version of this type light which was beamed directly up at a 90-degree angle.

The transformation of Class E-2 Pacific 2903 into a high-stepping E-2-a that made the 400 famous: As delivered from Alco (above), 2903 and its brethren had 75-inch drivers, 4-wheel-truck tenders and an overall well-proportioned appearance. After rebuild (below), 2903 and three sister locomotives sported 79-inch Boxpok wheels, a larger, clean-lined tank on 6-wheel trucks, and other appliances. The result was a locomotive of imposing, but still classic, proportions. Lower photo is 2903 as it appeared after having been reconverted to coal.

swath 1400 to 2000 feet ahead of the locomotive. This was the direct prototype of the Mars lights used almost universally on diesel road locomotives for many years. The relationship between C&NW and Mars continued through other developments. In 1944 a headlight which could be reversed to show a red indication, as well as the usual white, was created—as had been the original oscillating light—by the railway's assistant to vice president of operation, Charles H. Longman, and engineered by Mars. This was undoubtedly inspired by the stationary red front-end warn-

ing lights which had been used on the Class E-4 4-6-4's and Class H 4-8-4's for several years. In 1945 and 1946, the theme of signal lights was carried even further by the partnership with the development, first, of a rear-end oscillating red light manually controlled by the flagman, and then a system under which the red warning lights at both ends of the train were linked to the train air brake line. The red warning lights would automatically be activated any time an emergency stop was made. The first installation was on the parlor-solarium cars of the *Twin Cities 400*, and later applied to most other North Western trains.

In June 1937, North Western, for the seventh time, won first place among class A railroads for safety, and for the second time received the Harriman gold medal from the American Museum of Safety. The Mars light on the *400* helped secure these distinguished awards.

The E-2-a's were the first steam locomotives called upon to extensively match or exceed the performance of new diesel streamliners. Initially, they exceeded the performance of the diesel lightweights and throughout their *400* assignment, they equalled the achievements of internal combustion. They reversed the general impression that steam power lacked the ability to compete, and without question influenced other roads in their continued use of the original form of locomotion. Much favorable newspaper publicity accrued to North Western because of the 2900's, and the railway was not at all bashful in informing the fourth estate of the accomplishments of its Pacifics and their conventional train.

Describing that first run of January 2, 1935, *The Milwaukee Journal* pointed out that the improved 4-6-2's showed plenty of reserve power as they made up time lost because of slowing to pass crowds of spectators jammed close to the right-of-way. A few months later, *Railway Mechanical Engineer* editorialized—its thoughts primarily based on the *400*—that steam was not dead yet, and that it was determined to fight to the last ditch against the diesel.

With on-time performance, *400* speed was in the 80–95 mph range. One engineman stated, "You could get an E-2-a up over 100 mph without much trouble, but not as easily as the Milwaukee Class A *Hiawatha* Atlantics."

One well-documented instance of speeds above 100 mph is known. On a fall evening in 1935, a late train 400 raced from Milwaukee to Chicago in 65 minutes (which is probably *the* minimum time for any C&NW train between these metropoli), arriving C&NW Terminal on time. The train reached speeds in excess of 108 mph between Highland Park and Evanston.

The high speeds were especially remarkable considering the line between Milwaukee and Chicago was interrupted by speed restrictions through several of the larger communities. Speeds of

The 2908 in full 400 regalia— "400" signs on nose and flanks, angled Mars light, large C&NW herald on tank. Compare with the lower photo on the facing page— the 2908's tender is for oil-burning service; note how 2903's oil tender was modified when that locomotive returned to coal. Note also 2908's spoked pilot wheels, nickeled cylinder heads.

R. J. Foster

85–90 were common between South Milwaukee and Carrollville and frequently 97 to 100 mph between Kenosha and Waukegan. Between Waukegan and North Western Terminal, a distance of 35 miles, train 400 was allowed but 34 minutes despite other rail traffic and the passage through population centers. In summer 1937, Neil Neiglick, very close to his retirement, at the throttle of train 400, was stopped by a red block signal at Asbestos, just north of Waukegan. Once underway again, the big Pacific (probably the 2908) was "flogged" up the hill into North Chicago, and in-cab recollections are that speeds of nearly two miles per minute were maintained on either side of Highwood.

When South Beaver Dam and later Wyeville and Racine (for 401 only) became stops for the *400*, the reserve potential of the E-2-a's was fully demonstrated. Each stop represented a minimum five-minute delay because of deceleration, standing time and restart; yet no running time was added to compensate. The E-2-a propelling the train simply had to work a little harder.

Unlike the E-2-b's, the four *400* steeds were not equipped with boosters, since the medium-length *400* consists did not require such an appliance, which had a limited speed potential anyway. Also, the terrain was basically level between Chicago and Eau Claire through Adams. The roughest part of the journey was between Eau Claire and the Twin Cities what with ruling grades approaching Knapp, Wis. from either direction, and the descent into and the climb from the St. Croix river valley at the Wisconsin-Minnesota state line.

After approximately 10 months of operation in their upgraded state, at least one E-2-a was subjected to close scrutinizing to determine if the new valves and super-heater installed in the November 1934 modernizing were satisfactory or whether the sub-class would undergo more shopping to improve efficiency. A cab resembling an oversize phone booth was placed on the left front pilot beam. Two technicians sat in the housing to read gauges indicating the efficiency of the generation and delivery of steam to the pistons; a third member of the team shared the locomotive cab with the engine crew and took additional notes. This process required six weeks; ultimately the tests determined that the four steeds were doing a fine job.

Early in 1937 Chicago & North Western announced it had ordered eight (later increased to nine) streamlined passenger steam locomotives of the 4-6-4 (Hudson) wheel arrangement, of which two would be used on the *400*, with the remainder running between Chicago and Omaha. That fall a sketch with striking resemblance to the E-4 class (as it emerged from Schenectady) appeared in newspapers and was captioned in such a way as to imply such locomotives would be assigned to the *400*. A national publication indicated the new Hudsons would enable 400 and 401 to better meet the competition of the *Hiawatha* and *Zephyrs* since the 4-6-4's would permit not only expanded consists but increased speeds.

Eminent industrial designer Otto Kuhler styled on his drawing board a bullet-nosed 4-6-4 lettered "400" CHICAGO & NORTH WESTERN with a two-tone color livery, with shrouding resembling that applied earlier to B&O's *Royal Blue* 5304 of 1937.

As winter eased into spring 1938, Omaha Railway Class E-3's, the world's heaviest 4-6-2's, were assigned to overnight trains

Class D Atlantic 126 and sister 125 worked the Minnesota 400 *early in its career. These locomotives were already in their thirties when they entered 400 service.*

Ten-Wheeler 1331, C&NW Class R-1, was usually given the duty of handling the Flambeau 400's *Watersmeet section in the steam years. It was ideal for the medium-speed, multi-stop run.*

between Minneapolis and Milwaukee. Use of these coal-burning Pacifics was described as the first step toward improvement of *400* service under which the existing heavyweight trains would operate on a morning schedule while the regular afternoon *400* became a streamliner.

The public read in the media that the Kinnickinnic River bridge would need strengthening to withstand heavier axle loadings, and of the need for extending roundhouse stalls and installing a new turntable in Milwaukee to accommodate the greater length of the anticipated power. The Omaha's bridges over the St. Croix at Hudson, the Chippewa at Eau Claire, and the Black near Black River Falls would also have required strengthening. Of course, the operation of any steam larger than the E-2-a's on the *400* never occurred.

There were frequent media references to use of the freight line between Chicago and Milwaukee to accomplish a one-hour running time between these metropoli. Also mentioned was the possibility of a 5½-hour schedule between the railroad capital of North America and the capital of the Gopher State. Columnists shrugged off railway rebuttals by reminding their readers that similar repudiations preceded the coming of the *400* which stole the show from the Burlington and Milwaukee Road streamliners.

In May and June 1939, the splendid E-2-a pacesetters were eased out of their *400* assignment by newly delivered E-3 diesel units; but they enjoyed a brief respite during the few days in September when the streamlined trains, with their motive power, were on demonstration and exhibition tours.

Trains 418 and 419, the *Minnesota 400*, entered service behind highly polished Class D's. Their 4-4-2, or Atlantic, wheel arrangement represented the apex of high-speed locomotive design in the opening decade of the 20th century.

Atlantic 125 apparently had no difficulty with its four-car first-trip consist of train 418, but luck was not always that good even with the more normal two-car consist of the time. An observant railfan present for the departure of 418 from Onalaska, Wis., one afternoon in 1936 vividly remembers sister 128 having trouble moving out with its combine/cafe-lounge consist. After the handful of passengers were aboard, the engineman confidently opened the throttle but to his amazement he only spun those 81-inch drivers. He had to put his charge in reverse, take slack, and then jack-rabbit away in the direction of Wyeville.

The service span of the variously numbered turn-of-the-century products of Schenectady on the *Minnesota 400* was from June 1936 to August 1937.

C&NW obtained a large number of Pacifics upon the development of that wheel arrangement. Class E comprised 168 members, acquired from 1909 until the arrival of the Class E-2. Class ES were those which became stoker-equipped, otherwise there were no subclasses even though some members of the clan varied in specifications.

Of all of these engines, only two definitely served regularly in *400* assignments. In the fall of 1941, in anticipation of the *Minnesota 400* becoming a streamliner and due to the nature of its medium-distance route (which did not justify use of a diesel locomotive), 4-6-2's 1617 and 1620 were converted from straight E to ES. They received shrouding similar to that already on the much larger Class E-4 Hudsons in use between Chicago and Omaha. Unlike the nine 4-6-4's, the duo—which were marking up a quarter-century of heading North Western varnish—received a bright color treatment corresponding to the modern cars they would pull.

The upper portion of the casing that fully enclosed the stack,

212

bell, steam and sand domes was green, as was the jacket down to the running board and the cab to the lower edge of the windows. This green extended back along the top of the tender, fully covering the built-up coal bunker and edging the top of the tank. On the locomotives themselves, the green swooped down the nose, terminating in a point just above the front coupler housing. The yellow flowed back across the nose below the green, across the wide skirting below the running board and the flank of the tender. Black stripes separated green from yellow, and a black stripe through the middle of the yellow band corresponded with that on *400* rolling stock. The pilot was green, as was the tender skirting, and both were edged with a black stripe. Cylinders, which were mostly exposed, were black. The characteristic shield above the headlight lens remained.

Initially at least, 1617 sported the C&NW emblem on its nose, while 1620 lacked the adornment. At time of upgrading, both engines had CHICAGO AND NORTH WESTERN spelled out across their tenders, but apparently not too many months later, that script was replaced by the North Western trademark on the 1617. Much later, the 1620 appeared with its tender carrying the herald, although it's possible the tenders could have been switched—some later photos of 1617 show a tender with lettering. Also later in its career, the 1620 received the nose-mounted symbol.

Engines were changed in Winona. Usually 1620 handled the Mankato-Winona round trip, while 1617 ran east and, because of the relatively short mileage of its Wyeville "turn", also negotiated the Tunnel District on a nocturnal round trip to Elroy with trains 514 and 515.

Other class ES engines saw occasional service on some *400* trains. At holiday times throughout the 1940s, it was customary to expand the consists of *Shoreland/Valley 400* trains 153 and 216 with heavyweight cars, but there were no extra diesel units to handle the extra loads (seven cars were the maximum for a single E7 in *400* service). Consequently, a 1600 would be coupled ahead of the "growler". In those instances, steam engines were changed in Milwaukee and Green Bay. During occasional diesel failures, the lanky Pacifics took turns on *Flambeau 400's* 153 and 216 north of Green Bay. These standard North Western ES passenger engines handled the *Minnesota 400* in its heavyweight steam-powered extension into Chicago in 1937–38 and in the train's remaining pre-streamlined years.

Class-R1 Ten-Wheelers were also assigned to *400* service on a regular basis: on the Monico-Watersmeet segment of the *Flambeau 400*. There was no fast running, stops were frequent and the total distance short, so 15 and 16 were within the capabilities of 4-6-0's built between 1901 and 1908. Unlike steeds of the same wheel arrangement used in northern Wisconsin by Milwaukee

Road's *North Woods Hiawatha*, the elderly power was not shrouded to conceal its age.

One of the first pronouncements relative to the use of diesel locomotives on trains 400 and 401 was that they negated the need to strengthen bridges between Chicago and the Twin Cities, as would have been required had the contemplated use of Hudson or steam-turbine locomotives been given the go-ahead.

Electro-Motive E3A models 5001-A/5001-B were received May 28, 1939, at Milwaukee, and their very first revenue-producing service was the handling of a 52-car freight from Butler (the city's freight terminal) to Proviso. The next morning they came again to Milwaukee with train 119, the *Commuter*, a 2-hour 5-minute air-conditioned schedule with diner and parlor, with eight regular and two conditional intermediate stops. The two cab units were broken in on other passenger trains, and their first run on the trains for which they were intended was to Milwaukee only on 401 Memorial Day.

On June 1, the 5001-A and 5001-B made their first trip through to Minneapolis on train 401 and returned to Chicago on Friday the 2nd. The consist was no problem at all for the 4000 h.p. machine, as train 400 was into Milwaukee 6 minutes early. Some hurried publicity must have preceded this first expedition, for a crowd estimated at 1000 turned out to witness the passage of the "double ended" locomotive through Eau Claire that Thursday evening.

Duplicate 5002 was delivered in Milwaukee Sunday, June 11, and pulled a 50-car Proviso-bound freight away from Butler at 11 a.m. Monday. It went into *400* service on the 14th; and by the end of the month, the two-unit locomotives had rolled up over 37,000 miles in their daily round-trip routine of stepping fast with a *400* in the afternoon, and lulling passengers to sleep on the *North Western Limited* at night.

These four were the only units ever constructed by EMD to incorporate Timken roller bearings in their trucks instead of the usual GM Hyatts. They were heralded as the first "double-ended" diesel locomotives placed in service on a "Western" railroad, and the first non-articulated road diesel locomotive northwest of the Windy City. Thusly, were the E-2-a's—one of the most heroic groups of Pacifics—dethroned.

Although the new units were delivered in livery identical to the forthcoming streamlined *400*, news items made no mention of the color combination, nor of its deviation from the previously announced yellow and brown. In fact, the first reference to the revival of North Western yellow and green for the impending streamliner was in an EMD Styling Section drawing bearing a May 1939 date. Interestingly, this same artwork, depicting a locomotive set composed of two A units back-to-back, gave them individual unit numbers of 5001 and 5002. Was it planned to

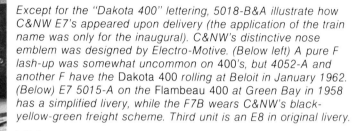

Except for the "Dakota 400" lettering, 5018-B&A illustrate how C&NW E7's appeared upon delivery (the application of the train name was only for the inaugural). C&NW's distinctive nose emblem was designed by Electro-Motive. (Below left) A pure F lash-up was somewhat uncommon on 400's, but 4052-A and another F have the Dakota 400 rolling at Beloit in January 1962. (Below) E7 5015-A on the Flambeau 400 at Green Bay in 1958 has a simplified livery, while the F7B wears C&NW's black-yellow-green freight scheme. Third unit is an E8 in original livery.

C&NW   C&NW

Jim Walter

Brad Kniskern

operation made possible the quick change of duty each evening at Chicago and Minneapolis from speed demon to Limited.

Faster average speeds of diesel-powered trains presented new problems in spring suspension. The problems were overcome by providing the new locomotives with a new treatment of load suspension that improved ride quality and greater stability in negotiating curves. Four hydraulic shock absorbers and carefully designed springs on each unit dampened sway and also eased the body load against the truck frames as the locomotive entered and left curves. When the diesel entered a curve, there was no usual

number the other pair 5003 and 5004, with the use of suffixes for each two-unit combination an afterthought?*

Things taken for granted now relative to dieselization were explained in considerable detail in the vernacular of the era. The new units were actually independent 2000 h.p. locomotives which could be operated separately if desired. Of course, back-to-back

---

*An EMC builder's photo, too, shows E3's 5001 and 5002 back-to-back (see Chapter 2). Details are shrouded in history, but it is possible the 5002 was renumbered 5001-B upon delivery; or that the two "A"-series units were lashed together only for the purpose of taking the builder's

photo, while their "B"-series counterparts waited on the sidelines. Also, early action photos of the E3's show the 5001 and the 5002 without "A" suffixes. It is presumed the "A" designation, initially at least, appeared on roster records only and not on the locomotive itself.

Diesel locomotives

Model	Builder	Year	Road numbers	Total units (combinations)	Wheel arrangement	Horsepower per unit	Comments
E3	EMD	1939	5001-5002	4 (A-A)	A1A-A1A	2000	Timken bearings; scrapped 1958-59
E2	EMD	1937[1]	5003	1 (A)	A1A-A1A	1800	Was UP-C&NW LA-1
E6	EMD	1940[2]	5004A	1 (A)	A1A-A1A	2000	Was UP-SP-C&NW SF-4
E6	EMD	1941	5005-5006	4 (A-A)	A1A-A1A	2000	Scrapped 1958-59
E7	EMD	1946[3]	5004B	1 (A)	A1A-A1A	2000	Was UP-C&NW 927; scrapped 1959
E7	EMD	1945-49	5007B-5020A	26 (A-A)	A1A-A1A	2000	Many scrapped or traded for high-h.p. hood units during 1960's; 5019B upgraded to E8 in 1953
E8	EMD	1950-53	5021-5030 / 5031A	20 (A-A) / 1 (A)	A1A-A1A / A1A-A1A	2250 / 2250	All E8's and E7 5019B converted to Cummins
F7	EMD	1949-50	4052A-4100C	43 (A)	B-B	1500	Some traded or scrapped, but several still on roster at start of Amtrak
Erie	FM	1947	6001-6002	4 (A-A)	A1A-A1A	2000	Lettered for CStPM&O: Scrapped 1957-59
DL109	Alco	1941	5007A	1 (A)	A1A-A1A	2000	Scrapped 1956
RSD4	Alco	1951	1515-1517	1 (hood)	C-C	1600	One of these units used on Watersmeet branch

[1]C&NW acquired full ownership 1948, scrapped by 1953
[2]C&NW acquired full ownership 1948, scrapped 1959
[3]C&NW acquired full ownership 1948
NOTE: On E units, all were cab units and suffixed "A" or "B"; F7 cab units were "A" and "C"

sudden jerk (as with steam locomotives) when the wheels started to curve while the engine attempted to continue straight ahead. Instead, the weight of the body was shifted against the side springs and the car-body was gradually eased into the path taken by the wheels through the curve.

Each unit carried 1200 gallons of "ordinary" fuel oil of the type used in household furnaces, and 1100 gallons of boiler heating water. With full supplies, each two-unit locomotive weighed approximately 600,000 pounds. Dimensions were: total length, 140 feet; height, 13 feet, 11 inches; width, 9 feet, 10 inches.

The 5001 and 5002 were provided with the same type of Mars signal light as was developed for the E-2-a's, flashing upward and sideways in the form of a figure eight, at night warning motorists and pedestrians up to five miles distant of the approach of a super-speed train. Super speed it was—the units reached speeds of 112 mph on their first "try-out" run on train 401.

The pair of two-unit E3's performed well. Each set was on the road 16½ hours out of every 24, and in their first two years of service only one trip was missed by one unit. The 1939 La Grange products rolled 900,000 miles before any of them entered the shops for general repairs in May 1942.

Between August 15 and 31, 1941, four current model E6 cab units were acquired from EMD in anticipation of the forthcoming expansion of *400* service. Units 5005A-B and 5006A-B in regular operation held the Chicago-Minneapolis daily round trip, with the E3's being bumped to the newer trains in Wisconsin and Michigan.

At this same time, the lone passenger unit contributed by Alco-GE to *400* service rolled out of Schenectady to be inscribed on the roster as 5007-A. The classic "needle-nose" DL109 was given the honor of pulling one of the demonstration trains preceding inauguration of the *400* fleet. Each of these five new 2000 h.p. machines cost in the neighborhood of 175,000 just-out-of-the-depression dollars.

C&NW now had nine passenger diesels. The four new E6's were assigned to 400 and 401; two of the bumped E3's went into *Peninsula 400* service (209 and 214 had the heaviest consist, and therefore required two units) while the remaining two E3's and the lone DL109 rotated on the two smaller (usually seven cars) *400's* which made short trips into Wisconsin. The "extra" unit made it possible to accomplish fast turnarounds with the little *400s* in Chicago. The five units averaged 517 miles daily, while the four units running to and from the Twin Cities wheeled over 800 miles in each 24 hours. In their first year of service they totalled nearly one million miles with virtually no interruptions; additionally they rolled several thousand miles on conventional trains during the three months preceding commencement of the *400* fleet.

Initially the Alco ran on the short-distance *400's* much of the time, but was soon paired with various EMD's to handle the two-unit assignment of the *Peninsula 400*, and it became familiar to residents of Ishpeming, Escanaba, Marinette, et al for at least a decade. It managed to roll up nearly 2 million miles before finally being retired because of a broken underframe and being considered beyond economical repair.

The success of the E3 and E6 units led North Western to opt for additional EMD power to replace worn steam locomotives as passenger unit production began again in 1945. It was one of the first recipients of the new bulldog-nose E7 model, with the 5007-B arriving on the property in April. Its number provided the unusual circumstance wherein—if one follows the usual reasoning of A-B suffixes—the two units comprising the "same" locomotive were constructed by rival builders and at a considerable time gap.

Eleven other E7's were received during the second half of September 1947, and they operated on regular trains as well as the *400* fleet. In March 1949 the final six 2000 h.p. EMD's were received and lined up for the postwar expansion of *400* service which they highballed a year later.

Next in line from "the home of the diesel locomotive" was the E8, which boasted a 250 h.p. increase in horsepower. C&NW's first four E8's arrived July 1950 just after the final extension of *400* service. A pair of them were quickly assigned to *Dakato 400*, trains 518–519, which had eight-car consists for part of their route and thus had been assigned two E7's. The other E8's, which were joined by more of their type during the construction era of that model, handled most trains on the system at some time or another. They were often combined with E3's, E6's, and E7's when North Western began to team up units without regard to model.

In October 1958, four E8's were outfitted with Cummins head-end power systems for train lighting, heating and air-conditioning for the bilevel *400's*. The same type of equipment was introduced into Chicago suburban service, so all E8's eventually lost their steam generators to Cummins sets. In fact, at the time of the demise

of the *Twin Cities 400,* only three E8's still carried their boilers.

EMD F7's, originally built for freight service, were also outfitted with Cummins generators, for substitute service in the long-distance bilevel *400* trains. When North Western made the decision to convert all suburban cars to head-end power during its suburban train modernization policy, additional F7's were "electrified," and many of them survived into the 1980's along with the E8's. As the use of bilevel cars spread to other *400* services, any one of the upgraded F7's was apt to be seen powering an intercity train, as was the case when the E8's were converted.

In 1948 certain of the jointly owned (with UP and SP) cars and locomotives for the *City* streamliners were acquired individually by the Overland Route partners. North Western acquired locomotive 921A (nee LA-1), one of two E2 cab units—part of the very rare custom-styled A-B-B locomotive sets built for the first 17-car streamliner. This ex- *City of Los Angeles* team-member, which became C&NW 5003 (no suffix), saw service on a variety of C&NW trains. The unit was painted *400* yellow and green, and was used on trains 153–216, the *Flambeau 400*, between Chicago and Ashland in 1951. It was off the roster by 1953, destroyed in a head-on collision near Rhinelander.

North Western sampled the opposed pistons of Fairbanks-Morse by delegating a quartet of Erie-built cab units to the Omaha Railway. In practice though, the deep-rumbling A-1-A's spent most of their time on the C&NW proper, working singly on smaller *400* trains, and later being multipled with EMD's in the same manner the 5007-A had been. They were the shortest-lived *400* diesels, lasting barely a decade.

Road-switchers were seldom used on *400* trains. A six-axle 1600 h.p. steam generator-equipped Alco RSD-4 was for a time assigned to the Waters meet section of the *Flambeau 400* in that train's final years of operation on the branch north of Monico. The same unit made a second round trip with trains 10 and 11, which connected with the *Ashland Limited.* Generally, EMD Geeps (GP7's and GP9's) were used in *400* service only in extenuating circumstances. For example, a GP7 was used on *Commuter 400* 152 out of Milwaukee one summer morning in 1954. The final trip of *Peninsula 400* 209 between Green Bay and Ishpeming required a Geep when 800-series coaches were substituted for the usual bilevel cars. And on June 1, 1969, GP7 1650 was used on Sunday & holiday-only train 239 with five 800-series coaches. On a related note to this last operation, there was one example of a Geep being regularly assigned to haul a *400*, albeit, the train was actually unnamed at the time: In the final months of operation of trains 239/168's Sunday-only extension beyond Green Bay to Menominee, Mich., (a remnant of the *Valley 400* northbound, *Shoreland 400* southbound), a geep was assigned north of Green Bay to facilitate fast turnaround at Menominee.

The 400 Story

Only days away from the end of Chicago-Twin Cities service, train 400 swings through Wiscona interlocking on Milwaukee's north side on July 6, 1963.

Jim Scribbins

Rolling stock

THIS LISTING includes only those cars constructed specifically for streamlined *400* service; all cars were built by Pullman-Standard. Streamlined coaches built for the original *Challengers* were used on *400* trains during the war years of the 1940's, and after 1955. C&NW-owned equipment which had been designated for and assigned to the *City* Streamliners saw *400* service. Descriptions of these non-*400* cars appear in the appropriate chapters. Smoking rooms are not included in the seating capacities of coaches and parlor cars. Dispositions of cars are indicated as of the establishment of Amtrak on May 1, 1971. No attempt has been made to trace equipment after that date except for bilevel cars purchased by Amtrak.

Parlor-solarium (2)

General notes: 12 parlor seats, bar service area, 20 lounge seats, 9 solarium seats

Car number	Manufactured	Service notes	Disposition
7200-7201	1939	Used exclusively for *Twin Cities 400*	Sold to National Railways of Mexico (NdeM) in 1964; 7200 became *Club Isaac Romero Malpica* (374), 7201 became *Club Jose Maria Cardenas* (375)

Parlor (17)

General notes: 22 seats, drawing room; all parlors off roster by 1966 except as noted

6500-6505	1939		6500 and two others off roster by 1961
6506-6507	1941		6506 off roster by 1961; 6507 off roster by 1965
6508-6516	1947		6508-6510 off roster by 1965; 6511 became club-lounge 6700 in 1961[1]; 6512 off roster by 1965; 6513 off roster by 1966; 6514 became coach-club-lounge 553 in 1959[2]; 6515 became coach-club-lounge 555 in 1959[2]; 6516 became coach-club-lounge 510 in 1959[2]; all other parlors off roster by 1966.

Dining (6)

General notes: all 56 seats, except 6955 (48 seats)

6950	1939		To NdeM, 1963: *Mocambo* 3646
6951	1939		To NdeM, 1963: *Comanjilla* 3647
6952	1941		To NdeM, 1964: *San Jose Purua* 3649
6953-6954	1941	First service, *Twin Cities 400*; converted for bilevel operation, 1958	Off roster by 1971
6955	1950	First service, *Dakota 400*	To NdeM, 1964: *Agua Azul* 3653

Baggage-cafe-lounge (4)

General notes: 6 counter seats, 30 table seats

7625-7628	1950	First service: *Flambeau 400, Shoreland/Valley 400* of 1950, Chicago-Milwaukee *400's*	7625 off roster by 1961; others, 1965

Baggage-tavern-lunch counter-lounge (3)

General notes: 16 tavern seats, 10 counter seats, 10 lounge seats

7500-7501	1939	*Twin Cities 400*	Off roster by 1961
7502	1941	*Minnesota 400*	Converted for work-train service as X-3009 by 1961

RPO-baggage-tavern-lunch counter (2)

General notes: 16 tavern seats, 9 counter seats

7600-7601	1941	*Peninsula 400, Shoreland/Valley 400* of 1942; 7601 rebuilt for bilevel operation, 1958	7600 became crane tender car at Butler, Wis.

Baggage-tavern-lunch counter (1)

General notes: 16 tavern seats, 9 counter seats

7602	1941	*Capitol 400;* rebuilt for bilevel operation, 1958

Cafe-coach (1)

General notes: 12 booth seats, 4 counter seats, 36 coach seats

7000	1950	*Flambeau 400,* Watersmeet (Mich.) section[3]	Off roster by 1965

Coach (4)

General notes: stewardess room, 48 coach seats

3400-3401	1939	*Twin Cities 400;* 3400 upgraded as 807[4]; 3401 upgraded as 836[4]	807: R; 836 off roster by 1969
3402	1941	*Minnesota 400;* upgraded as 805[4]	Off roster by 1969
3403	1949	*Dakota 400;* upgraded as 829	R

Coach (67)

General notes: 56 seats

3410	1939[5]		Off roster by 1965
3411	1939[5]	Upgraded as 847	Off roster by 1971
3412	1939[5]		Off roster by 1965
3413	1939[5]	Upgraded as 839	Off roster by 1971
3414-3415	1939[5]		Off roster by 1965
3416	1941[6]		Off roster by 1965 (note A)
3417	1941[6]	Upgraded as 843	Off roster by 1965 (note B)
3418	1941[6]	Upgraded as 818	R (note A)
3419	1941[6]	Upgraded as 809	R (note A)
3420	1941[6]	Upgraded as 845	Off roster by 1971 (note A)
3421-3422	1941[6]		Off roster by 1965

3423	1941[6]	Upgraded as 824	R (note A)
3424	1941[6]	Upgraded as 846	R
3425	1941[6]	Upgraded as 816	R
3426	1941[6]		Off roster by 1965 (note B)
3427	1941[6]	Upgraded as 840	R
3428	1941[6]	Upgraded as 800	R (note A)
3429	1941[6]	Upgraded as 803	Off roster by 1971 (note A)
3430	1941[6]	Upgraded as 804	R (note A)
3431	1946	Upgraded as 823	R
3432	1946	Upgraded as 825	To Great Northern, 1963: 1098
3433	1946	Upgraded as 819	To Great Northern, 1965: 1076
3434	1946		To Great Northern, 1961: 1095
3435	1946	Upgraded as 834	To Great Northern, 1964: 1078
3436	1946	Upgraded as 806	To Great Northern, 1966: 1082
3437	1946	Upgraded as 810	To Great Northern, 1963: 1086
3438	1946		To Northern Pacific, 1961: 518
3439	1946	Upgraded as 821	To Great Northern, 1963: 1089
3440	1946		To Northern Pacific, 1961: 519
3441	1946	Upgraded as 815	R
3442	1946	Upgraded as 811	To Burlington, 1964: 4653
3443	1946	Upgraded as 812	To Burlington, 1964: 4654
3444	1946	Upgraded as 808	To Great Northern, 1963: 1097
3445	1946		To Northern Pacific, 1961: 520
3446	1946	Upgraded as 837	To Burlington, 1964: 4657
3447	1946	Upgraded as 817	R
3448	1946	Upgraded as 802	To Burlington, 1963: 4652
3449	1946	Upgraded as 842	To Great Northern, 1964: 1080
3450	1946		To Great Northern, 1961: 1090
3451	1947	Upgraded as 831	To Great Northern, 1963: 1088
3452	1947	Upgraded as 833	R
3453	1947	Upgraded as 801	To Great Northern, 1963: 1096
3454	1947	Upgraded as 832	To Great Northern, 1964: 1079
3455	1947	Upgraded as 813	R
3456	1947	Upgraded as 838	To Northern Pacific, 1963: 525
3457	1947	Upgraded as 820	To Burlington, 1963: 4651
3458	1947		To Northern Pacific, 1961: 521
3459	1947		To Great Northern, 1963: 1093
3460	1947	Upgraded as 822	To Burlington, 1961: 4650

3461	1947	Became suburban coach 440 *Northwest Passage II*, 1960	
3462	1947		To Great Northern, 1962: 1092
3463	1947	Upgraded as 844	To Northern Pacific, 1963: 526
3464	1947	Upgraded as 814	R
3465	1947	Upgraded as 826	To Northern Pacific, 1963: 524
3466	1947	Upgraded as 835	R
3467	1947	Upgraded as 848	To Burlington, 1964: 4656
3468	1947	Upgraded as 849	To Great Northern, 1964: 1081
3469	1947		To Great Northern, 1961: 1091
3470	1947	Upgraded as 830	To Great Northern, 1965: 1087
3471	1947	Upgraded as 827	To Great Northern, 1965: 1077
3472	1947		To Northern Pacific, 1961: 522
3473	1947	Upgraded as 828	To Burlington, 1961: 4655
3474	1947		To Northern Pacific: 523
3475	1947		To Great Northern, 1961: 1094
3476	1947	Upgraded as 841	To Great Northern, 1963: 1099

RPO-baggage (2)

General notes: 15-foot RPO, 64-foot baggage

| 8202-8203 | 1950 | Used briefly on *Dakota 400*, then transferred to *Flambeau 400*[8] | Off roster by 1965 |

Bilevel cars (13)

600	1958	30 parlor seats, 48 coach seats[9]	Amtrak 9600
700-709	1958	96 coach seats	Amtrak 9611-9620
903	1958	48 coach seats, 32 tavern seats[9]	Amtrak 9601
6400	1958	60 parlor seats[10]	

R = Car remaining on C&NW roster as of Amtrak start-up on May 1, 1971

[1] Some sources give 6700 the name *Deerpath*

[2] Used in suburban service

[3] Originally intended for Sioux City section for never-instituted *Corn King 400*

[4] When upgraded, stewardess room removed and capacity increased to 56 seats

[5] All coaches built in 1939 for *Twin Cities 400* and reassigned to other *400* runs in 1942

[6] Six coaches of 1941 order assigned to *Twin Cities 400*, replacing 1939-built cars

[7] See details of upgrading following roster

[8] Re-equipped to operate with bilevel cars in 1958, but did not have false roof applied

[9] Converted to snack-coach in 1970

[10] Converted to suburban coach 225 in 1967

NOTE A: Coaches 3416, 3418-3420, 3423, 3428-3430 converted to coach-lounge for *City* train service in immediate postwar era and painted in Union Pacific colors; returned to full coach when upgraded.

NOTE B: Coaches 3417 and 3426 painted in UP colors for *City* train service in immediate postwar era

In latter years some ACF-built diner-lounges, full lounges, full diners and coaches were used occasionally in 400 service, but these cars are not included in the listing since they were not originally intended for *400* trains.

Car 7602 (left side of car, upper photo; right side, lower) as built in 1941 had the external appearance of an RPO-baggage-tavern-lunch counter. However, interior mail facilities were never installed, nor was the partition between the "RPO" and baggage space. Later, the RPO door and window were closed. Booth section featured murals of Wisconsin vacationland scenes. This car played an important role in the bilevel era when, after modification, it went to work on the Flambeau 400.

(Above right) Car 3445 built in 1946 typified most C&NW 56-seat coaches. (Above) Interior of coach 3419, a 56-seater built in 1941 for the Twin Cities 400. For a time it and several other cars in the series were modified for service on the joint UP-C&NW City trains. (Right) Coach 3403 was built for the Dakota 400 in 1949. It contained 48 seats and a stewardess room, identified by the fourth, single, window from the left end of the car. (Far right) As delivered, 400 cars had full-width diaphragms.

CHICAGO AND NORTH WESTERN

C&NW, collection of Patrick C. Dorin

(Below) Parlor 6510 was one of nine such cars Pullman-Standard outshopped for C&NW in 1947 for 400 service. (Left) Parlor 6502 was one of the original six 400 parlor cars built in 1939. The round drawing-room lavatory window was a distinctive identifying feature of these cars.

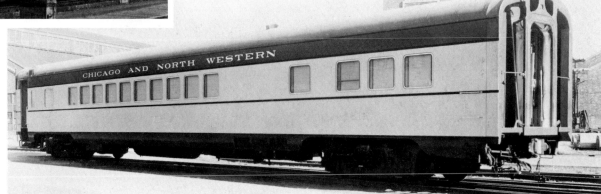

(Below) Diner 6955, shown here in Milwaukee in 1961, was built for the Dakota 400 in 1950. Its seating capacity of 48—versus 56 for all other diners built for 400 service—made it a one-of-a-kind item on the C&NW roster.

Owen Leander, collection of William Stauss

C&NW

Jim Harper

A number of C&NW cars built by American Car & Foundry for joint UP-C&NW-SP City train service found their way onto various 400's. Diner 7801 (above right) frequented the latter-day Twin Cities and Dakota 400's. (Right) Club-lounge 7900 at Milwaukee in 1964 for use on train 160, the Streamliner 400.

Jim Scribbins

Brad Kniskern

Coach 709 was one of the ten bilevel long distance cars built in 1958. In spite of its high capacity (96), seating was spacious and comfortable. Unlike Santa Fe Hi-Level cars and Amtrak double-deck Superliners, passage from one car to another was on the lower level.

Robert P. Schmidt

A bit of the Twin Cities 400 survived into the 1970's in Mexico. Club Isaac Romero Malpica (ex-C&NW parlor-solarium 7200) brings up the markers of NdeM's Aztec Eagle near Mexico City in 1972.

Jim Scribbins

The Upgrading

Between February 1958 and May 1959, 50 of the 3400-series coaches were upgraded or remanufactured by Pullman-Standard, an undertaking which the company hoped would stimulate a flow of business from most major passenger-carrying railroads. Initially, coach 3428 retained its number, but eventually became the 800. The other rebuilds all received numbers in the 800 series.

Mechanically, the coaches were returned to good-as-new condition, minus frills. Rigid steps replaced folding ones in the vestibules, and skirting and wide diaphragms were removed. A simplified livery, omitting the black stripes and substituting yellow for the silver words, CHICAGO AND NORTH WESTERN, on the letterboard, became the only changes in exterior color during the life of the *400* trains. Car numerals were black and the mid-car *400* design was removed.

Interiors lost some luxury appearance. Leather pier panels between windows disappeared, along with shades and blinds. The new windows were heavily tinted green. Seats received a plastic-leatherette covering in place of upholstery. The cars remained comfortable and smooth-riding until the introduction of Amtrak.

C&NW